1972

The Modernist Idea

The Modernist Idea

A Critical Survey
of Brazilian Writing
in the Twentieth Century

Wilson Martins

Translated by Jack E. Tomlins

New York • *NEW YORK UNIVERSITY PRESS* 1970

TRANSLATOR'S DEDICATION TO

Albert Richard Lopes:

MASTER TEACHER AND PIONEER

Acknowledgments

Acknowledgment is made to the Editôra Cultrix of São Paulo, Brazil, for their kind permission to translate this volume into English. Especial gratitude is due Wilson Martins, whose patience and guidance are as endless as his knowledge of Brazilian letters. The Research Fund of the Language and Area Center for Latin America at the University of New Mexico and Marshall Rutherford Nason, its director, have followed this project from the beginning with aid and encouragement that I deeply appreciated. To my colleagues Robert Deupree Herron and Gerald M. Slavin, Brazilianists of good faith, go my thanks and appreciation. My chairman and friend, William Holloway Roberts, saw this task to its conclusion with good cheer and reassurance. Finally to my wife, my finest editor, goes the gratitude that only an accurate typist deserves.

Preface

This work first appeared in Brazil in 1965 as the sixth and final volume of the collective history *A Literatura Brasileira* (São Paulo: Editôra Cultrix). It bore the Portuguese title *O Modernismo (1916–1945)*; and, thus delimited chronologically, it studied the crucial six years prior to the Week of Modern Art (São Paulo, February, 1922), the revolutionary and iconoclastic years of 1922 through 1930, and the years which represented the maturation of Modernism, from 1930 to 1945. Brazilianists immediately welcomed Wilson Martins's work as the first—and only, up to the present—intelligent, informed, and comprehensive statement made of Brazil's Modernist Movement after the promising introduction of Mário da Silva Brito, who in 1958 so thoroughly studied the antecedents of the Week of Modern Art. An indispensable foreword to the study of Brazilian letters from the mid-forties to the present, this volume is presently in its third and updated edition (1969). In this form it now comes into English. As it serves the specialist in its Brazilian version, hopefully the translation will serve the English-reading public as a proper introduction to the rich literature of the Brazilian twentieth century.

The present study departs from the fundamental postulate that the history of Brazilian Modernism is essentially the history of the idea of modernism—or modernity—as that idea riotously penetrated the Brazilian literary mind around the time of the Week of Modern Art. As he charts the evolution of Marinettian Futurism through Modernism to a sense of the modern, Wilson Martins delineates the historic, esthetic, and political perspectives of Brazilian writing in the first half of the twentieth century. Against this complex background, he views Brazilian literature coming of age as the European vanguards stormed the tropical beaches soon after World War I.

The literary activity that ensued was chaotic, often awkward, frequently flawed, but—like the young poet and esthetician Mário de Andrade—alive! Wilson Martins investigates this peculiar aspect of vitality through those representative works without which the Movement cannot be properly comprehended: Mário de Andrade's colorful and noisy masterpiece *Paulicéia Desvairada* and his ars poetica *A Escrava Que Não É Isaura;* Oswald de Andrade's poem-manifesto *Pau Brasil;* three Brazilian portraits (all out of focus) from the year 1928: *Retrato do Brasil, Macunaíma,* and *Martim Cererê;* the Indianist mysticism and mythology of *Cobra Norato;* and finally Gilberto Freyre's Gargantuan masterwork, *Casa Grande & Senzala,* which revolutionized sociological studies in Brazil.

A clear distinction is made here between the representative work and the basic author. They may be—though not of necessity —mutually exclusive. According to Wilson Martins's analysis a basic author may never have composed a representative work, just as the author of a representative work may never have attained the stature of a basic author. This approach to the problem is especially enlightening in the discussion of Gilberto Freyre and Jorge Amado (the two twentieth-century Brazilian writers perhaps best known to English readers) and the roles they played in the so-called Regionalist Movement. Wilson Martins throws abundant new light on this old problem and settles the issue in the juxta-position of *paulista* "Futurism" and the Northeasterner's longing for a dead past. Thus the Regionalist Manifesto is given a new reading, and a small but significant chapter of Brazilian literary history is rewritten in the light of new evidence and a new perspective.

This combination of historical accuracy, a sense of history, keen literary discernment, and unfailing wit readily identifies the lively critical personality of Wilson Martins to a generation of Brazilianists. He has recorded here the birth pangs of Brazilian letters, paradoxically in the twentieth century, and—likewise paradoxical—the expression of Brazil's truest Romanticism. In so doing, it has fallen to him to paint the authentic portrait of Brazil.

Jack E. Tomlins

Albuquerque, New Mexico

Wilson Martins

In the midst of a distinguished career in law and letters, Wilson Martins came to the United States in 1962 from the Department of Romance Language and Literature of the University of Paraná (Brazil). He spent that academic year as visiting associate professor at the University of Kansas. From 1963 to 1965 he served as visiting professor of Brazilian literature at the University of Wisconsin. Since 1965 he has lectured as full professor at New York University in the field of Brazilian literature. Prior to his arrival in the United States Wilson Martins offered a series of lectures on the Brazilian Symbolist poet João da Cruz e Sousa at the Institut de Hautes Études de l'Amérique Latine of the University of Paris in 1958, and he was a regular lecturer in Brazilian literary criticism in the joint program of the University of Wisconsin and the University of Rio Grande do Sul (Pôrto Alegre, Brazil) in 1962. In addition to his regular academic duties, in 1963 and 1964 he offered a course in Brazilian civilization and culture for the Peace Corps training program held at the University of Wisconsin.

Wilson Martins read for the law at the University of Paraná, where he took the degree in 1943 at the age of twenty-two. That university also awarded him the Ph.D. in 1952. As a grantee of the French government he studied Romance literature in Paris in 1947 and 1948, where he carried out his researches at the École Normale Supérieure and the Collège de France. Since 1954 he has served as a leading literary critic for the prestigious *O Estado de São Paulo* (São Paulo, Brazil) and other newspapers and journals both in Brazil and abroad.

He is a corresponding member of the Academia Mineira de Letras and an associate editor of the *Revista Iberoamericana,* the *Luso-Brazilian Review,* and *Compromisso* (Brasília). He is a frequent reviewer for the principal North American, South American, and European literary journals, and for some years he has acted as consultant for the publishing firm of Alfred A. Knopf, Incorporated.

Long active in cultural affairs, Wilson Martins has been a member of the first and third Congressos Brasileiros de Escritores (São Paulo, 1953 and 1954); of the Brazilian delegation to the "Rencontres Intellectuelles" of UNESCO (São Paulo, 1954); of the first and second Congressos Brasileiros de Crítica e História Literária (Recife, 1960, and Assis, São Paulo, 1961); of the ninth International Congress of Literary Criticism and Literary History (New York University, 1963); of the third, fourth, fifth, and sixth Colóquios Internacionais de Estudos Luso-Brasileiros (Lisbon, 1957; Salvador, 1959; Coimbra, 1963; and Harvard University, 1966), all colloquia for which he has often contributed official reports.

At the present time Professor Martins is involved in research on Brazilian intellectual history, which he projects as a work of several volumes.

Major Works by Wilson Martins

Interpretações (Critical Essays). Rio de Janeiro: Livraria José Olympio Editôra, 1946.
Introdução à Democracia Brasileira. Pôrto Alegre: Editôra Globo, 1951.
Criação de uma Cadeira de Crítica Literária (a plan presented upon invitation to the French authorities of the Ministère de l'Education Nationale). Curitiba, 1952.

Imagens da França (Books, Men, Things). Curitiba, 1952.

Les Théories Critiques dans l'Histoire de la Littérature Française, Curitiba, 1952.

A Crítica Literária no Brasil. São Paulo: Departamento de Cultura, 1952.

Introdução ao Estudo do Simbolismo. Reprint from *Letras.* Curitiba, 1953.

Poesia e Prosa. Reprint from *Letras.* Curitiba, 1954.

Um Brasil Diferente (an essay on the phenomena of acculturation in Paraná). São Paulo: Editôra Anhembi Limitada, 1955.

Código de Processo Penal (suggestions for its reform). São Paulo: Editôra Anhembi Limitada, 1956.

"A Literatura e o Conhecimento da Terra," in *A Literatura no Brasil,* ed. Afrânio Coutinho. Vol. I, Part I. Rio de Janeiro: Editorial Sul-Americana, 1956.

A Palavra Escrita (a history of books, printing, and the library). São Paulo: Editôra Anhembi Limitada, 1957.

"50 Anos de Literatura Brasileira," in *Panorama das Literaturas das Américas (De 1900 à atualidade),* ed. Joaquim de Montezuma de Carvalho. Vol. I. Angola: Edição do Município de Nova Lisboa, 1958.

O Teatro no Brasil. Reprint from *Hispania,* Vol. XLVI, No. 2 (May, 1963). Lawrence, Kansas. (English text in "The Theatre Annual," 1963, Vol. XX. A publication of Information and Research in the Arts and History of the Theatre. Cleveland, Ohio: The Western Reserve University Press, 1964.)

"Literature and Society in Brazil," in *Literature and Society,* ed. Bernice Slote. Lincoln: University of Nebraska Press, 1964.

Teatro Brasileiro Contemporâneo (in collaboration with Seymour Menton). New York: Appleton-Century-Crofts, 1966. 2nd edition: 1968.

"A língua simbólica de José Lins do Rêgo." Introduction to *Usina,* 6th ed. Rio de Janeiro: José Olympio, 1967.

"Brazilian Literature: The Task of the Next Twenty Years," in Raymond S. Sayers, ed., *Portugal and Brazil in Transition.* Minneapolis: The University of Minnesota Press, 1968.

"Guimarães Rosa na sala de aula." Introduction to Mary Lou

Daniel, *João Guimarães Rosa: travessia literária.* Rio de Janeiro: José Olympio, 1968.

"Linhas de Fôrça na Literatura Brasileira." Reprint from *Revista Iberoamericana,* No. 68 (May–August, 1969), pp. 285–302.

Contents

Part One
Perspectives

Introduction

Literary history, in so far as I understand it, is made up of exclusions and may as legitimately be defined by what it rejects and omits as by what it embraces and enshrines. History cannot exist apart from criticism and the selective spirit. To study the past, especially the literary past, is to understand it in its profoundest nature, to discover in it a meaning and a significance. At the same time, literary history, like criticism, can only be justified as long as it exists consciously under the sign of *quality*. It matters little that the notion of quality varies from one person to another, from one era to another. What matters is that the awareness of quality should be present and that it not be corrupted at the hands of the historian or literary critic.

By the same token, on the purely factual plane, literary history cannot ignore the spiritual climate or the basic trends of a given epoch. These are the factors that *condition the concept of the esthetic,* which is the essence of critical judgment, while, at the same time, such judgment is simply an attendant phenomenon within the total perspective. As an aspect of culture, literature cannot ignore these trends; and this is the reason that esthetic appreciation will always be relative, since it is immersed in a universe so broad and diffuse that it becomes imperceptible to the observer, just as the circulation of the blood is as imperceptible as the nutritional virtues that it bears with it. Every epoch in the historiography of art includes or excludes different names and works, just as each age evaluates them in diverse ways. From that fact the critical faculty gains its creative force and its stimulating nature.

For that very reason, contrary to what the manuals tacitly admit or insinuate, in each literary period *representative works* and *basic authors* are two totally different matters. The truly great writer, the one who attains the level of genius in the annals of literary history, is the one who not only presents himself as *fundamental* to the destiny of a particular school but who also publishes at least one work that is eminently representative of the tendencies and principles of the school in question. Nevertheless, a basic author does not always leave behind books that are representative or typical of the esthetic current to which he has definitely linked his name. On the other hand, many representative works were written by authors who, viewed in this light, never reached the level of writers of the first rank. In other words, in literary history a representative work is often associated with a decisive date: 1922 with the *Paulicéia Desvairada*; 1928 will always be linked with the *Retrato do Brasil,* with *Macunaíma,* and with *Martim Cererê. Casa Grande & Senzala* represents, in 1933, a new orientation in our studies of sociology and social history. Each one of these dates and each one of these titles signifies a break with the past or a new program aimed at the future, no matter what their specific qualities or defects might have been. Mário de Andrade wrote about *Catimbó*: "Originality is not enough to give a work real value." The converse is equally true, as it cannot be denied that a work can be an artistic failure, as in the case of the *Paulicéia Desvairada* and *Macunaíma,* and at the same time eventually come to play a role of considerable historical and esthetic significance. As a matter of fact, that has been precisely the case with all the Modernist literature produced in the twenties. This does not mean, however, that this literature was not cast in the same font as numerous works of great value which were published subsequent to the twenties.

The basic author is the author who is typical of or inseparable from a literary school. Very frequently he will be a minor writer who is more important to literary history than to literature. He will have lived through the artistic battle in all its tumult and rapture although he may have been incapable, for one reason or another, of creating the work that theoretically might have lain within his capabilities. In the annals of Brazilian Modernism, I view Oswald de Andrade more as a basic author than as the author of a representative work, but Mário de Andrade will have a place in both categories. Strictly speaking, Graça Aranha wrote nothing that could be called representative of Modernist literature; still, he is undeniably a basic author. Without the basic author and the representative work there can be no literary school, nor indeed can there be a spiritual movement with loud repercussions and long-lasting influence such as Modernism was. It simply happens that the same person is not always a basic author and the author of a representative work.

In Brazilian Modernism a first attempt to distinguish basic authors and representative works might give the following results:

BASIC AUTHORS, ACCORDING TO THE DATE OF THEIR DEBUT

1902	Graça Aranha
1914	Jorge de Lima
1917	Manuel Bandeira
	Menotti del Picchia
	Guilherme de Almeida
1919	Ronald de Carvalho
1920	Oliveira Viana
1922	Mário de Andrade
	Oswald de Andrade
1926	Plínio Salgado
1927	Alcântara Machado
1928	José Américo de Almeida
	Augusto Frederico Schmidt
1930	Carlos Drummond de Andrade
1932	José Lins do Rêgo
	Jorge Amado
1933	Gilberto Freyre
	Graciliano Ramos
	Érico Veríssimo

REPRESENTATIVE WORKS, ACCORDING TO THE DATE
OF PUBLICATION

1922   *Paulicéia Desvairada*
1925   *A Escrava Que Não É Isaura*
        Pau Brasil
1928   *Retrato do Brasil*
        Macunaíma
        Martim Cererê
1931   *Cobra Norato*
1933   *Casa Grande & Senzala*

This book attempts to present a history of the Modernist *idea*—of its advent, characteristics and transformations through the years—rather than a literary history of the Modernist period. The latter would require several weighty volumes, as can be seen from the considerable research initiated by Mário da Silva Brito.[1] On the other hand, an ideological and artistic synthesis can effectively be contained in a small panorama like this present one. The reader should not expect to find here exhaustive studies of authors and works. This book represents a balance sheet and attempts to evaluate Brazilian Modernism rather than to describe it. What the reader may demand of the author is an exhaustive study of Modernism as an intellectual process of artistic creation and thought or as a specific state of mind. We might say, in the broad sense of the word, that there exists a Modernist *ideology*. That ideology will be our main interest. On the whole the facts are sufficiently well known, but the spiritual perspectives of the Modernist Movement are frequently confused and jumbled. In the best sense, a change of perspectives might lead to a reappraisal of the facts and of their nature and significance. But this will be a task to be undertaken later.

Chronology

More than a simple literary *school,* or even a period in our intellectual life, Modernism in my opinion was a whole *epoch* of Brazilian life inscribed within a wide social and historical process, the source and result of transformations which far overflowed their esthetic frontiers. Here as elsewhere a new society necessarily required a new literature. From the very first moment the theoreticians and the artists never tired of repeating this statement. In Brazil, as well as outside Brazil, the new art and the new literature were clearly far in advance of society, which was transforming itself much more slowly. As is natural, writers and artists understood much earlier than others what the technical and scientific progress of the early part of the century signified. They immediately realized, as we shall see, that the very nature and quality of the human spirit were bound to change under the impact of the machine. The machine not only represented something added to daily life, but it was also a catalytic agent of unforeseen magnitude.

It is natural, then, that in imitation of what was happening in Europe the initial disquietude resulting from that state of mind should have repeated itself in Brazil from the first years of the century. In his inauguration speech in the Academy in 1909, João do Rio spoke vaguely and confusedly of a "new esthetics." [2] Still it would be erroneous to consider sporadic eruptions, devoid as they were of any specific meaning, as historically precursive signs of the Modernist Movement. Among these were an article by E. Bertarelli in the *O Estado de São Paulo* (1914) concerning Italian Futurism and the first exhibition by Segall in São Paulo. Such isolated occurrences cannot properly be linked to the *history* of Modernism. If we move the date of birth too far back into the past or too far in the opposite direction, we run the risk of depriving the Movement of its specific shape and form. The same error has been committed by those who, at one time or another, have hastened to record the death of Modernism.

As a consequence, every effort should be made to observe social and spiritual junctures which are marked enough to allow us to think that at a certain moment the Modernist epoch began or that likewise at another point it began to draw to an end. As it sprang forth from a characteristic state of mind and disappeared with the advent of another state of mind, it does not seem difficult to recognize, in our social and intellectual history, the indisputable occurrences that distinguish one moment from another.

In the first place it is undeniable that a series of facts—literary and extraliterary—make, or might conventionally make, of the year 1916 a kind of locomotive turntable. The *Revista do Brasil* was founded under the joint editorship of L. P. Barreto, Júlio Mesquita, and Alfredo Pujol, in the name of the nationalism that, in the guise of various avatars, would be one of the most imperious dogmas of Modernism and of Brazilian life then and to come. At long last the Civil Code was promulgated, which thereby implied a new social age. Some attempted to organize a company in São Paulo that would sell shares for the purpose of publishing the works of São Paulo writers. This was, of course, the beginning of the tremendous growth in the publishing industry during the twenties. The September number of the *Revista do Brasil* initiated publication of *O Dialeto Caipira* by Amadeu Amaral, thus revealing a preoccupation with language which from Rui Barbosa to Mário de Andrade and Mário Neme came to be one of the main characteristics of Modernism.

Along the same lines of "discovery of Brazil," Roquette-

Pinto's *Rondônia* was published in 1916, while on the purely literary plane the *Casos e Impressões* by Adelino Magalhães presaged a revolution still lurking over the horizon. Properly speaking, the *Revista do Brasil,* down to the editorship of Paulo Prado (1923), was a vaguely academic journal, at first indifferent and later generally hostile to the Modernists. One of its most notable intellectual lights, Alfredo Pujol, in 1916 also initiated in the Sociedade de Cultura Artística a famous series of lectures on Machado de Assis, published in book form the following year. We should observe, however, that contrary to the fate of Coelho Neto and Rui Barbosa, the Modernists never openly repudiated Machado de Assis, owing no doubt to the fact that Machado's work at no point entered the dispute between the "old" and the "new" which determined the polemical attitudes of the time. On the other hand, if it is true that Olavo Bilac suffered from the intense campaign of denigration initiated by the Modernists (who confused Parnassianism with sub-Parnassianism and false Parnassianism), it is no less true that Bilac had set into motion the extraordinary nationalist campaign which resulted in the creation of the Nationalist League and the League of National Defense, both of which inspired broad social repercussions and the development of a characteristic frame of mind, as we shall later observe. The Modernists, whether they desired it or not, were the heirs of those nationalist aspirations. The Civil Code had as one of its most evident sociological aspects a recognition of the emancipation of woman, and that advance came together with nationalism in the book by M. F. Pinto Pereira, *A Mulher no Brasil,* also published in 1916.

These were the pseudopodia which the year 1916 put out toward the future and which contained a certain "futurism" in so far as they repudiated the past and reflected para-revolutionary aspirations. Thus an atmosphere was created that was extremely favorable to the Modernist campaign, and this fact allows us to understand why the vanguardists were often violently attacked more for their tactical excesses than for their strategic positions. In a study of the atmosphere which surrounded the Week of Modern Art, we can verify the fact that there occurred, at its inception, a kind of shock when it was learned that not all the

"Futurists" (Graça Aranha or Ronald de Carvalho, for example) were as "futuristic" as it had been feared.[3]

Parallel to these positive signs of 1916 are two negative occurrences worthy of mention: first, the death of José Veríssimo. This was the passing of the last great critic of the nineteenth century, perhaps the only great critic of the nineteenth century. Henceforth, Brazilian criticism would either be Modernist or it would not exist at all. By a singular chronological coincidence his book the *História da Literatura Brasileira,* the last great historiographic and critical treatise of the nineteenth century, was published in 1916. There was something symbolic in all of this: Veríssimo's book unquestionably struck a balance and in large part served as a manifesto against Sílvio Romero. It was, in truth, the end of the nineteenth century in Brazilian literature.

After that moment Modernist history began. I have already observed that Modernist history extended over three decades and successively sapped its energies in various literary genres. According to one point of view that I have long upheld (and which today seems generally accepted, especially after the vigorous confirmation it received in the *História do Modernismo Brasileiro* by Mário da Silva Brito), the Week of Modern Art was the apex of an entire intellectual process, rather than a point of departure. Modernism now took a serious look at itself. As it always happens, the vanguard then represented the group that first understood, however obscurely and contradictorily, the true nature of the random anxieties and manifestations which had been recurring with ever-increasing insistence since the first years of the new century. When the Week of Modern Art took place, I wrote in the *Panorama das Literaturas das Américas,*[4] Modernism was already *mature;* and if it was not so accepted by the general reading public, it was so recognized at least among the literati who at that time composed the most lively and creative sector of the Brazilian intelligentsia. The Week "officially" introduced a new state of mind and most assuredly was the most profound of all our literary revolutions.

In that Week our "literary century" began. Brazilian writers of the three decades that followed that Week lived under the sign of Modernism and created, even unwittingly and unintentionally, a "Modernist literature." It is not unreasonable to include here, in an organic view of Modernist chronology, some observations from that *Panorama*. Modernism, which was a movement crammed with theories and ideas, a revolution which in its early years was a revolution of manifestoes, set forth a system of programs which were slowly carried out, partially and successively, with no apparent connection among the several parts. So it was that in the first ten-year period Modernism was a poetic movement. The great names are names of poets (or of writers who expressed themselves in verse); the great books are books of poetry. The second ten-year period was marked by a depletion of the more specifically "Modernist" poetry; the ideological and technical conquests began to take root and attain greater equilibrium as they became less preoccupied with novelty and developed a certain gravity (which the first generation had lacked to a degree) in the creation of a poetry that we might call "definitive." Poetic Modernism was then dead, in so far as the distinguishing marks of its first years were dead: the critical spirit, the joke-poem, gratuitous exoticism, and the desire to shock. The new ten-year phase was marked by the appearance of the novel, which had been so rare in the first phase, and more especially by a certain kind of novel which lent the period an unmistakable stamp. The years between 1930 and 1940 are the years of the social and "Northeastern" novel. Initiated in 1928 by *A Bagaceira*, a novel of the droughts, that period saw the famous cycle written by José Lins do Rêgo, the proletarian novel of Amando Fontes, the political novel of Jorge Amado, and the psychological novel of Graciliano Ramos, to mention only writers of the first rank. Such was the power and popularity of that current that it tacitly rejected, for their marginality, novelists such as Octavio de Faria and Érico Veríssimo. The third decade of Modernism belonged to criticism. In the first period only one exceptional critic distinguished himself: Tristão de Athayde (the pseudonym of Alceu Amoroso Lima). In the second period some Modernists—novelists and poets—like Mário de Andrade, for example, created an admirable body of criticism; but it was subsidiary to their other activities and was deliberately a "criticism by the artist for artists." The forties saw the appearance of a distinguished "generation of critics," among whom Álvaro Lins and Antônio Cândido were outstanding.

It is evident that in all these periods there were interpenetrations. The outline just suggested is meant merely to emphasize the lines of force and the predominant tendencies. Of course, a moment finally arrived when the Modernist spirit disappeared; and its "death," periodically recorded since 1930, was finally accepted and the literary conscience clearly understood that it was beginning to live in a different era. This constituted one more crossroad similar to the one we observed in 1916. In my opinion, the significant facts of that transformation can be located in 1945. In that year, also in São Paulo, the first Congress of Brazilian Writers took place, which constituted a simultaneous affirmation of the professional and political spirit of the class. In an interview granted to Homero Senna,[5] Mário de Andrade called the Congress "admirable" and further added that it was a "true legitimation of the dignity of the Brazilian intelligentsia." If the Modernist spirit in literature dates from the Week of Modern Art in 1922, it may be thought that the *modern* spirit resulted, to a large extent, from the first Congress of Writers which, in that regard, repressed and mingled sources which could be identified from some years back.

Leaving aside the *Poesias Completas* of Manuel Bandeira (Rio de Janeiro: Americ-Edit) which, on the historical plane, means little because Bandeira had since 1924 been in the habit of periodically gathering all his works in collected editions, it was also in 1945 that the first great "balance sheet," "inventory," or "testament" of a typical Modernist was published: the *Poesias Reunidas* of Oswald de Andrade,[6] which contained *Pau Brasil, Primeiro Caderno do Aluno de Poesia Oswald de Andrade, Cântico dos Cânticos para Flauta e Violão*, and *Alguns Poemas Menores*. Another "inventory" by the same author, this one of his critical work, was *Ponta de Lança*, published by the Livraria Martins, a strange conglomerate of Modernist apostleship (already an anachronism), of settlement of disputes, and literary politics. Simultaneously, the Editôra José Olympio issued *Chão*, the second volume of *Marco Zero*, the Modernist novel which just missed achieving greatness.

Two years earlier, revealing an evident transformation in the

intellectual spirit, Mário Neme had initiated a series of provocative interviews with young writers in the *O Estado de São Paulo*.
But it was not until 1945, under the title of *Plataforma da Nova
Geração*, that these interviews were published in book form by the
Editôra Globo in Pôrto Alegre, an obvious and direct answer to
the *Testamento de Uma Geração* by Edgard Cavalheiro, which the
same publishing house had issued in 1944. Testaments and plat-
forms in various guises increased in number around 1945. *Brigada Ligeira* (São Paulo: Martins) by Antônio Cândido, published
at this time, is also a platform of the most recent criticism. It is
no surprise that we find in it the first critical balance sheet of any
importance on the novels of Oswald de Andrade.

Reflecting the two divergent orientations that poetry either
had taken or would take in the future—the political and the esthetical—some significant volumes appeared in 1945: *A Rosa do Povo*
by Carlos Drummond de Andrade, the beloved son of Modernism
(Rio de Janeiro: Editôra José Olympio), and *O Engenheiro* by João
Cabral de Melo Neto, the precursor of all the poetic engineering
of the subsequent years. Also religious or "spiritualist" poetry,
situated midway between those two main tendencies, was represented in 1945 by *Mundo Enigma* by Murilo Mendes (Pôrto
Alegre: Globo) and by *Mar Absoluto* (Rio de Janeiro: Livros de
Portugal) by Cecília Meireles.

On the negative side, the sudden death of Mário de Andrade
at this time was the symbolic catastrophe which concluded the
"Modernist era," for he was the only writer who had truly identified his own intellectual destiny with the fate of the Movement.
He was the "conscience of Modernist literature," just as, on higher
planes, he had been an exemplary literary conscience.

We can see how the web of events, literary and extraliterary,
contributed in 1945 to bring the Modernist process to a close just
as, in 1916, it had served to set that process in motion. Thus, in
the main, Modernism identified our intellectual temper during
the period between the two world wars. It was born of the state
of mind shaped by the Great War out of the spiritual disquietude
of the first decade of the century. It disappeared with the new state
of conscience that resulted from World War II and, as a consequence, reflected a particular kind of artistic civilization which was

initially the Brazilian manifestation of the "roaring twenties" and later served as the expression of political unrest. Finally, in its last moments, it was the instrument of return to literature with no esthetic or political ax to grind.

These landmarks save us from the error of looking too far into the past for the origins of Modernism, which would be no more than a bookish illusion, and they also prevent our prolonging the Movement or killing it out of season (which has been, and still is, the commonest tendency). To bring this aspect of the matter to a close, let us say that if the so-called "generation of 1945" did deserve the sarcasm of Oswald de Andrade [7] and if it does not appear to have earned the right to take the place of Modernism, it is nonetheless certain that the generation vindicated, by its mere existence, the presence of different ideals in literature.

With Modernism thus delimited between 1916 and 1945, this present study will be concerned with the works published between those years as well as with the writers, Modernist or not, who preceded the Movement or lived past it.

Toward a Definition

Modernism was the reflection of a disquietude and a dissatis-
faction. The vanguard of the Brazilian intelligentsia was obviously
dissatisfied in 1916 with the frightening literary anemia which had
resulted from the weakening of Parnassianism and Symbolism.
From that time to 1921, literary vanguard above all else in Brazil
meant Monteiro Lobato. Ideally he ought to have been the natural
leader of Modernism. Oswald de Andrade recognized this in the
forties when he wrote: "But you, Lobato, are at fault for not having claimed your lion's share in the violent, but definitive, changes
that have been developing since the Week of Modern Art in 1922.
You were the Gandhi of Modernism. You fasted and produced
very likely in that and in other areas the most efficacious passive
resistance in which a patriotic vocation might take pride." [8] To a
far greater degree than Anita Malfatti, he was the "protomartyr
of Modernism," in the sense that the new generations at first
ignored him and later combatted him and usurped a role that he
might have legitimately claimed as his own. The entire sad spectacle of his frustration, of his undeniable literary resentment, dates
from here.

From his pen we have our first documents against traditionalism. Word for word, his famous article of 1915, "Urupês," could
and should have been the first Modernist manifesto:

The balsamic Indianism of Alencar has crumbled to dust with the advent of the Rondons who, quite the contrary of depicting Indians in a drawing room with reminiscences of Chateaubriand in their heads and with *Iracema* open on their knees, rather take to trudging through the backlands while clutching a Winchester. Peri has died, the incomparable idealization of natural man as Rousseau conceived him, the prototype of such great human perfection who, in the novel, shoulder to shoulder with the highest civilized types, surpasses them all in beauty of soul and body. The cruel ethnology of the present-day backlanders has set a true savage over against him, ugly and brutal, angular and uninteresting, as incapable physically of uprooting a palm tree as he is morally incapable of loving Ceci. To our joy—and to that of D. Antônio de Mariz—Alencar did not see these creatures. He dreamed them as did Rousseau. Otherwise we would have Araré's son roasting the beauteous maiden on a pyre of good Brazilwood instead of following her adoringly through the jungle like the beneficent Ariel of the Paquequer.

Who could fail to recognize in these words the immediate source of Oswald de Andrade's Cannibal Manifesto of 1928? That well-known document, which set out at that time to represent the artistic vanguard, was quite obviously nearly fifteen years behind the times. The expressionist style of the manifesto was, at several junctures, a mere paraphrase of Lobato's text: "Only cannibalism unites us. . . . Against all catechisms . . . Against the Indian bearing a firebrand. The Indian who is the son of Mary, godson of Catherine de Medicis and son-in-law of D. Antônio de Mariz." [9]

Creating in that article the character of Jeca Tatu, Monteiro Lobato proposed the first type of literary "hero," in opposition to Peri, Alencar's idealized Indian, which our modern literature saw. At the same time he unleashed the campaign against sham regionalism which the Modernists soon after expropriated for themselves, a campaign in which Jeca himself became embroiled. But it was not only the Cannibal Manifesto that Lobato presaged in "Urupês." It was also the central postulate in the *Retrato do Brasil*:

In the midst of Brazilian nature—so varied in form and color, with the foliage of the cedars burgeoning under the first rains of September, the blue-backed manikan takes flight, the bees dart like streaks of sunshine, living emeralds flutter, and locusts, a dionysian life in constant flow—the backlander is the melancholy mushroom on the rotting log, silently drowsing in the dark recesses of some dank grotto. He alone does not speak, he sings not, he laughs not, he loves not. He alone, in the heart of all this bustling life, lives not. . . .[10]

Thus two significant works of Modernism—both of which appeared in the crucial year 1928—or, rather, the total development of one of the most important underground currents of the Movement had already been expressed in 1915 in the article by Monteiro Lobato. On the more immediately literary level, in 1918 he had the opportunity of striking the crucial literary balance regarding the lack of originality then reigning when he wrote the preface for Borges Netto's book, No Silêncio:

. . . when Eça, then a novelty, was all the rage in Brazil, unconscious imitation produced the most disastrous effects. Eça killed many a promising vocation. He made pale satellites out of talents otherwise quite capable of producing their own light. He gave birth to a mechanical imitation as a result of which every fat man issued from the mold of the Counselor, all the women were Louisas, the bohemians were all like Egas, which made of the author a mere sheet of carbon paper. After that sickness came "fialhitis." Everything reeked of Fialho. The powerful orchestration of Fialho's style was dazzling. That polychromatism of the idea, his art which was a composite of all the arts, his style which painted and sang, sculpted and symphonized, cursed and wept, battered and lulled to sleep, his new language wherein all the resources extorted from sister tongues could be found . . . turned the heads a thousandfold of youths who were suffering the pangs of artistic puberty. . . . Infected by these two fads, our young writers on the threshold of their careers coughed their whooping cough until prose went out of style. We suffered from versophilia. To debut came to mean to appear before the public with a slender volume of sonnets in one's hand whether out of sloth—it always requires less effort to hack out the fourteen lines of a sonnet than to construct a short story, a novella, or a novel—or out of sluggishness fostered by Bilac's brilliance, the truth is that prose fell into disregard as though it had little or no value at all. Freed from all epidemic influences, the prose that is still being written—if it does not reveal outright imitation—also does not shun the old national vices. Loose, obese, lazy, insipid, with no control over the bounteous qualities which make of Camilo's prose the marvel of the Portuguese language that it is, this prose, under the treatment of the novice, turns to jelly. The adjective takes on the function of the birdie in the field: lavish and excessive as it underplays the design in order to lay on the color with a heavy brush stroke. The progressive verb which enervates the action—"he went around doing," "he was in the course of doing," etc.—is used and abused for the express purpose of vitiating the sentence. Naturalistic description, a disease caught from Zola, is preferred apparently because it annoys the reader. One sets out to say badly in ten words what might better be said in two. We see smaller and smaller doses of ideas, the stupidity of torture, entangling complications. . . . These vices have made of our prose a colorless and tasteless tapioca pudding with little nutritional value. If we add to this bad habit of excessive psychologizing —picked up, no doubt, from Bourget, Goncourt, and other talented bores—the static short story, the motionless novella, the novel that is from start to finish little more than puff paste, then we can clearly understand why the reading public rejected this dull prose as a useless art form which labored much and gave birth to mice.

No Modernist ever wrote any more merciless criticism than this against the "literature of the past." Because all the Modernist critics preferred the brilliant discussion of great literary principles and theoretical ideas, none of them left behind any analysis that could be compared with the objectivity and sense of stylistic technique found in these words by Lobato. In a similar vein, Marques Rebêlo, recalling the predominant state of mind of the years of his youth, wrote: "We were children who bore in our untutored hearts a restless craving for new things, a longing to soar to uncharted heights, a whole new set of hopes. We were living in an age of political, social, and esthetic upheavals. The colossal erosion which the war of 1918 had incited in the exhausted bourgeois world finally came crashing in upon the distant beaches of Brazil in mighty breakers." [11] Young intellectuals, as we see, keenly sensed the exhaustion of literature on the national level; and after 1917 this tedium was heightened by the unrest caused by the new esthetic experiments in Europe before, during, and immediately after the war. These new currents were beginning to reach our shores at this very time.

Why 1917? Because 1917 is a date of signal importance: it was the year of the second exhibition of paintings by Anita Malfatti (1896–1964) and of her violent clash with Monteiro Lobato. It marked a turning point for the Modernist generation as well as for Monteiro Lobato himself, who had already attained considerable stature as a writer. That year induced in the Modernists an attitude of defiance, which they maintained throughout the early period of their revolutionary heroics. It led Monteiro Lobato to undertake the "passive resistance" which Oswald de Andrade would later mention. Therefore, it is of the greatest importance that we study and correctly understand this event in Brazilian intellectual history.

The Anita Malfatti Affair

The Anita Malfatti affair has come down to us charged with so much emotion that even today it is virtually foolhardy to attempt to face the event objectively. For the Modernist and post-Modernist generations, Anita Malfatti was exactly as Lourival Gomes Machado summed her up many years after the fact: the "protomartyr of modern art in Brazil." At the same time Lobato, author of an article which was much more violent in its title than in its content,[12] came to symbolize the lack of understanding on the part of the reactionary forces. We must point out from the beginning that it is incorrect to say that modern art was received with hostility in Brazil: the opposite was closer to the truth. Mário da Silva Brito, in his invaluable *História do Modernismo Brasileiro,* writes that Lasar Segall was treated with extreme kindness in 1913 on the occasion of his first exhibition. The same is true of Anita Malfatti, who apart from Lobato's truculent behavior, was always received with considerable sympathy, even by the most conservative periodicals. It is enough to read what Nestor Rangel Pestana (presumably) wrote in May of 1914 on the occasion of her first appearance in São Paulo:

Senhorita Malfatti is unquestionably in possession of a splendid talent. Her studies have a spontaneity, a vigor of expres-

20

sion, and a breadth of execution which only true artistic temperaments have at their disposal. In these artists the power of synthesis is immediately evident in the least of their studies and sketches. In addition to that, her sense of color is rich and balanced. Her means of expression—which are still hindered by a beginner's technique which is the more notable considering the short time of her apprenticeship—are nonetheless powerful for the emotion they succeed in awakening.[13]

Since these words appeared in the columns of the prestigious *O Estado de São Paulo,* they could only be interpreted as being extremely encouraging and we can see that Anita Malfatti initiated her career under exceptionally favorable auspices. It was even true that Lobato's article attracted attention more because of its provocative and polemical title than because of what it said. Lobato's text, after all, contained nothing exceptional, considering that it constituted an unfavorable review. In all events, the article is no more incomprehensible and sarcastic than Mário de Andrade's guffaws when, *before* Lobato's review appeared, he attended Anita's exhibition for the first time.[14] It is no less a false notion to depict Monteiro Lobato blindly attacking all modern art. In the first place, the tone and the style which he adopted against Anita Malfatti in no way differ from his usual expression in other polemical writing, including his criticisms of *academic artists.* It is sufficient to recall his notes in the *Revista do Brasil* concerning plans for the erection of the Monument to Brazilian Independence. Beyond that, Mário da Silva Brito recalls that he was from the beginning one of Brecheret's greatest enthusiasts; and Brecheret, at that stage of our artistic history, had the same renovative significance as Anita Malfatti.

Just as in literature he had created the character of Jeca Tatu, it was Lobato who first had the idea of depicting in a work of art the imaginary character of the imp Saci, another of Modernism's literary myths. To that end, in 1917 he instigated a research project and a competition. Anita Malfatti herself entered the latter along with several fellow artists. In November of that year, in the *Revista do Brasil,* Lobato closely examined the works on view in the Saci Exhibition and wrote, even before the appearance of the slanderous article of December 20, 1917, his first attack on Anita's style. From that article one can conclude that his quarrel was aimed more at the new schools in painting rather than at the artist:

> Senhorita Malfatti has also contributed her own -ism. A rider and his horse, placidly meandering along a red road, fall down in terror when they happen upon a creature from the other world hanging from a cane of bamboo. The rider topples down, the horse topples down, the horse's head topples down as it attempts to leap from its neck, ridiculously elongated as if it were made of the Amazon's best rubber. I call this genre "topple-ism." Like all the -ism genres in painting—cubism, futurism, impressionism, marinettism—it is *hors concours*. It is no good for critics to talk about these -isms because they do not understand them. In this regard critics run neck and neck with the public who also do not understand. We can only believe that the author-artists understand them as well as critics and public. In the midst of this general non-understanding, one is well advised to tip one's hat and pass quickly by.

This congenital hostility, which almost immediately produced the grapes of wrath of Modernism, does not necessarily mean that Lobato was a partisan of strict academism, of which he has so often been accused. On that same note, even before his adverse criticism of Anita Malfatti's work, Lobato had written the following words with regard to the artistic problems created by the competition:

> To paint a character type who is purely subjective, unstable in form, filled with variation, existing only in the imagination of the backlander is a task that requires from the artist slightly more talent than that needed to paint a burgeoning melon, portray a blustering Cavaliere Ufficiale, or copy the background of the Tabatingüera, a favorite subject for our landscape artists who grow delirious on a few extremely attractive brush strokes borrowed from Venice. It requires inventiveness, it requires composition, an excellence of composition that has no ready-made points of reference or, rather,

former works of the same genre which have long since been hallowed, points over which the painter mounts his own work without the public's taking notice. Perhaps for that reason our Brazilian painters of Britannia and Cavaliere Ufficiale have abstained from entering the competition. As they were talented painters of Absolutions, Salomes, and Tabatingüeras it did not befit them to lower their masks—Regnaults of the Café Paulista and Corots of the Várzea do Carmo—long enough to participate in the dangerous adventure of *algo nuevo.* They stuck by their *algo viejo* and were wise to have done so. One of the ways to have talent is to feign talent.

Anita Malfatti's exhibition, which opened practically at the time of this skirmish, furnished Lobato with the opportunity of settling his accounts thoroughly with the *-isms,* rather than with the artists. Still, we lack an element which would be of considerable importance: the personal and verbal reactions of Anita Malfatti and her friends to Lobato's first note. However, it is enlightening to recall that Nestor Rangel Pestana (presumably), in the *Revista do Brasil* of January, 1918, wrote a detailed criticism of the exhibition which discussed the artistic problems involved. The tone was sympathetic, but the review was not without a certain disagreement which was exactly the same as Monteiro Lobato's:

NEW MOVEMENT IN THE ARTS: MALFATTI EXHIBITION. The young São Paulo painter, Anita Malfatti, can be proud of the fact that she has disturbed our stagnant artistic waters with her latest exhibition. That disturbance never went beyond a small circle of amateurs and some reviews in our daily press, which were not entirely favorable to the artist. At all events, one discusses only that which exhibits true value. Senhorita Malfatti possesses that value to a considerably high degree. Her first exhibition in São Paulo gave high hopes to all lovers of art. In the works of her apprenticeship one could already sense the assertion of an individuality, a rare vigor in her artistic touch and a general conception of painting which announced a genuine "artistic temperament." In the canvases recently exhibited these same quali-

ties are still displayed. However, besides the good qualities
certain flaws appear and these seem very serious to us in that
they betray a deviation from an original orientation which
could well be fatal to the promising career of so talented a
painter.

Senhorita Malfatti has allowed herself to be "emballée"
by the excesses of the so-called "futurists," and she has placed
her splendid talent at the service of that artistic trend which
cannot even be called a school.

Her good faith and the very inexperience of her youth
preserve the illusion for her that she is making "futurism."
There does not exist, in her new manner, the slightest trace
of sincerity, although her intent is perfectly honest. However, Senhorita Malfatti, under the pretext of breaking with
the conventions of established art, without questioning has
adopted the entire preposterous conventionalism of a false
art whose only exhibitors are the "ratés" and the unbalanced.

The adepts of the "new school" labor under the crazed
presumption that they are reproducing movement according
to the reality of our sensations.

We should recall that all movement operates in nature
with a rapidity very often greater than the most rapid of our
means of expression. We can easily see the absurdity of any
attempt to reproduce this movement integrally by means of
the image.

Art can never integrally reproduce movement. The role
of art is to suggest to those who contemplate a work—a figure,
for example—the series of movements which that figure would
make in the execution of a given intention or to create the
illusion of life, since life is movement.

For this purpose it was not necessary to invent futurism.

All the modern schools, especially those which have developed since the triumph of "open air" and Impressionism,
have tended toward that end and have attained extraordinary
results. The substitution of the theory of values and of luminous painting based on the fusion of colors revealed by the
solar spectrum for conventional shapes and shadows offers
limitless resources to artists.

None of them, however, can dispense with the notion
of form and design which is the basis for everything, the

indispensable framework for any artistic construction. Now, the futurists suppress design and give themselves over to the most daring fantasia of color. Their painting speaks a language that is incomprehensible because it is illogical and irrelevant. Rodin knew, as no one else, how to create the supreme expression of movement in sculpture. No sculptors of any age have been more realistic or more unaffected than this brilliant artist whom France has just lost. In every human body that he brought to life in clay the arms are a prolongation of the shoulders and the legs support the trunk.

The futurists are not in the least troubled by joining an arm to a head or by causing a leg to sprout from an armpit as long as they "create" the impression of movement, the tremor of life.

Senhorita Malfatti has adopted the liberties of this pseudo-school in the creation of her "Negra Baiana" which is to us poor normal souls a teratological case study. However, to one side of the Negress she has placed some pineapples which are so well drawn and so perfect that they would delight a botanist. . . .

Where is the school, the method, the system?

On the head of a man lustily painted, with a masterful indication of the planes, perfectly in accord with the laws of normal painting, she has tinted the face green and yellow . . . and she is convinced that she has created futurism.

Moreover, in her etchings, which are indeed splendid, she reveals a careful technique without the slightest trace of evil influence, such as the "Cabeça de Egípcia" which is delightfully fresh and spontaneous.

Every time she has attempted to affect her art, to adapt it to the tenets of futurism, she has committed serious errors in design and she has employed purely conventional colors. In those works only some sections can be saved, those in which the artist's sincerity, reasserting its rights, has prevented her employment of the extravagance of futurism.

There is not enough space in this review for a meticulous examination of Senhorita Malfatti's work. It would not be difficult, however, to demonstrate, canvas by canvas, what has been said above as general statement.

It is one's duty to say it because few artists have had so triumphant a debut as Senhorita Malfatti: it would be profoundly lamentable to see an artistic organization such as this painter possesses lose itself in a repudiation of her esthetic orientation. Senhorita Malfatti has reached a decisive moment in her career. If she does not completely forsake her new trend to devote herself more seriously to the study of design, she will risk total failure. We hope we are wrong in this forecast. Nonetheless, we believe that the facts corroborate our opinions.

We can reproach this criticism for its lack of foresight with regard to the subsequent fate and development of the plastic arts in the twentieth century. We cannot, however, argue with its informed point of view and the solid foundations of its esthetic analysis. The great historic import of Anita Malfatti's exhibition lies in her having introduced into Brazil the monumental esthetic debate which had dominated artistic circles in Europe since the turn of the century. What came to be our modern artistic turmoil, the cosmopolitan and international side of our Modernism, came in through a little door on Líbero Badaró Street. Guilherme de Almeida attributed the name "Futurists," which was originally given to the Brazilian Modernists, to a misunderstanding stemming from an article written by Oswald de Andrade, "O Meu Poeta Futurista" (1921).[15] From what has been said, it is easily seen that such an observation has little bearing on the truth. All the confusion over modern art, bound up in the burning question of Futurism, dates from Anita Malfatti's second exhibition.

However, Guilherme de Almeida's error did serve the purpose of demonstrating that the Modernists did not attribute to the Anita Malfatti episode the decisive and symbolic importance that later was granted to it. Moreover, Nestor Rangel Pestana, as well as Monteiro Lobato, cast some doubt on the artist's sincerity and on the esthetic viability of the new school. In the same vein as Monteiro Lobato's review, "Paranoia or Hoax," Menotti del Picchia, who came late to Modernism and for a few months became the Movement's ostensible militant leader, wrote in 1920, long after the first two critics, an article of violent attack on modern art. This was published in the *Correio Paulistano*:

In that gallant and daring psychopathy of the unprecedented, some have taken to the morbid, the bizarre, the hermetic. The mediocre, in their delirium, have engendered idiotic gongorisms; the geniuses, in their creative acts, have gone past the portals of the nebulae which the fanatical have accepted as they pretend to understand the absurd. Hence the appearance in art of a sickly creation which is called cubism and of an enigmatic and crazed school which is called futurism. Nothing, however, is lost. The actions of the new artists have gone to such extremes that the conservative elements have been rallied into action. . . . Our lack of critical sense lifts up the merciless sledge hammer of contempt to destroy that entire patrimony of glory. Out of a kind of decadentism which has ignominiously flourished since the war's end, in a growing frenzy to reshape the face of the world, our modern-day artists mock the past and, by way of irritating irony, create a puerile art, absurd and ephemeral, which they deify under the aegis of primitivism and candor. Admirable artists, infected by this new current, make a cult of this sickly art which tomorrow, through the same reaction of less radical artists, will be merely a ridiculous memory in the history of art.[16]

Obviously, Monteiro Lobato by himself has settled accounts for many others—and often they are the best minds of his time—but it must be clarified at this point that along with the historical significance of Anita Malfatti's exhibition goes the uncommon importance of Nestor Rangel Pestana's article. The fact is that he moved the debate across the ocean to Brazil and literally repeated what the theoreticians of Futurist painting had been saying about "simultaneism" since the turn of the century. As Pär Bergman has written: "during the teens there were in Paris many debates and arguments on the ideas of 'simultanéité,' 'simultaneità,' 'simultanéisme,' 'simultanisme' and other terms of this type." [17] That sensibility, he adds (p. 147), should be considered in its relationship to the Futurist cult of speed, but "the first futurists who attacked the technical problem of 'simultaneità' were the painters" (p. 158). In an interview of 1912, Marinetti stated that Futurist painters "wish to paint movement." In the "technical manifesto,"

La Pittura Futurista, we read these words: "Everything moves, everything runs, everything turns. A figure is no longer static before our eyes. Rather it appears and disappears endlessly. Because of the persistence of the image on our retina, things succeed one another like vibrations in the space through which they pass. Thus a race horse does not have four legs: it has twenty legs and their movements are triangular." [18]

The problem of the plastic rendition of movement, raised by Anita Malfatti's paintings (or by some of them, because we should not forget that a number of the canvases in the exhibition were not Futurist), was discussed at length by Mário de Andrade some years later (1925) in his notable "treatise on certain tendencies in Modernist poetry," *A Escrava Que Não É Isaura.* Note N in that volume reveals that the polemical support lent to Anita Malfatti by the Modernists at that particular point in time was purely tactical: "The spatial work of art aspires to immediate equilibrium. For that reason simultaneity in a painting is nearly always flawed, anti-esthetic, ultra-impressionistic, and nearly always destructive of true pictorial qualities. The temporal work of art aspires to mediate equilibrium. Simultaneity can very well exist in this art form because the very comprehension of a temporal work of art constitutes a simultaneity of acts of memory. The interaction of simultaneity of sensations is a phenomenon which we observe in life every day."

This was exactly what Anita Malfatti's first critics wrote. It happens, merely, that these critics had not yet experienced the impact of the cinema, whose influence on the arts in general, and on the plastic arts in particular, was incalculable. Mário de Andrade, who wrote in the *Escrava*: "The Malherbe of the modern history of the arts is cinematography" was, of course, less in the right than Nestor Rangel Pestana and Monteiro Lobato when he refused to admit any viability whatsoever for simultaneist painting. In light of that fact, everything seems to indicate that the "trauma" suffered by Anita Malfatti as a result of Lobato's intemperate criticism was a subsequent rationalization to explain certain details of her career. The Modernists themselves seem to have forgotten her completely in the theoretical debates which ensued. Between 1917 and 1924, when the first doctrinary books of the

new school appeared, Modernism had already passed two fundamental stages of its history: on the one hand, it had accepted
esthetic internationalization and had sought to reconcile it to
nationalism of theme; on the other hand, it had definitely rejected
any compromise with Futurism and had declared itself purely
Modernist.

The rejection of Futurism indicated at least a tacit forswear-
ing of Anita Malfatti. The approval of the international put
painting back into the ideal picture of the patron saints. As a
matter of fact, what Modernism most vehemently wished to cast
into oblivion was its suspicious origin in the pictorial arts. If the
Week of Modern Art was the "four arts ball," it is no less certain
that after that date each of the arts sought its own specific destiny.
As she purposefully opened her doors on Líbero Badaró Street in
1917, Anita Malfatti unwillingly and unwittingly also opened
the doors of the Municipal Theatre in 1922.

The Theoretical Foundations

Marinetti committed his gravest error when he gave the name of Futurism to his movement. As a matter of fact, what he as well as the other Futurists wanted was to discover the artistic style that best represented modern life, i.e., the present: Futurism wished to be a kind of "presentism" or, as the Brazilian Futurists soon discovered, a kind of *modernism*. Pär Bergman speaks of the "cult which the futurists made of what they believed to be 'modern,' i.e., their 'modernolatry,' a word which was probably coined by Boccioni in 1914 and which considerably gratified Marinetti." [19] Marinetti later referred to the term as a "magic word" and a "fruitful word." Because Marinetti burned his bridges in 1910, he abandoned all possibility of return, which might have metamorphosed his Futurism into Modernism after the manner of the Brazilians.

The fact is, there existed a latent but conscious "modernism" prior to the advent of Futurism. From the opening years of the century, Pär Bergman recalls, references to "life," to the "present," and to the "future" abounded in poetry, as did the word "modern." These references were always linked to mechanical techniques and inventions which, at that time or in any other, represented the point of departure of modernity. It is a well-known fact that after 1905 the vanguardist group began to create the entire "modern" movement, which World War I for a brief spell interrupted and cut short. The generation of the twenties harvested the crop that was planted in the teens. Seen in that light, far from being a catastrophe, the war was providential because it lent time for maturation and divulgation to the very techniques that justified and gave meaning to Modernism: the cinema, the airplane, the automobile, and the machine in general.

Reflecting the "modernist age" much more than the Futurist delirium, Rubens Borba de Moraes wrote in 1924 that "our age is materially superior to all others," and he added a statement that might easily have surprised those who had not witnessed the subtle transformation from Futurism to Modernism: "But that is of no importance to us." What was important, according to Modernism's first treatise writer, what mattered to the modern artist was *to translate our age and its personality*. He himself italicized that postulate, and since immediately after that he added that "a day will come when our artists will be considered old-fashioned," he consequently prepared a way for the transition from Modernism to the modern, which has been the fundamental characteristic of the third phase of the Movement.[20] Of course, the most evident symbol of "modern life" was *speed*, an external manifestation of an essential and profound fact: man's understanding of the deepest implications of the concept of time. Rubens Borba de Moraes, with great acuity, or at least acuity more notable than that of the first Futurists who had mistaken the cloud for Juno, immediately identified the singularity of the concept and traced it correctly to its source: the theory of relativity, which was itself the first document of that new phase in the intellectual history of mankind.

Viewed in this light, the central chapter of the entire Modernist theory might well be read in the words that he wrote in part eight of his book:

The factor which has most deeply influenced the development of the new esthetics is Time. Einstein tells us that time does not exist. Accordingly, time *in itself*, metaphysical time, perhaps does not exist (we knew that a good long while before Einstein). But material time does exist. Just ask anyone who

has missed a train. For the mystic of the French thirteenth
century, for the Hindus, for the Indo-Chinese of the Khmer
Empire, time did not exist. Men who spent two hundred
years in the building of a cathedral, sculpting the façade of
a palace, had no notion of time, of passing life. We think
differently. The intensity of modern life has sharpened our
notion of material time. The North American businessman
is acutely aware of the minute; the engineer on any railroad
except the Sul-Mineira Line is also aware of the minute. The
backlander is aware only of day and night; the Eskimo of
winter and summer. The man who, in the midst of rapid
business transactions is aware of the minute, in the backlands
knows only the hour.

It is not difficult to note that under that guise of typically
Modernist irony Rubens Borba de Moraes was pointing up the
absolute intellectual revolution along with Brazil's inability to
keep apace of world time, an inability which, in large measure,
continues down to the present day. That for the most part
explains, indeed truly does explain, the immense *mental* resistance
(not only esthetic and literary resistance) which Modernism encountered. The vanguard opened doors onto a new world which
the men "of the past" did not choose to enter. The vanguard
foretold the unknown and thereby established *cosmic terror,* of
which Graça Aranha spoke in the midst of general incomprehension, including that of the Modernists themselves. Rubens Borba
de Moraes continues his reasoning in these words:

Modern-day inventions have transformed our senses. Man no
longer has merely five senses: he has hundreds and thousands.
The speed of modern life forces the artist to depict quickly
what he felt quickly, before the intellect intervenes. From
that condition was born the synthesization of modern art.
Time! . . . Besides cinematographic synthesization, the diz-
zying whirl of modern life also creates in the artist a facility
of close analysis produced by the multiplicity of different
facts which occur over a short space of time, almost simultaneously. Proust spends 229 pages describing his arrival at a

ball given by the Princess de Guermantes. And Proust is one of the greatest representatives of modern literature.

Proust is a result of the tumult of contemporary life. Speed sharpened his senses to such a degree that he sees and feels what man from the pre-speed era could never feel. His incredible sensitivity is not only a consequence of his illness but also of his perception stimulated by the intense life that today's man leads. The charm of Proust lies in his telling us everything and suggesting to us what he cannot tell owing to his lack of *time*. In the future, when critics wish to cite a representative of our age, they will name Proust.[21]

All of this is much more trenchant and far better expressed than the famous book by Jean Epstein, which the Modernists had made their vade mecum. However, the proof that really new states of mind require a certain amount of time to enter the current of conscious thought can be seen in the fact that it took eight years for Renato Almeida, one of Graça Aranha's two favorite disciples (the other was Ronald de Carvalho), to publish a volume with the significant title of *Velocidade* in 1932.[22] Its opening words were the following: "If one element can characterize civilization, which has transformed Humanity after the discovery of steam power, it is speed." One of the theses of the book, repeating what at that time the rest of the theoreticians had already comprehended, was that speed had changed human psychology and conditioned modern life: "Speed is the modern spiritual category" (p. 48). And referring more directly to literature: "Speaking of speed and its reflection in letters, in certain expressions, we must not fail to mention one of the most beautiful poems to that new beauty, and that is the Futurist manifesto *A nova religião moral da velocidade* by Marinetti. It is a vigorously dazzling canto to the new heroism, a prayer to the divinity with which we are fused when we make a mad dash in automobile, train, or airplane." [23]

The cinema was the means of artistic expression that provided the Modernists and Futurists with the instrument for creating a temporal art, or an art in motion. Renato Almeida said that "with the cinema a new language was born" (p. 85), and although he asserted that the cinema still awaited "its artist of true genius," he did not hesitate to name it as the art form typical of modern times (times which the cinema, as a matter of fact—which was, in Jean Epstein's words, "beyond Descartes"—mocked in 1936 in the Chaplin film *Modern Times*). The same Epstein, in his book which became the bible of the first Modernists, *La Poésie d'Aujourd'hui*,[24] wrote an important chapter entitled "Le cinéma et les lettres modernes," which opens with these words: "The cinema saturates modern literature. Likewise that mysterious art form has taken to itself a good deal of literature" (p. 169). It is there that we should locate the immediate and direct source of the well-known selection from *A Escrava Que Não É Isaura*:

A WORK OF ART IS A MACHINE FOR PRODUCING EMOTIONAL TUMULT. And we have come to discover that truth because Malherbe has arrived. The Malherbe of the modern history of the arts is cinematography. As it depicts the immediate features of life and nature with more perfection than the plastic arts and the word (and take note that cinematography is still an art form in its infancy; no one can tell what development it will have in the future), as it depicts life as no other art form has in the past, it has become the Eureka! of the pure art forms. Only then was it understood that painting could be and ought to be only painting, balance of colors, lines, shapes on a surface; a synthetic, interpretive, and stylizing deformation and not an imperfect commentary, and nearly always a merely superficial commentary, on life. Only then could we understand sculpture as dynamism of light on shape or the architectural and monumental character of its interpretation.

The problem of speed and dynamism, which was artistically solved by the cinema (accepting this evidence, Mário de Andrade once more disclaimed all attempts to establish "movement" in painting, thus taking the side of Nestor Rangel Pestana against Anita Malfatti), is closely allied to the new vision of the world symbolized by the airplane. As early as 1918 Jean Cocteau minutely described in *Le Cap de Bonne Espérance* the dizziness (in the medical and the figurative sense of the word) unleashed by the airplane's take-off and the spectacle of the world seen from the air. The fact that in 1936 Flávio de Carvalho, in *Os Ossos do Mundo,* still thought it necessary to describe the same sensation merely reiterates Brazil's backwardness, to which I have previously alluded. However, in the second number of *Klaxon* (June 15, 1922), Luís Aranha perhaps created in the "Poema Giratório" the only poetic work of Modernism that expressed *movement,* speed, gyration, psychological and even geographical simultaneity, thus reflecting his reading of Cocteau, as in a poem like "O Aeroplano":

> I would like to be an air ace and fly high
> Over the city of my birth!
> Higher still than the bronze laments
> Of the cataleptic cathedrals:
> Close, close to the blue almost disappearing in the sky
> Far from the houses growing tiny
> Far, far away from this asphalt pavement . . .[25]

This is merely a paraphrase of Cocteau. But the "religion of speed" came soon after:

> If one day
> My body should fall from the airplane,
> I would passionately spread my arms
> For the blue plunge into the transparent afternoon . . .
>   .   .   .   .   .
> My sudden fall would draw a line 'cross the sky
>
> Rapid and precise,
> Cutting the air in an ecstasy of space
> My body would sing
> Whistling
> The symphony of speed . . .[26]

In number 6 of *Klaxon* (October 15, 1922), Sérgio Milliet, who at that time was the French poet Serge Milliet, put the dream of speed in his "Rêverie":

> Ah!   the automobile century
> airplane
> 75
> Speed above all SPEED [27]

Speed and the view of life represented by the cinema and the airplane were obviously linked to simultaneism, which was the
guiding esthetic principle of the Modernists in all the art forms.
The "esthetic and technical" postulates expressed by Mário de
Andrade in *A Escrava Que Não É Isaura* were the following:

> TECHNICAL—Free verse, free Rhyme, victory over the
>   dictionary
> ESTHETIC—Substitution of the Subconscious Order for
>   the
>   Intellectual Order
>   Speed and synthesis
>   Polyphonism

And he added: "I use the term Polyphonism for the Simultaneity
of the French, using Epstein as my authority, the Simultaneism
of Fernand Divoire, the Synchronism of Marcello Fabri." Farther
on he adds:

> Speed and Synthesis.
>
> They are intimately conjoined.
> Some wish to relate the speed of the Modernist poet
> to the very speed of modern-day life . . .
> It is true.
>
> .   .   .   .   .
>
> For the most part Modernist poets write short poems. Short
> on inspiration? enough inspiration for gigantic "Colombos"?
> No. What we have is a need for synthetic speed which re-
> linquishes useless details.

The short poem was, then, as he himself wrote in capital letters:
INEVITABLE RESULT OF OUR TIMES. And he adds: "A
consequence of electricity, the telegraph, the marine cable, wire-

less telegraphy, the railroad, ocean liners, the automobile, the airplane." It is quite obvious that Oswald de Andrade's "blue Cadillac" had, in Modernist mythology, a far deeper significance than we might at first think.

Mário de Andrade wrote the following concerning simultaneity:

> Because I was forced, at the mistake of friends and one enemy, to write a preface for the *Pauliçéia Desvairada,* I did so and included in it some remarks about *Harmonism* to which I later gave the more apt name of *Polyphonism.* At that time I knew nothing of Epstein's *Simultaneity* or of Divoire's *Simultaneism.* I have still not been able to secure a proper explanation of Marcello Fabri's *Synchronism.* However, I think that it all amounts to many names given to the same child. I knew of Soffici, but what he calls *Simultaneity* leaves me unsatisfied. I knew of cubist and futurist theories from painting. Also the experiments of Macdonald Right. I only wish to say that I have no intention to create anything at all. *Polyphonism* is the theory behind certain processes employed daily by some Modernist poets. Polyphonism and simultaneity are one and the same. The name of *Polyphonism,* which is characteristically artificial, derives from my knowledge of music, which I shall not qualify as meager, out of humility.

In spite of the fact that he asserted that "polyphonism and simultaneity are one and the same," he did, as a matter of fact, distinguish between the two: *"Simultaneity* is the coexistence of things and events at a given moment. *Polyphony* is the simultaneous artistic union of two or more melodies which have the fleeting effect of clashing sounds as they contribute to a *total final effect."*

The Modernists would perhaps have been surprised if they had been told that, even in Brazil, the perception of an age of speed had not waited for them but had already found expression in the first decade of the century. João do Rio, in his inaugural address at the Academy, exclaimed in 1909:

> A new esthetics appears on the horizon, the esthetics of the stimulating miracle. Nature is changed as it is utilized by

man and viewed in the automobile race. . . . The landscape with its vegetation of factory smokestacks, the fleeting
shadows of airplanes and the headlong dash of automobiles,
oceans rapidly crossed, disemboweled by submarines, the
dramas that such a new atmosphere gives to our steel-crossed
cities, gushing out, from above and below, rushing throngs,
the display of luxury, the neurosis of magically lit advertisements, commerce, character, passions, customs in which the
feeling of distance disappears, the increasing destruction of
the useless, the fearful flora of parasitism and vice, love, the
hundredfold life of the nerves: all of this makes it necessary
for the artist to see and feel in a new way, to love in a new
way, to reproduce in a new way.[28]

Before the airplane became an accepted mode of travel in Brazil,
it was the automobile that gave the Modernists a sensation of
speed and simultaneity. Oswald de Andrade had one of his characters come down the Santos road at two hundred kilometers an
hour, which seems a bit exaggerated. In number 1 of *Estética*
(September, 1924), under the title of "Velocidade," Guilherme de
Almeida wrote a poem at a more modest speed of "ninety-six
kilometers an hour":

Do you recall the giant with the seven-league boots?
There he goes: dashing, in a flight of blind wings,
across distances . . .
    He bolts,
        won't halt,
            won't look
    aside,
        ahead,
            behind . . .
                Like an outcast he goes . . .
He carries a tangled skein of ribbons:
ribbons
    blue,
        white,
            green,
                yellow . . .
                    unforeseen . . .

He cuts the wind:—and the wind increasing in ferocity,
untangles the skein, combing with fingers of air
the fine sheaf of strips,
                    bands,
                        ribbons,
                            strands,
                                stripes . . .
And stretches them out,
    pulls them out,
        straightens them out,
            strings them out far far back:
And the taut colors rise, fall SLOW-LY,
parallel-ly,
    parallel-ly,
                horizontal,
above the frightened head of Tom Thumb.[29]

We thus see that, well before Graciliano Ramos's character
played anagrams with Marina's name, Guilherme de Almeida had
already invented Concretism in 1924.

Style

Such preoccupations with theory, and such an atmosphere, could find in no other style than Expressionism their natural form of artistic fulfillment. Modernism was basically in its first phase and, in a general way, in its other phases a movement which was expressionist in nature. Its *nationalist* content, which had been developing since 1916, as had also its desire for *modernity,* led stylistically to Expressionism; and thus it compared to the state of mind of international art, which had been developing in Europe since before the war, but which during and after the war (in the twenties) became all the more intense.

Ilse and Pierre Garnier [30] wrote that Expressionism "is, in the first place, an atmosphere, that of Germany and Europe on the eve of the Great War and during the War; after the conflict youth begins to breathe and react against an atmosphere which it finds unbreathable. In other words, it is the outcry of that youth in the face of the strictures of the present." Let us avoid, they add, "one possible error: there is no expressionist 'school' or 'group': there is an expressionist 'climate.' No program, no master; a total liberty of form and content for the different poets and influences as diverse as those of Nietzsche, Rimbaud, Whitman, Hölderlin, and the baroque poets." [31]

The language "of the heart," of the "true passion" is, according to the Garniers, the natural style of Expressionism: brief, incisive sentences, stripped of adjectives, jolting, replete with exclamation points. Add to this the rhythmic intent, the omissions, the lack of development or justification, the succession of statements which, although they are apparently calm, really have the force of invectives (p. 26). Poems cease being ecstatic and take on movement: it amounts to the conjoining of speed and the poetic creation. Thus, structures and processes must be altered: "the adjective which, in the time of Impressionism, had reigned supreme is now eliminated or at least is no longer employed except as a point of support: the type-words of Expressionism are the noun and the verb. . . . To that is added rhythm: everything becomes impulse, activity, dynamics, violence; sentences are simplified, freed of all dead weight. Little by little, the meaning itself is lost and one reaches the absurd, a series of outcries and babblings which do not cover over the vacant spaces. It has already been said that Expressionism is an art of trend: in the name of the expression one moves away from reality; finally only the expression is left, that is, a kind of precocious *'lettrisme' "* (p. 29).

In 1934, in answer to Manuel Bandeira's inquiries, Mário de Andrade offered definitions of Expressionism which coincided quite naturally with the comments just recorded: "A trend in the arts of German origin which submits the facts of reality and the rules of techniques to the personal expressive vision which the artist has of the world." Dissatisfied with this first offering, he suggested the following: "A modern trend in the arts (of German origin) which attempts to submit any other artistic elements to the personal expressive vision which the artist has of the world." [32] This definition could serve for Modernism itself as far as artistic attitude is concerned; and the highly esteemed Epstein, in commenting on a poem by Cendrars, had formerly given the correct answer: "The caricaturesque, deforming, anti-photographic part of all art appears here as a simplification by excess which, in order to be sure of reaching benumbed, worn-out, civilized sensibilities (usually difficult to take unawares), yells through the loudest megaphone." [33]

Expressionism is, then, the superstyle that ends up being the anti-style and even the absence of style: here we note the main point of the entire Modernist dilemma, which up to the present commentators seem not to have perceived the importance of and which for that reason has been the source of grave errors. That point is that, on the whole, Modernism (like Expressionism) *was a school that fostered flawed works.* In another letter to Manuel Bandeira, Mário de Andrade recognized that *Macunaíma* had been the masterpiece that failed as a masterpiece. The same can be said of all the representative works of Modernism. One outstanding modern critic even went so far as to write that Modernism had not left behind a single work of importance, which is true, but not in the sense which he gave to that observation. Soon after the publication of *Ulysses,* T. S. Eliot answered for all time that kind of judgment: it was indeed a flawed work but one of incalculable literary significance. More particularly concerning Expressionism and, as a consequence, Modernism, Ilse and Pierre Garnier also emphasize: "Not always is it the works that represent the essential part of what an era leaves behind. It is quite possible that the works themselves are of the least importance. . . . What an era passes on to history is its presence: the Napoleonic era was something grandiose, it nourished an entire century, but what work did it bequeath to posterity? This means simply that there are literary movements which are doubtless more important for their atmosphere, which we continue to breathe through the successive years, than for their works. In that case, what is recorded in books is no more than the parliamentary minutes of a great presence." [34]

This is especially the case of Modernism: the atmosphere that it created was its characteristic contribution, more relevant than the works it created. The proof lies in the sense of creative freedom that it definitively established in Brazilian literature. Later, even non-Modernist or anti-Modernist works were possible only because they were able to benefit from that atmosphere. Thus the "memorable catastrophes" of Modernism (to recall Virginia Woolf's remarks on *Ulysses*)—*Paulicéia Desvairada, Marco Zero, Cobra Norato*—are paradoxically its great triumphs, the victory of a literary idea, of a concept of literature, and of a new vision of the world.

It is also this peculiarity which explains the marked Modernist tendency toward experimentalism. Contrary to what one might think, contrary to what the artist with an experimentalist bent might think, this tendency was for the most part the result of an insecurity, of a lack of technical competence. In 1941, in the moving although somewhat polemical pages of his "Elegia de Abril," [35] Mário de Andrade denounced this internal contradiction: "If we contemplate the artistic landscape, what immediately comes to our attention is the imperfection of technical competence. The experimentalism of the 'Modernists' of my generation in several sectors was confused with ignorance and was the self-defense of many a writer." Of Mário himself it would not be wrong to say that he sacrificed his creative possibilities to experimentalist curiosity. In a general way our Modernists, according to a famous dictum, "wanted to find out to what extent it was possible to go too far." ORIGINALITY OR DEATH, Cassiano Ricardo proclaimed sometime around 1927.[36] That heartfelt cry from all of modern art, which has more often led to death than to originality, was nevertheless modern art's essential implicit postulate.

That extreme content of theoretical foundation-laying made of modern art, and especially of literature, the area of choice of intellectual abstraction: it is not without reason that Expressionism ended up by leading to Abstractionism. Such an evolution had been clearly foreseen by Jean Epstein: "Modern literature, in spite of a certain tendency to schematize and settle for approximation, is not characterized in the least by simplicity. Precisely because they schematize the moderns demand of their audience, in order to be understood, a complementary intellectual effort, and they will be appreciated only by a certain kind of savant who forms at the same time a 'neuropathic aristocracy' (Professor Babinski)." More than the art of the past (for all of the arts demand of their respective audiences adequate indoctrination) the great artistic repository of Modernism necessitates on the part of the spectator or reader the prerequisite of culture, if not of erudition and professionalism. That was the great barrier that was erected in our time between the artist and the audience. The hostility which surrounded Modernism as a consequence, especially in its early years before the present-day institutionalization of the vanguard, resulted for the most part from an insurmountable difference in level between the producer and the consumer once the work of art had lost its traditional role as communication between writer and reader.

The phenomenon was felt by Jean Epstein as early as 1921:

> The fact is that today the reader who lacks literary habits and culture will not be able to follow modern authors whom he casually attempts to understand. They will sorely tax the reader who does not bring two or three thousand previous readings with him. As for the writers, at the expense of pursuing ambiguous interpretations and strange associations, they have come—quite logically, moreover—*to consider the word merely for its possibilities of association, meaning, and sound, its ability to admit intellectual games, symbols, and even puns.* The word is no longer the designation of a precise object; rather it is a kind of peg, as universal as possible, *destined to unite the most disparate of images.*[37]

São Paulo! *Tumult of My Life...*

If art and literature have always been by-products of urban civilization, for many reasons it was proper that this should be the case with Modernism, as it was so closely allied to the machine and technical progress. The spiritual process of the Modernists aimed at two different integrations on the part of the artist: first, in his own country, and in that regard he implicitly and irreparably rejected the cosmopolitan and international nature of Futurism; second, and contrariwise, he reclaimed that universalization because he also wished to be the expression of a time, of a historical moment. The first form in which that tendency manifested itself was the identification of Modernism with the city, that is, with a fact of civilization but also with the city of São Paulo. Facing that problem, Mário de Andrade stated in the famous spiritual testament which was his lecture *O Movimento Modernista*:

> But the Modernist spirit and its mode were imported directly from Europe. At that time São Paulo was much more "in the know" than Rio de Janeiro. And, socially speaking, Modernism could really be imported only by São Paulo to break out later in the provinces. There was a vast difference,

45

now less noticeable, between Rio and São Paulo. Rio was much more international, as far as the external norm of life was concerned. Obviously: seaport and capital of the country, Rio possesses an inborn internationalism. São Paulo was spiritually much more modern, however, the necessary consequence of the coffee economy and our concomitant industrialism. Up-range yokel still preserving a servile provincial frame of mind quite evident in its politics, São Paulo was at the same time, because of its up-to-date commercial activity and its industrialization, in closer spiritual and technical contact with the modern world. It is truly surprising how Rio maintains, in the oscillating cunning of the international city, a kind of ruralism, a traditional backward character which is much more pronounced than that of São Paulo. Rio is one of those cities in which not only the national "exoticism" remains indissoluble (which is, moreover, proof of the vitality of its character) but also the interpenetration of the rural and the urban. It would be impossible to find such a manifestation in São Paulo.[38]

The truth is that from the beginning a "ridiculous rivalry" [39] (also Mário de Andrade's expression in a letter to Manuel Bandeira) grew up between São Paulo and Rio; in the first place, for the establishment of a Modernist priority and later on for the establishment of greater Modernist purity. One year later, tired of so many caustic remarks, Mário poured out his heart to Manuel Bandeira: "Good Lord, what a bore this business of vanity is! You people in Rio will never forgive São Paulo for having rung the liberty bell." As a matter of fact it was not only Rio: the Northeast in general and Recife in particular even today show little inclination to forgive the *paulistas* for their impertinent bell-ringing. We will deal with that matter later. Be that as it may, the Modernists, before they progressed to "ruralism"—which was, as a matter of fact, introduced into literature by the poets and novelists of the Northeast—made the city their basic literary theme. Mário de Andrade stated that "the first book of the Movement sings regionally of the native city." However, in addition to the *Paulicéia Desvairada*, the creations which in prose and verse celebrate the machine, asphalt, and skyscrapers are quite numerous.

The classical literary review of Modernism bore the fundamentally urban name of *Klaxon*; it was only after the Movement had begun to disintegrate and take off in several contradictory directions that magazines appeared with such names as *Verde* or *Terra Roxa e Outras Terras*. There was even a simulation of Modernism in minor writers who adopted those themes with no creative authenticity. As a kind of premonitory reproach, Mário de Andrade wrote in the "Extremely Interesting Preface" to his *Paulicéia Desvairada*: "In my opinion, to write modern art never means to represent modern life through its externals: automobiles, movies, asphalt. If these words frequent my book, it is not because I think that I write 'modern' with them; but since my book is modern, these things have their reason for being in it."

It is interesting to recall that as early as 1917 Alceu Amoroso Lima foresaw that São Paulo would be the home of a renovative movement in literature:

> Today, the same law of history, which we have seen to have full confirmation among us, authorizes us to foresee that the future intellectual movement in Brazil will originate in São Paulo. Living in the very heart of the regionalist idea, enjoying one half of the national income, possessing a landed gentry, having sons who have inherited the pride and good sense of the *"paulistas"* of Piratininga, São Paulo is preparing for the grandeur of the Republic. This is not the case of petty envy; let us make an effort merely to see that regionalism, instead of stifling nationalism, will breathe new vigor into it. The sixteenth century belonged to Pernambuco, the seventeenth to Bahia, the eighteenth to Minas Gerais, the nineteenth to Rio de Janeiro. The twentieth is the century of São Paulo.[40]

São Paulo, which the journalistic penchant for metaphor had dubbed the "Milan of South America," thus unwittingly repeated, as a symbolic coincidence, the literary fate of the Italian city and thus confirmed the identification of Modernism with the great industrial complexes. In that respect Pär Bergman writes: "It seems of interest to us to note the fact that the movement takes on form in Milan, the first industrial city of Italy, which was rapidly expanding at the beginning of the century. To be sure, Milan is one of the least 'poetic' cities in Italy, but still the city had some literary 'traditions' which have considerable importance for Futurism, notably the anti-bourgeois nonconformity of the 'Scapigliatura' which frequently recalls the 'bohème parisienne.' " [41] The similarity to São Paulo is obvious. The ideal triangle of Milan–Paris–São Paulo furnishes us the perfect historic and esthetic frame for Brazilian Modernism.

This theme is obviously linked to the cult of the machine: instead of taking pleasure in "dead cities," or of celebrating them as the Symbolists did, the *"modern poet* should express the brutal life and the cacophony of collective living, of machines, and great cities." Bergman also writes: "Instead of the solitary and inactive man, the 'modern' poet should sing of modern man, that is, the active and 'dynamic' man of his own time, like the motorist and the aviator." [42] The first indication that the Modernists had won the wager came precisely when São Paulo perceived that, at least from the artistic point of view, it was retrograde in relation to other great centers of culture. One journal, which to that point had been conservative and indifferent to Modernism (that is the least one can say), marked an important transition in 1923 when Paulo Prado assumed its editorship. In April of that year the editorial of the *Revista do Brasil* said the following, among other things:

In this artistic capital Art lives in bitterest exile. Save for one group or another, which is ignored or aggressive, except for one individual or another languishing in sickly indifference, in this capital of Art, there are no artists. What we call Art is a crude caricature of the divine Muses.

We are more than fifty years behind the times in music; we have not yet progressed past the babbling age of the little girl who toys at the piano, and we spend mountains of money to sit solemnly trussed up and listen to the mustiest operas of the ancient Italian repertoire. In 1923 one still remarks, in a pitiful effort to make jokes, that Wagner is the musician of the future. . . . We heed painting solely for the repugnant exhibition of the bad taste of our new rich. The last

word in this genre is still the likeness or the affecting anec-
dote narrated by the treakly brush of realistic painters.

In sculpture, were there an artistic ethic, our innocent
children should be forbidden to be perverted by the contemplation of the monstrosities scattered about the streets and
squares of our city. This hideous collection, which resembles
the *musée des horreurs* of Courteline—only two or three
works distinguish themselves, and one of them is admirable—
is lost in the midst of public indifference. If we suddenly
found a Rodin *Balzac* in our city, or canvases by Cézanne
and Matisse, or heard Ravel's *Heure espagnole* at the Municipal Theatre, what a Homeric guffaw would rock the
sadness of our balderdash-spouting public! How those masterpieces of true Art would stir up the hatred of our philistines!

It was also through the offices of Paulo Prado in 1923 that
Mário de Andrade assumed the position of art critic on the *Revista
do Brasil*; no other occurrence could have been so expressive of a
transformation in spirit. In June of 1921, when it published his
article "Debussy e o Impressionismo," the noteworthy journal
introduced the writer with the following words: "The Author is
one of those youths, full of rare vigor and gallant independence,
who are revolutionizing ideas in the field of literature and art in
São Paulo. This study of his should be read with pleasure and
profit by those who are not indifferent to questions relating to the
artistic evolution of modern times." The coincidence of these
small facts corroborates Mário da Silva Brito when he says that
"1920 was a year of plans and options; 1921 of combat, of outbreak of hostilities, of affirmations, of conquest of terrain and
preparations for the victory of 1922." [43] But it seems premature
to call the uncertain battle of 1922 an outright victory: everything
indicates that it came one year later when the evolution was
decided in favor of the Modernists. From then on the battle of
Hernani was transformed into the Modernist Austerlitz: it is
sufficient to recall that, even in November of 1922, when it
reviewed *O Homem e a Morte* by Menotti del Picchia, the *Revista
do Brasil* said that the book had been eagerly awaited as the
"Cromwell's preface" of the new and revolutionary esthetics.

Seven Days That Shook the Literary World

In effect, the Modernists marched seven times around the walls of traditionalism before they came tumbling down in the wake of outcries, grimaces, and strident trumpets. The history of Modernism, down to the book by Mário da Silva Brito, was more in the nature of a mythology, a battle between Olympus and Hell. On the contrary, the facts reveal that prior to the Week of Modern Art, particularly after 1916, *everybody was a Modernist* in the sense that everybody agreed that Parnassianism and Symbolism were passé and that it was necessary to create something new. The fact is that, as usual, the majority of those who declared themselves in favor of a revolution wanted at the same time to be sure that the renovations would essentially alter nothing. The Modernists were simply the first to recognize that it was not really a question of *renovation* but of *revolution,* or at least they knew that there had never been esthetic renovations that were not to some degree revolutionary. On the eve of the Week numerous critical reviews were published which ridiculed the pseudo-Parnassians and insisted on the anachronism of that school. Equally numerous were the manifestations of an obscure and vague longing for any other school whatsoever.

When the matter is viewed in this light, it might be thought that in its earliest moment the Week of Modern Art, because of its provocative and scandalous nature, destroyed everything. In reality, the Week generated considerably more resistance to Modernism than it would normally have provoked had it expressed itself not with fewer manifestoes but with fewer manifestations. At any rate, it is a good idea, before all else, to avoid falling into the trap of the literary columnists who were nearly always ingenuous and exaggerated the violent attacks of the traditionalists against the Modernists. Such attacks, many of which were petty like that of Aristeu Seixas, were less numerous and, moreover, less significant than one might imagine. In the strictest sense, it was not the traditionalists but those minds totally unreceptive to literature and the arts that truly rose up against Modernism and transformed it into a peculiar question of honor in which the famed "São Paulo pride" was involved. However, when we observe, name by name, who exactly was involved, it is virtually impossible to contain our laughter. It would have been embarrassing if they had declared themselves in favor of the vanguard. The one who seemed to have understood this from the very beginning, owing to his incomparable tactical sense, was Oswald de Andrade, if it is true, as Mário Guastini maintained in 1926, that Oswald went from editorial room to editorial room of the conservative papers (practically all papers were conservative) asking them to attack the Week and the Modernists.

The strangest fact is that Oswald's Machiavellian plot failed, as we shall see. Newspapers were traditionally classicist and, therefore, artistically conservative, like *O Estado de São Paulo*, dealt with the Modernists and the Week with considerable kindness and even with sympathy. In fact, everything stood in favor of the emergence of a vanguardist movement, although, no doubt, in favor of a movement less radical than Modernism. When the echo of the battles had long since faded away, Sérgio Buarque de Holanda and Prudente de Morais Neto, reviewing the volume of Manuel Bandeira's *Poesias* in *Estética*, II (January–March, 1925), wrote: "The year 1917 signifies for our literature something more than a date of promise and a little less than an era of brilliant fulfillment. . . . For example, we would be almost unjust if we said of Senhor Manuel Bandeira's first book, which was published in 1917 when Guilherme de Almeida and Mário de Andrade also gave us their first books, that it was for the moment a promise, even a 'splendid promise,' as some critics of the time ought to have said." Three years later in 1920, Mário de Andrade wrote in its entirety the first version of the *Pauicéia Desvairada*, as he asserted in the famous "Open letter to Alberto de Oliveira." [44] It is significant that, once the Modernist campaign was underway, he should in the beginning have refused to publish his revolutionary book, which shows clearly that, even in the spirit of the vanguardists, creative daring sought to limit itself. As Mário da Silva Brito has it, the point of rupture was Oswald de Andrade's speech, delivered on January 9, 1921, at the conservative banquet in honor of Menotti del Picchia, in which he declared that he was speaking "in the name of half a dozen young artists of São Paulo, which explains my warm and overflowing pride." [45]

Contrary to what has been thought for so many years, as a consequence of an understandable error in perspective, it was the Modernists who created the Week of Modern Art and not the Week of Modern Art that created Modernism. However, before this last word became current, the fashionable name was "Futurism"; this term was so widespread that it rendered meaningless the tardy proofs of priority by which the writers from Rio de Janeiro, for example, justified themselves. In 1921, Paulo Mendes de Almeida recalls in his memoir of the literary sections of the review *A Cigarra*,[46] that "one spoke a great deal about Futurism. Under that pretext the *A Cigarra* published an editorial launching, as 'the most interesting of our new futurist poets,' a certain Mário Flama, 'pseudonym of a young invalid who has been paralyzed for the last ten years.' Gifted with a 'prodigious genius,' it was probable that in Brazil he would take up 'the baton of the new school,' adding that Marinetti, in Milan, had been the first to 'proclaim him genius.' Following that statement, he reproduced some works by this unknown literary luminary. Among them, the following:

> tall, straight, fine and thin
> with your shoulders in a straight line,
> you give to him who sees you
> the impression of a gigantic T.[47]

Rubbish. Evidently, it was a joke. Its author: Júlio César da Silva."

In so far as I know, the literary generations that constitute Modernism have not yet really been differentiated, particularly that generation which the Movement, in a sensitive psychoanalytical process, tried to reject and forget. On September 8, 1921, Benjamin de Garay wrote an article in the journal *La Unión* of Buenos Aires, which bore the title "O Movimento Paulista na Literatura Brasileira." It was transcribed in January of the following year in the *Revista do Brasil*. Here is the main passage:

> Brazilian literature reveals at the moment, in that prosperous State, one of its most characteristic aspects. Breaking with the prejudices of the generation of writers who, at the beginning of this century, made fashionable a horror for national subjects, habits, customs, and idiosyncrasies of their temperament, the modern writers of São Paulo have followed the example of Afonso Arinos and Euclides da Cunha and have reestablished the traditions of the Indianists of the second half of the nineteenth century. Instead of imitating third-rate foreign literature—the novels of Jean Lorrain, the paradoxes of Oscar Wilde, the negativist philosophy of Nietzsche, the scandalous manner of the French naturalists— as their predecessors did with greater or lesser success, they have sought to extract from the voices of the earth, from the natural landscape and the peculiarities of the national atmosphere, the themes of their works. . . . They have concretized their customs by stressing the virtues and the defects of the race as they stigmatized, when necessary, the vices, tics, and errors of their education and pointed out the remedies that might cure them, the means to combat them. . . .

That panorama is of interest not only because it demonstrates that there already was a "Modernist" Movement *before* the Week, observable in concrete works and in a tacit but clear program, but also because it demonstrates that the first "Modernist" generation had little in common with the warriors of 1922. That also is in agreement with the terms of an article by Breno Ferraz to which I shall later make reference. The center of that first generation,

which today—given the direction taken by literary history—we can
see only as a pre-Modernist generation transformed by the force of
things into an anti-Modernist generation, was Monteiro Lobato:

> Congregated around Monteiro Lobato were novelists and
> poets of worth like Léo Vaz, Hilário Tácito, Godofredo
> Rangel, Menotti del Picchia, Paulo Setúbal, Veiga Miranda,
> Waldomiro Silveira, Ribeiro Couto, to mention only those
> who present a modality which is the offspring of the earth.
> . . . The influence of this literature on Brazilian letters is
> already making itself felt. It is sufficient to note the interest
> provoked by the several editions of Monteiro Lobato, sold
> by the thousands in four hundred different places in Brazil-
> ian territory. . . . Moreover, the São Paulo group is not
> isolated. Throughout Brazil all the new writers reveal this
> same care in describing the things of their homeland. They
> research its history, drag heroes, soldiers, men of thought
> and action out of centuries of obscurity. They bring to life
> the past of the Brazilian race as they point up the *beaux
> gestes* and serene attitudes of the Brazilian nation.

The enumeration of that first modern—if it was not yet
Modernist—generation exactly coincided with the list of Breno
Ferraz, as recorded in an article written in reply to an article by
José Maria Belo which had appeared in the *O Jornal* of Rio de
Janeiro in order to deal with the "literary movement in São Paulo
and national literature," and so was denied the existence of any
activity of importance in the capital of the state of São Paulo. The
article by Breno Ferraz appeared in the *Revista do Brasil* of February, 1922, at the exact moment when the Week of Modern Art was
in preparation:

> Seven years ago, at the most critical moment in our history,
> the *Revista do Brasil* appeared as the vigorous blossoming
> of the best our nation had to offer, born for glorious fulfill-
> ment. It was a petulant gesture made by provincials, but
> among its leadership figured Pereira Barreto, Júlio Mesquita,
> Alfredo Pujol, Pedro Lessa, Bilac. . . . This daring under-

taking went through its golden age. It produced two great names, indisputably its own products: Monteiro Lobato and Martins Fontes. *Urupês* and *Verão* were published in its pages. The fate of the *Revista* was therein mapped out: the work was successively edited and thereby gained solidity and was expanded before it was published in book form. *Idéias de Jeca* and *Cidades Mortas* followed. The list of authors published grew in length: Léo Vaz, with his *O Professor Jeremias*; J. M. Toledo Malta with *Mme. Pommery*; Godofredo Rangel with *Vida Ociosa*; J. A. Nogueira with *Amor Imortal.* . . . Then . . . Then, the highest number, up to 150,000 copies last year.

Benjamin de Garay, as well as Breno Ferraz, failed to mention the names of Mário de Andrade or Oswald de Andrade, of Ronald de Carvalho or any others who came to be typical Modernists; and if the name of Menotti del Picchia appears on the list, it is for the well-known reason that he was "converted" late to Modernism—like Saul—after he had fiercely attacked the Movement.

José Maria Belo, seeing dimly or from afar, observed in São Paulo "three or four poets or writers, whose books I have had the good fortune to know intimately: Senhor Amadeu Amaral, Senhor Monteiro Lobato with his admirable *Urupês* and the ironist who wrote *Professor Jeremias* have truly shown me excellent examples of the talent and literary ability of the São Paulo youths." To which Breno Ferraz retorted:

As a matter of fact, Amadeu Amaral is an exceptional personality, an exceptional poet, an unmistakable poet who, with *Espumas,* sets a new direction for our poetic art. He stands outside and above the "regionalist" mode. Monteiro Lobato is also a renovator. Léo Vaz, another original individual. Are they regionalists? Menotti del Picchia goes from *Juca Mulato* to *Máscaras* with a cosmopolitan profession of faith.
But that is not all.
Vicente de Carvalho is one of our nation's great names. He retains that unique glory which Euclides acknowledged in no man. Francisca Júlia is the sublime poetess, indeed

master poet of São Paulo and Rio. Júlio César da Silva, blood brother in art, has for thirty years been a highly refined poet. Batista Cepelos, the epic poet of the *"bandeiras."* Martins Fontes, the symphonist of the great orchestrations of the mother tongue. Guilherme de Almeida, a whole Paris in the soul of a citizen of São Paulo. Manuel Carlos, a conqueror who allows himself to be conquered. Gustavo Teixeira, the artistic miracle of a town whose mayor is an Italian, as are also the priest, the tax collector, and the political boss. Paulo Setúbal, the first edition of 6000 copies now out of print: *Alma Cabocla.* Ricardo Gonçalves, a regionalist like the preceding, the most beloved of all. Afonso Schmidt, the poet most representative of São Paulo, the singer of the anonymous masses, the sidewalks of D. Sancha, the city neighborhoods, finally, of the city. Ribeiro Couto, a modern expression in poetry.

Senhor J. M. Belo does not recognize, then, even one sixth of the poetic production of São Paulo. He appears to know only two authors or, rather, two books: *Espumas* and *Juca Mulato.*

He does no better for prose. These are our writers: Alfredo Pujol, Amadeu Amaral, Léo Vaz, Hilário Tácito, Godofredo Rangel, J. A. Nogueira, Oliveira Vianna, Waldomiro Silveira, Amando Caiuby, Cornélio Pires, Albertino Moreira, Martim Francisco, Veiga Miranda, Sud Menucci, Thales de Andrade, Mário Pinto Serva, Cláudio de Sousa, Benedito Otávio, Agenor Silveira, A. de Freitas, A. E. Taunay, Fernando de Azevedo, all with a book; and Plínio Barreto, Roberto Moreira, Sampaio Dória, J. Mesquita Filho, Heitor Morais, Moacir Piza, Lourenço Filho, Armando Rodrigues, Eurico Sodré, and Alcântara Machado.

The first part, signed with the initials B. F., is followed on the second of March by another article, this one signed with the full name. The last paragraph of the second article revealed one of the great differences between that first generation and the group more legitimately called Modernists. The former attempted to maintain and continue a literary tradition, although renovating it on one hand and on the other attempting to surpass nationalism in the achievement of universalism: "To the work of Monteiro

Lobato, shot through with legitimate realism, the literature of São Paulo owes the epithet of 'regionalist,' by which they falsely attempt to qualify it. *Urupês,* however, with its Jeca and the dramatic quality of its characters, is 'regional,' in the old or modern sense, as the masterpieces of world literature are 'regional.' "

Although Breno Ferraz would deny it, it is obvious that in that period "modern" literature was identified with regionalism: that may explain, at least in part, why the Modernists, with an attitude that at first seems contradictory, should furiously attack regionalist literature. What we must emphasize, however, is the fact that Monteiro Lobato, at that moment, enjoyed the privileged position of undisputed leader of all literary renaissance and could not, as a consequence, adapt himself to the role of disciple after 1922. There, quite naturally, is the reason for his strange repudiation of literature, inexplicable to so many and which he himself, many years later, interpreted as a corollary of his disinterest in literary activity. That happened well before 1925, contrary to what we read in official hagiography, and is an opinion adopted also by Arthur Neves in the preface to the omnibus edition of 1943; the bankruptcy of his publishing firm was merely a dramatic symbol of a career which had come to a close precisely with the publication of *A Onda Verde.*

The strictly literary career of Monteiro Lobato might be graphed as a failure: a rising straight line between 1915, the date of Jeca Tatu, and 1918, the date of *Urupês;* and a descending straight line from 1919, the date of *Cidades Mortas,* to 1926, the date of *O Choque das Raças.* It would be enlightening to superimpose on that graph the much more complex figure of the rise and apex of Modernism, which can be practically included between the same dates. The exemplary case of Menotti del Picchia might serve to demonstrate the correctness of this analysis: as a writer who was already famous in 1922, but who was merely a common seaman in the vast armada of which Monteiro Lobato was the commander, it was not only likely but also inevitable and natural that he should adhere to Modernism where his reputation might give him—as indeed it did—the title of leader in its first weeks. So the two apparent incongruities resolved themselves with relative ease owing to the fact that the Modernist "insincerity" of

Menotti del Picchia (immediately indicted in criticisms and verbal commentaries) corresponded symmetrically to the nationalist and therefore regionalist "sincerity" of Monteiro Lobato.

The same names already mentioned by Breno Ferraz also appeared in the article by Plínio Salgado, who listed "the São Paulo poets of this Centennial year," [48] among whom the name of Mário de Andrade appeared for the first time in an accounting of some importance and in a position equivalent to that of writers then renowned:

> The latest novelty, the "prat [sic] du jour" of São Paulo poetry (it is still too early to say São Paulo urban poetry), is seen in the person of Mário de Andrade. We shall have to speak more in detail at another time about this poet who deserves an important place in this new movement in our literature, owing to the profundity of his thought which albeit arrives in the company of a host of nonsense. The author of the *Paulicéia Desvairada* is an adept of radical futurism, although he denies it, and he garbs his thoughts in the clay of good-natured expressions peculiar to the Brazilian character of our first years of nationality. This serious matter cannot be discussed in a short space, in a work that is more reportage than criticism, rather a balance sheet listing materials than a profound and detailed study of species. Our opinion is that Mário de Andrade is more reformer than artist. His ideas have exercised an influence on notable artists, and the day is not far off when his influence will be felt on Brazilian poetry and prose.

We could hardly ask for clearer discernment. On the other hand, by that time the Week of Modern Art had already taken place.

The Spirit of Harlequin

If one had read only the *Revista do Brasil* down to 1923, he would have run the risk of never knowing that the Week of Modern Art had occurred in São Paulo. In April of 1922 in a review of Pedro Costa's *Alaor e Ocede*,[49] that solemn journal mentioned merely in passing the legend composed in "Modernist" verse: "As one can see, from his retreat in the backlands of Bahia comes a full-scale poet who asks no quarter of the leaders of our ultra-civilized futurism. 'I go forth to the field, to the heart of nature, the storehouse of beauty. . . .' There it is. No such image ever erupted at the Municipal Theatre with such vigor of realism and such a sense of the future. . . . The new futurist leader has written pages that make our poets envious, outclassing by leagues the best pages of the *Paulicéia Desvairada*. Here is something like the dance of the manakins:

> The canary "crackles"!
> —Warbles! Warbles! Warbles!
>   Chaotic!
>   Exotic!
> And the parakeet "chirrups"
>   (He's the village bard!)

But another winged creature flies and repeats a "rosary":
—Husband! . . . Husband! . . . Husband-is-it-day?! . . .
   Husbandzitday?! . . .
   Husbandzitday?! . . .
(And how his song matches the hour!)
   And there's one who says to the light
   —In flight! In flight! In flight!
   And while this bird calls out
   Another bird bawls out
   I-saw-thee! I-saw-thee! I-saw-thee!

   Ah! when all Nature wakes up
   The storehouse of beauty it makes up! . . ." [50]

Moreover, this ridiculous asininity poses a strange problem, because it is dubious that the Week of Modern Art could have reached the interior of Bahia in such a short space of time and allowed for the composition and publication of Pedro Costa's poem. Rather, all evidence points to its being a spontaneous creation.

We have seen that under the editorship of Paulo Prado the *Revista do Brasil* nonetheless abandoned its former attitude of cold hostility and was transformed into a moderately Modernist organ. Two years after the Week, in February of 1924 (which leads one to suspect some commemorative intention), Paulo Prado published a complimentary article with regard to Brecheret, in which the historical significance of the Week was made abundantly apparent:

Within a short time—perhaps a very short time, indeed—what in February of 1922 was called in São Paulo the Week of Modern Art will go down in history as a memorable date in the literary and artistic development of Brazil.

That endeavor—which was ingenuous and daring in its reaction against Bad Taste, the Cliché, the Déjà-Vu, the Old Saw, Decrepitude, and Mercantilism—led to unforeseen and far-reaching results. It outraged the philistines in their idleness; it introduced doubt into the minds of people of good faith and caused a sad and solemn public to break up in raucous laughter. It had the obvious defects and inevitable flaws always found in enterprises of that type that are carried out in the restrained atmosphere of a provincial city, in spite of the splendid contingent that Rio sent to us. But throughout it all, the note of talent and youth echoed clear and vibrant. To that note we owe the fact that the doors of the Municipal Theatre have been opened wide for a blast of fresh air that has cleared the stage and corridors of the illustrious house, still reeking of the rancid breath of the Mocchi Opera Company and the disreputable Coty of Monsieur Brûlé's plays. And, for the first time, São Paulo has taken an impassioned interest in an artistic problem. For the first time, in the midst of our industrial capital, the daily routine of our material preoccupations and our usual cheap talk have entered the arena of ideas in general.

At this point we reach the really rough ground. The true history of the Week and its many surprising reversals has not yet been written: Mário da Silva Brito has still not published the continuation of his researches. And Mário da Silva Brito himself— whom Oswald de Andrade called, with his usual malice, one of the grandsons of the first Modernists—falls victim at times to the traditions of the mock heroic literary columns which have cropped up around Modernism with the passing years. We might say that the best synthesis of that historiographic mythology is the short article written by Carminha de Almeida for the *Revista Anual do Salão de Maio,* 1939:

Once upon a time there was a man named Jacinto Silva who, in 1921, had a bookstore on Fifteenth of November Street, a publishing firm called "O Livro." Every afternoon a poet, a novelist, and a painter met there. Guilherme de Almeida, Oswald de Andrade, and Di Cavalcanti. One afternoon the poet read his book of the year in a room at the back of the bookstore. Later other writers read other books. More and more people arrived. Painters and sculptors (they discovered Brecheret) held exhibitions. Musicians played. It was then that they conceived the idea of celebrating, on that very spot, a grand exhibition of modern art, illustrated with concerts of modern music and recitation of modern poetry. Everything modern. Guilherme, Oswald, and Di spoke with Paulo Prado and Graça Aranha, and the latter not only supported but also spread the idea; however, they substituted the Municipal Theatre for the back room at the bookstore. René Thiollier went to the governor's palace to speak with Dr. Washington and when he mentioned at the Automobile Club that he was going to collect money for the Week, everyone laughed. . . . Rubens Borba de Moraes left no stone unturned in order to book the theatre free of charge. It seems he succeeded. Menotti del Picchia called the meeting to order. And the whole thing became a reality much to the great—the greatest—chagrin of the bourgeoisie. It was then February of 1922, the rainy season here in São Paulo, which did not prevent crowds from rushing to the scene of the crime. Canvases, sculptures, and sketches in the foyers and corridors; lectures, recitations, concerts and ballets in the main hall. Ivone Daumerie performing a modern dance as a butterfly . . . Guiomar Novaes, who intended to play Chopin, was forced to play Villa-Lobos. And play she did. All that to an angry audience ceaselessly booing. Mário de Andrade, Graça Aranha, Anita Malfatti, Di Cavalcanti, Villa-Lobos (who up till then had played only in movie houses in Rio), Sérgio Milliet, John Graz, Zina Aita, Brecheret: all reciprocated with good-natured smiles. Not really all of them, because they say that Ronald de Carvalho and Renato de Almeida suffered greatly from the booing and hotly protested while someone asked for more "because he required the booing as accompaniment for his speech." The ladies looked angrily at Anita Malfatti's "Yellow Man." The gentlemen attacked the works on view with insult and cane; one poked out the eye on a portrait by Segall. A stupid and petty lady tried to involve Zina Aita in a sordid affair when she telephoned the wife of one of the organizers to report that even then the artist was in the arms of her husband. It is easy to see that it went so far as to reach vilification. It is not necessary to say that the press, with the exception of the *Correio Paulistano,* attacked the entire affair sys-tem-a-ti-cal-ly. The *Estado de São Paulo* published a note as follows: "The columns of the classified section of this newspaper are hereby

open to anyone who wishes to attack the Week of Modern
Art in a defense of our national artistic heritage."

It would not be unjust to say of that pious history exactly
the same thing that Prudente de Morais Neto wrote about
Joaquim Inojosa's book: "The Week of Modern Art, as he tells
it, has retained the truth only in the booing." Since it was the
source, confessed or not, of numerous other narratives regarding
the Week, it is a repository of legends and heroic myths which
gradually grew up around a truth which was considerably less
complex.

We need to say before all else that the original idea of the
Week of Modern Art really seems to belong to Di Cavalcanti, as
he so claims in his memoirs.[51] Recalling the episode, Renato
Almeida wrote: "One afternoon at the *Monitor Mercantil*, Graça
Aranha called us together—Elysio de Carvalho, Ronald, and myself—and told us that Di Cavalcanti had suggested a wonderful
idea to him. It was to stage a grandiose art festival with modern
elements: lectures, recitation of poetry, concerts, and exposition
of modern ideas. Graça Aranha felt obliged to promote the gathering; but he thought it preferable to hold the occasion in São
Paulo, especially since there was in São Paulo a vigorous group of
Modernists—not only writers and poets, but also painters and
sculptors." [52] Thus the "caravan" of writers and artists from Rio
grew, among them the composer Villa-Lobos who, although he
was not famous at that time, "was very well established in Rio,"
according to Renato Almeida's declaration, which discredits
Carminha de Almeida's version concerning his modest activities
in motion picture houses.

But this is not all. Research into back issues of the *O Estado
de São Paulo* (February–March, 1922) revealed that it was impossible to locate the famous statement about the classified section.[53] By all indications not only was such a note never published,
but also no attack on the Modernists can be found either in the
editorial section or in the classified section, with the exception
of three small attacks mentioned below and the ironic account of
one of the festivals. In the long run, the newspaper coverage of
the Week was generally sympathetic, as we shall soon see.

It is equally incorrect to state that Guiomar Novaes had intended to play Chopin but had been forced (by whom?) to play Villa-Lobos. The Brazilian composer's pieces were part of the scheduled program which had been published in the issue of February 15; along with those pieces, Guiomar Novaes was to play, and indeed did play, E. R. Blanchet and Debussy. The confusion seems to have resulted from an incident in which the pianist became embroiled as a result of the violent direction events were taking. At any rate she protested against the intolerance of the Modernists, but this did not prevent her taking part in the music festival, as we have noted before.

The Week of Modern Art, as is widely known, took the form of three "festivals" held in the Municipal Theatre of São Paulo on February 13, 15, and 17, 1922. The first account of the Week, which was sufficiently enlightening, was published in the *O Estado de São Paulo* in the edition of February 3:

Week of Modern Art. The news of a projected "Week of Modern Art" in São Paulo has excited the liveliest interest in our intellectual and social circles. The governor of the state and the municipal mayor have promised their complete support to the members of the organizing committee. The festivals of the "Week of Modern Art" have been designated: the first, "Painting and Sculpture"; the second, "Literature and Poetry"; and the third, a "Festival of Music." The following will participate: in literature, Senhor Graça Aranha, who will deliver a lecture on "Esthetic Emotion in Modern Art," and Senhores Ronald de Carvalho, Mário de Andrade, Álvaro Moreyra, Oswald de Andrade, Menotti del Picchia, Renato de Almeida, Luís Aranha, Ribeiro Couto, Moacir de Abreu, Agenor Barbosa, Rodrigues de Almeida, Afonso Schmidt, Sérgio Milliet, Guilherme de Almeida and Plínio Salgado. In music: Guiomar Novaes, Villa-Lobos, Octavio Pinto, Paulina de Ambrósio, Ernani Braga, Alfredo Brecheret, Frutuoso and Lucília Villa-Lobos. In sculpture: Victor Brecheret, Hildegardo Leão Veloso and Haarberg. In painting: Anita Malfatti, Di Cavalcanti, Ferrignac, Zina Aita, Martins Ribeiro, Oswald Gueld ([*sic*] for Goeldi), Regina Graz, John Graz and Castello.

The demand for tickets to these festivals has been great.

On February 11, the same newspaper printed the following notice: "Day after tomorrow at 8:30 P.M., at the Municipal Theatre, the first festival of the 'Week of Modern Art' has been set. Numerous artists from São Paulo and Rio will participate." On the thirteenth the inaugural program was published. On the fourteenth the opening session was reported along with the complete text of Graça Aranha's address. The following final remarks were added:

The gathering, which was loudly applauded, was entertained with several musical numbers by Modernist authors performed by Senhor Ernani Braga and with poetry declaimed by Senhores Guilherme de Almeida and Ronald de Carvalho, all of which evoked a splendid reaction on the part of the audience.

The words delivered by Senhor Graça Aranha more than sufficiently explain the objectives of that artistic undertaking and render useless further details on our part.

Let us proceed to the performance of the musical section which followed. The music was entrusted to talented artists like Alfredo Gomes, Paulina d'Ambrosio, and F. Lima Vianna, so that we were treated to the compositions of a full-scale artist of exceptional personality: Senhor Villa-Lobos.

The second half of the program opened with two piano numbers by Senhor Villa-Lobos beautifully executed by Senhor Ernani Braga.

Immediately following, Senhor Ronald de Carvalho delivered an essay on modern esthetic currents in Brazilian painting and sculpture. That interesting disquisition in which the author, with great modesty, attributed his own ideas on art to a group of young artists, thus affirming the eclectic nature of modern Brazilian painting, which was simultaneously national in its basic characteristics and in its conception—if we understand his words correctly—seemed to some in the audience somewhat contradictory, owing to the statements of some of the leaders of this modern movement which many have called futurist. Obviously, we alone are to blame for this confusion.

In this second part of the program, music played an outstanding role. The impression aroused by the African dances was profound. Without wishing to detract from the merits of the author, we may say that the dances contributed no little to the general success of the evening.

Obviously, in these journalistic accounts, it is impossible to find any signs of that fierce hostility mentioned by the pious histories of the Week. As the reader has certainly perceived, there was more than vague relief after Ronald de Carvalho's words that, after all was said and done, Modernism was not so hideous as it had been depicted. On February 15 came the first, and moreover the only, internal crisis of the Week: [54] the "illustrious Brazilian pianist, Senhora Guiomar Novaes," as she was called by the *O Estado de São Paulo,* delivered the following letter to the members of the organizing committee:

Considering the fundamentally exclusivist and intolerant nature assumed by the first festival of modern art, which took place on the thirteenth of this month at the Municipal Theatre, with regard to the other schools of music of which I am an interpreter and admirer, I cannot fail to declare here my disagreement with that kind of thinking. I was sincerely saddened by the public performance of pieces which satirized the music of Chopin.

I admire and respect all great manifestations of art independent of the schools they represent, and it was in accord with my own point of view that, in accepting the invitation that was extended to me, I took part in one of the festivals of Modern Art.

At that point, however, some vague hostility became evident in the newspaper account, but without insistence. This occurred in the notice of February 16:

Yesterday at the Municipal Theatre the second festival of the "Week of Modern Art" took place. A splendid gathering, owing in great part to the inclusion on the program of the name of our illustrious pianist Guiomar Novaes. The evening opened with a lecture by Senhor Menotti del Picchia. Little by little, the atmosphere of the theatre altered to such a degree that it brought to mind the famous opening night of Tortola Valencia. That perhaps was the intention of the meeting's promoters, although it did not appear on the program. Whether it was a spontaneous manifestation from the gallery or a new kind of claque, the fact is that the least respectful phrases and attitudes were sometimes directed at artists, totally respectable for their talent and past performance, who took part in the festival. But for the "true Modernists," a nation's past or an individual's past counts for nothing. . . . In that, at least, we see that they have a certain logic. . . .

Only Senhorita Guiomar Novaes was heard in deep silence, even when she performed that "archaic musician" by the name of Debussy, who is naturally considered a complete nonentity by those who wish to open the portals of the New Age. . . .

On the seventeenth the newspaper published an article by Ronald de Carvalho, "The Music of Villa-Lobos," and on the following day devoted to the composer a sympathetic editorial notice: "Yesterday at the Municipal Theatre the final festival of the Week of Modern Art took place. The program was composed of several pieces by our distinguished national composer H. Villa-Lobos, which were beautifully performed by the talented artists, Ernani Braga, Alfredo Gomes, Paulina d'Ambrosio, Lima Vianna, Maria Emma, Lucília Villa-Lobos, Pedro Vieira and Antão Soares. The pieces performed deeply impressed the audience, although it was difficult, on a first hearing, to appreciate all the composer's qualities. Naturally, owing to their indubitable value, these works will be performed again in São Paulo under circumstances that will more easily facilitate the comprehension of the audience. This young and talented musician will then receive the laurels that his talent so justly merits."

The *Estado* did not publish a word against the Modernists during or immediately after the Week (certainly not the famous notice about the classified section); the newspaper rather expressed the hope that a Villa-Lobos concert would take place under better conditions so that the artist could benefit from a more objective judgment, and that concert did indeed take place on March 7, under the auspices of the Sociedade de Cultura Artística (which had nothing at all to do either with revolution or Modernism). On the eighth, the newspaper published a praise-filled review, glorifying the composer's qualities. Likewise, Ernani Braga performed in São Paulo in March as did also Guiomar Novaes. Simultaneously Zina Aita held an exhibition of her paintings in the hall of the publishing firm O Livro, which earned excellent publicity and the praise of newspapers.

In February and March only three small notes appeared in the classified section, hopelessly lost in the chaotic pagination of the time. On the seventeenth of February we read the first:

> FUTURIST WEEK. The right to boo and stamp one's feet is recognized in every civilized country. Does this country have no more rotten tomatoes? A PAULISTA

The assertion of the civilized right to boo and stamp could only issue from the thoughts of an angered and contradictory traditionalist. On the eighteenth, there appeared another small notice:

> FUTURISM. Wanted to hire an honest youth to write futurist poetry. Must present certificate of ignorance.

On the nineteenth, encouraged by the refined civilization attested by the boos of the preceding days, the Paulista struck again in the classified section:

> FUTURIST WEEK. Fortunately São Paulo's mettle has been vindicated. During the last spree of the Futurist Week, it was necessary to close the galleries lest the stage run red with the juice of rotten tomatoes. However, even with the galleries proscribed, the matter would have turned into an enormous stamping of feet if they had continued to present those visionary and pointless discourses as on the preceding

nights. The orchestra section was prepared to receive them as they deserved. On the final night there was only music, and it is not music that we are combating.

And that is all. Naturally, the name "Futurist" had by that time become a kind of insult to hurl at any adversary. Thus, for example, in another attack in the classified section of the *O Estado de São Paulo,* a rival of Counselor Antônio Prado called him the "Leo the Tenth of the Week of Modern Art"—this with regard to an obscure land question.

The columnists seem to revert to the time of the Week, and they concentrate on that period the immense reaction which the Modernists inspired over the years, especially after 1923. What happened was something quite different and, moreover, something much more natural. At first considered a mere student prank or an exhibitionist manifestation of young artists, the Week automatically suggested to the conservatives the tactic of silence and was at first simply ignored. Léo Vaz attempted this tactic in 1924 when he responded to Paulo Prado's article on Brecheret, which had been published in *O Estado de São Paulo* before its appearance in the *Revista do Brasil.* The journalist was surprised that in Paulo Prado's collaboration there should be "more than one reference to a certain week of art which by all appearances must have taken place here in São Paulo, leaving behind it a shining trail in our brain." And immediately afterward: "What seems to have happened some years back was a trip taken by a certain esthete gentleman who had business dealings here. . . ." [55]

It was around 1924 that not only was a Modernist esthetics formulated (after the period of confusion and initial indecision) but also the opposing hosts of Modernists and anti-Modernists became clearly distinguishable. The fact is that the latter discovered somewhat tardily that the former had come to stay and that they could no longer be ignored. By that time the attacks were of little or no importance: in the first place because it was impossible to discern the slightest doctrinal contribution; in the second place because Modernism was then the dominant note of creative literature; in the third place because the attacks inevitably were aimed at esthetic aspects which the Modernists themselves had long since surpassed; and finally because everyone felt that, for good or ill, the Modernist arts were the only ones that had anything of value to offer. The esthetic depletion of the traditionalists was by that time incontrovertible and irremediable.

From Futurism to Modernism

The evolution of Futurism into Modernism was reflected immediately in Mário de Andrade's artistic development; and it was Mário de Andrade who incarnated Brazilian Modernism after the early extravagant phase, identified with Oswald de Andrade, had passed. On the whole, it can be said that Futurism existed in Brazil before the Week of Modern Art, let us say, as a point of reference, between Anita Malfatti's exhibition of 1917 and the Week of 1922. The Week had tacitly suggested the adjective which reappeared in the subtitle of *A Escrava Que Não É Isaura* ("Modernist"), so that in effect Mário de Andrade's formulation of a poetics constituted the doctrinal repudiation of Futurism. It proved once and for all that the Brazilian arts were held to exist in a Modernist age.

It is not correct to say that Oswald de Andrade's article "O meu poeta futurista" put the word "futurist" into circulation. "Before that article," we read in *A Literatura no Brasil*,[56] "these words were known and current, but they did not inspire argumentation or polemic as they later did in the intellectual circles of São Paulo. Before Oswald de Andrade's article they were words that represented our reality and were not employed solely to describe the European situation." In fact, there were writers who

71

had long since mentioned Futurism, but it did not imply esthetic implantation as a literary movement, a school, or a vanguardist group. Since 1914, at least, Ernesto Bertarelli, in the *O Estado de São Paulo*, spoke of the "lessons of Futurism"; and in the reception of Goulart de Andrade into the Academy, Alberto de Oliveira alluded to the "Futurists or companions of Marinetti." Even in 1917, L. Xavier published *Oásis*, a book totally forgotten today, which came out with a legitimate (and blustery) Futurist manifesto in its preface: "In this century of airplanes in which we march toward denationalization, in which Esperanto comes forth as the leveler of languages and art advances toward Futurism, while thought advances toward anarchy like the canoe that has strayed off course, the current of *Nationalism* here—like the current of the *Enracinement* in France—casts its anchor at a propitious hour to the depths of the troubled sea of the modern idea, as if it desired to cling firmly to the traditions of the past. . . ." It cannot be said that the brain of the good Xavier was a model of logical thought, or even of literary information; at any rate, here is the proof, alongside many others, that before the Week everyone was more or less steeped in Modernism.

Mário de Andrade's very rebuttal, "Futurista?!" [57] showed that Oswald de Andrade, in his frantic search for novelty, was beginning to be surpassed because the author of the *Paulicéia Desvairada* (which had already been written by that time) [58] said that he had repudiated "the weird futurism of Europe" as well as "the vague futurism of Brazil." Furthermore, *Klaxon,* which was the only journal that could legitimately maintain itself as the official organ of Modernism, began by declaring: "KLAXON is not Futurist" (number 1 of May, 1922). The fact that it declared itself "Klaxist," and that Ramón Gómez de la Serna should have gotten into the picture when he included "Klaxism" among the universal -*isms,* is merely one more amusing aspect of the Movement's history. "Klaxism" was only an ironic appellation for Modernism, because the literary journal desired to "represent the period of 1920 forward." Forward—and not backward to the Futurism of 1910.

This Futurism had been so successful that it had to suffer the paternal claims of several progenitors: one of them, Gabriel

Alomar, around 1917 included in his book *Verba* (Madrid: Biblioteca Nueva, n. d.) the lecture "Futurism," which was delivered
at the Ateneo Barcelonés on June 18, 1904, and remarked and
emphasized that "as a consequence, this movement considerably
antedates Marinetti's Futurism." Alomar, however, employed the
word in its broad sense as an antonym of traditionalism and con-
servatism as these were "the two forms of human expression." He
did not imply the meaning of a new artistic or literary school.
That lecture proved that at the beginning of the century the
idea was in the air, which was obviously true, because at that time
Picasso and Apollinaire were working in Paris, but nothing came
of it. At that time Alomar could not really have known what he
was saying. The matter is interesting because many years later
Carlos Chiacchio, in the exercise of his critical activities on the
newspapers of Bahia, tried to claim for the Spanish writer a priority which in fact did not exist.[59]

Going from the biographical level on which the article "Futurist?!" was written to the broader level of literary history, Mário
de Andrade, who was then art critic for the *Revista do Brasil*,
published the following observations in that journal in August
of 1923:

As I reach this thoughtful reading, I begin to think that
convalescences are not uniquely the property of physical illness. There are also spiritual convalescences. The Futurist
incident in Brazil . . . That horrible period that came
around the middle of 1920 and lasted until the Week of
Modern Art—February, even March of 1922—was nothing
more than a serious, very serious, illness which some youthful Brazilian artists suffered. What fever! What delirium!
Were there excesses? There were. Then came convalescence.
Do the excesses continue? They do. But they have another
aspect and, mainly, another essence. The sudden abandon-
ment of certain preconceptions, which for many years have
been our faith, the internal struggle between them and the
new preconceptions and isolation in the midst of general
disesteem brought on the fevers of the first excesses. And
what were they? Fruitless delirium. Deliberate divorcement
from the traditionalist truth merely to anger future adver-

saries, desperate sadness, iconoclast; persecution complex in which we saw (I saw) in our defenseless language, in our indifferent homeland, enemies which were really only windmills. That is the origin of the wounding of the language by shattering its graceful nobility, the origin of those charges against the masters of the past and anger turned against one's homeland which at last harbors and reconciles Futurists and traditionalists.

.   .   .   .   .

We shall be restored in the bosom of the traditionalism without which no one can live. Brazilian traditionalism? That, too. Why not? Through the pantheistic penetration of the earth, through the historical comprehension of the race, and through the service of a language that is evolving, to be sure, but without excessive deformations. Our traditionalism, however, will be principally human and universal. In our *modern* hearts the struggle has exhausted the source of rivalry.

.   .   .   .   .

There is, in fact, in our *Futurism* a rupture in our Brazilian evolution. The fact of the matter is that it has been said at least a thousand times for almost a century: several lustra behind the times, we have been nothing more than a reflection of France. A golden reflection. But a reflection nonetheless. We Modernists broke the pattern of natural evolution. We leaped over the lustra of backwardness. We obliterated the reflection. We are today the voice of Brazil of the 1923 chorus in which all nations sing. I could document that fact. That is how the problem of the continuity of Brazilian artistic tradition has been solved. Not even the great Cruz e Sousa and one or two other decadent Symbolists suffice to justify our present. I confess that there is a rupture through which we seem shocking and apparently excessive to some cross-eyed elements in our audience. How is it possible to evolve from well-fed academism and Impressionism to the work of Anita Malfatti in a country which closed its eyes to the revolutionary work of Seurat, Van Gogh, and Cézanne? How is it possible to evolve from Bernardelli to Brecheret without Metzner, Milles, Mestrovic? A lacuna. And the distressed cry of the macaws. Must we look to other countries for our own evolution? Not even for that reason are we less the voice of Brazil which is today depicted as universal. Such overwhelming movements are rare. Renaissance. Romanticism. To a large extent owing to the facility and rapidity of present-day communication, only Futurism is universal, and that is as poorly named as the other -*isms* of the past.

That article may well have been the breaking point between the last "Futurist" and revolutionary nostalgia and the conscious acceptance of a change of fortune. In the following year, in February of 1924, the *Revista do Brasil* carried a letter written by Ronald de Carvalho to Jackson de Figueiredo, originally published in the *O Jornal* of Rio de Janeiro of January 29. After stating that Futurism had been a purely Italian phenomenon that was past, he concluded: "Down with virtuoso-ism, sádemirandism, dictionarism and all the other phantoms that drained our energies, by reducing them to a capricious and stupid game. Futurism is also traditionalism. Down with Futurism!"

Down with Futurism! That became the battle cry of all the branches of Modernism after 1924, the year of the great options, of the first schisms, of heterodoxy that installed itself in the name of orthodoxy. In the manifesto of Brazilwood Poetry, Oswald de Andrade assumed the tone of voice of the historian: "The work of the Futurist generation was cyclopean. To set the imperial clock of our national literature. Once that stage had been passed, the problem altered. To be regional and pure in one's own time." Writers and artists began to understand vaguely what Abguar Bastos expressed in 1944 in the *Testamento de Uma Geração* by Edgard Cavalheiro: " 'Modernism' appeared in the garb of Futurism. Futurism was, moveover, a pre-war manifestation; it was, so to speak, already traditionalist. That may explain why the 'Modernists' tried to give a different meaning to the campaign." Thus, there is a delicious error in the dispute between traditionalism and Modernism, since some accused in the name of dead truths while others defended themselves in the name of internal metamorphoses.

Still stranger is the fact that the Modernists themselves often were not aware of that slow underground evolution. In the same book by Edgard Cavalheiro, João Alphonsus pointed out that it was a kind of anachronism to attack Graça Aranha and observed that *A Escrava Que Não É Isaura* had been the definitive treatise of the rupture:

> Moreover, when Graça Aranha wrote his preface to the Futurist manifestoes in 1926, a much more interesting book for all of us had been published the year before in São Paulo: *A Escrava Que Não É Isaura* (treatise on certain of the trends in Modernist poetry), by Mário de Andrade. Take note: "Modernist" poetry. It seems to me that ever since the Week of Modern Art the use of this name had become inevitable: Modernism. Yes, no appeal to an understanding of the future; rather the honest objectives of a modern-day art, since it was an absolute certainty that our art was positively antediluvian.

For that reason Mário de Andrade's book was, above all else, an anti-Marinettian pamphlet. Thus, through a coincidence that was, after all, natural, the "Futurist" campaign, which preceded the Week, as well as the anti-Futurist campaign, which consolidated Modernism after 1924, had as a necessary point of reference the figure of Marinetti. And if in 1921 he was a beacon shining in the darkness of the present and the future, in 1925 he represented the compromising figure who might well have been the undoing of Modernism. In this regard, we have an important letter from Mário de Andrade to Manuel Bandeira which compares to the *Escrava* and provided it, so to speak, with a proper perspective:

> Besides, I was damned irritated with all that nonsense Marinetti was spouting, which was only reinforced by his later rot. The fellow came over here with a frightful message of fraternity that was virtually indecent, and it is almost certain that on this trip he was acting as a delegate of fascism. Don't be deceived by Viggiani. Here in São Paulo a lecture of his was arranged by the Italian ambassador, because Viggiani couldn't find a theatre, and the Casino where Marinetti spoke yesterday belongs to the Bonnacchi firm, Viggiani's mortal enemy. It's best to be on your guard. Viggiani came to invite

me to introduce Marinetti at the theatre. I refused and it
seems that everyone followed my lead.[60] I didn't go to yesterday's inanities, and it appears I did well not to attend. I know
from reliable sources that they had a good booing prepared
for me if I had gone. I know that the whole arrangement was
beneath contempt. Marinetti, as usual, proceeded with admirable serenity. Good Lord, man, I don't know whether it
really was admirable because, after all, it isn't terribly difficult
to remain serene in the face of a scandal that one has personally arranged. Besides that, what really provoked me in
all that nonsense was their having recourse to the natural
imbecility of school boys for purposes of advertisement and
profit. They wanted and they fabricated the scandal; but
since they only wanted the boos—because the rest, of course,
could be really harmful—I know that the police frisked the
boys as they entered the theatre. Just the same, they smug-
gled in rotten eggs, tomatoes, and radishes, all of which ended
up on the stage. And Marinetti, after two and a half hours,
left the theatre without even having spoken. I still haven't
seen the guy. Viggiani wired me that he was arriving on Sun-
day. I was at the station with an esthetics student of mine.
When he didn't arrive, I picked up a paper (my student insisted that he really wouldn't arrive that day because the
Fanfulla had announced the night before that Marinetti was
going to broadcast a lecture there); I grabbed a *Fanfulla* and
learned that he wouldn't arrive until Friday. I tried to visit
him just yesterday with Yan de Almeida Prado, but he arranged our meeting for 6:00 P.M. and I couldn't go at that
hour because I had a class at the Conservatory. I've already
missed two classes there this month because of him. So I still
haven't seen the man, and it seems that out of spite he announced at the theatre that all of Brazil's Futurists were in
Rio de Janeiro. I don't know whether that's true (it must be)
because all of today's papers have repeated the statement.
Anyway, tomorrow (Wednesday) I'll go visit him. If he
doesn't wish to receive me, that's fine because he will avoid
the argument we are bound to have, since I am determined
to speak sincerely concerning my opinion of his behavior
here; furthermore I'll tell him that I didn't go to the theatre
because I have little taste for performances of boos that have
more or less been prearranged.

I'll visit him also in order to return his courtesies. After
that he can go to you-know-where. I'm convinced that it's
best to deal with him with the greatest nonchalance, even
with affected nonchalance, so he won't think that we're all
jumping on his wagon. Even the dullest things I say to him
will be spoken with the greatest nonchalance imaginable, as
if I were long since accustomed to dealing with the Marinet-
tis of this world. This "Eye-talian" who came over here to
make us lose at least half the ground we've gained to date
needs to be dealt with strictly according to his just deserts.[61]

The man who wrote that letter in 1925 was the very man
who published *A Escrava Que Não É Isaura* in the same year;
however, we should not forget that although the original outline
was kept intact, the book had been written in April and May
of 1922, that is, immediately after the Week, still in the heat of
combat. Without going into details, he stated that between composition and publication his ideas had changed. He did not eluci-
date, however, on the problem that engages us at the moment:
whether or not the anti-Marinettian slant of the volume came
after the original composition. As long as we lack documents to
clarify this question (if such documents exist), it is impossible to
take the Futurist temperature of the *Escrava* at those two essential
moments.

At any rate, it is important to bear in mind that since 1921
Mário de Andrade had expressly repudiated any affiliation with
Futurism; and it would not be wrong to take as the central
postulate of the *Escrava* a fact that should influence our interpretation of the book, the well-known cry of relief: "I do not intend to be a rebel all my life, in heaven's name!" This was all
the more true considering that ever since 1922 the Preface to the
Paulicéia Desvairada mocked the excesses of all literary schools
and sardonically founded "Hallucinism" and added: "You will
have to excuse me if I am behind the times as far as current artistic
movements are concerned. I am a traditionalist, I confess." More
clearly in a rejoinder that was simultaneously directed against
Oswald de Andrade and Marinetti, he wrote: "I am not a Futurist
(after Marinetti). I have said so before and I repeat it. I have

points of contact with Futurism. When Oswald de Andrade called me a Futurist, he was wrong. That was my fault. I knew of the existence of the article, and I allowed it to be published. The uproar was so great that I wished to see everyone drop dead." And identifying the transition to Modernism: "To write modern art never means to me to represent modern-day life through its externals: automobiles, movies, asphalt. If these words appear in my book, it is not because I think I write modern with them; rather because my book is modern, they have their reason for being in it."

Let us recall that Luís Aranha, who was very close to Mário de Andrade, in 1922 had written in the "Poema Giratório":

> One day a journal
> Then I met Cendrars
> Apollinaire
> Spire
> Vildrac
> Duhamel
> All the modern writers
> But still I could not understand Modernism [62]

The least we can assume is that for Mário de Andrade, as for the writers and artists who were closest to him, the revolutionary movement had always been Modernist and never Futurist. The opposite was perhaps true for Oswald de Andrade, so that the two Andrades really represented the two divergent trends of the school. If we add what Mário de Andrade wrote about Luís Aranha: "Of the books by Blaise Cendrars, Max Jacob, Apollinaire, and Cocteau that I was receiving daily, often it was Luís Aranha who first devoured them," we can understand that it was the French (*horresco referens!*) who were the true masters of Modernism and not Marinetti and the Italians. They, therefore, guarantee the passage from Futurism to Modernism. After 1924, to adopt Futurism meant to be a traditionalist. A greater lack of true intimacy with the Movement was exhibited by Jorge de Lima when he mentioned the "futurism of the Modernists" in 1929 in his essay "Todos Cantam Sua Terra. . . ."

Quite the contrary of Jorge de Lima, because he pointed the true direction, was Mário de Andrade's praise of the "magnificent Folgore" who was "the greatest and truly the most modern of the Italian Futurist group." To be modern, among the Futurists, was to live *modernity* and modernism; to be Futurist among the moderns was to be merely a laggard.

Mário, Marinetti, Mallarmé

Taking Rimbaud as the source of all modern poetry, Mário de Andrade nonetheless categorically rejected the artist who, to a large extent, continued Rimbaud's experiments: Mallarmé. AVOID MALLARMÉ AT ALL COSTS, he shouted in the pages of the *Escrava*, because analogy, of necessity, led to paraphrase, which in literature represented the capital sin (in the Modernist's catechism as it had been in the Romanticist's). Such a view of Mallarmé was, no doubt, biased and incomplete. As the super-Modernists who came after the Modernists understood things, it was Mallarmé, rather than Rimbaud, who had divested the slave girl Poesy of all her useless tinsel.[63]

Of course, Mário de Andrade, who by that time had become the chief lawgiver of Modernism, maintained his greatest quarrel with Marinetti. When he created the "liberated word," we read in the *Escrava*, "Marinetti discovered what had always existed, and he was profoundly in error when he took as an end what was merely a transitory means of expression. His passages of liberated words are unbearable for their hermeticism, their artificiality and monotony." Also in the experiments with "association of images," Marinetti (in Mário de Andrade's opinion) took "the means as an end." But he kept his death blow for the conclusion: "Must I

81

say it again? The Marinetti whom many consider the crucifer in the procession, is way behind the times, preoccupied, as he is, with *upholding* Futurism, which is often rhetorical and always loud-mouthed.

Note that these words were obviously written between 1922 and 1924, that is, well before the disastrous and hapless visit of Marinetti to Brazil: Mário de Andrade's anti-Marinettism was, so to speak, congenital and irremediable. Because of all the Modernists he was the most modern and the least Futurist, and because he suffered little from the vanguardist malaise, or at least from the vanguardist idolatry of the vanguard (Oswald de Andrade's identifying mark), it is to Mário de Andrade more than to anyone else that we owe the swift passage from Futurism to Modernism, the main characteristic of the Brazilian Movement.

That is an important point which clearly identifies the origin of Modernist "Brazilianism" in that early phase and in later developments: one could imagine (although such thoughts have no meaning at all from the historical point of view) that the Modernist novel might have turned in the direction of estheticist cosmopolitanism or might have adopted Cocteau as its master, if in the midst of its first decade the school's perspectives had not suffered the anti-Futurist impact that we are now studying.

Of course, Mário de Andrade did not effect that change of direction all by himself; it even happened that, on the basis of what we have so far observed, he encountered rather pronounced "reactionary" trends within a certain Modernist group: the group in closer alliance with Graça Aranha, particularly Ronald de Carvalho. It is strange to recall that Mário de Andrade noticeably disregarded Ronald de Carvalho's estheticism and considerably disparaged his instinct as a popularizer. For his part Ronald found Graça Aranha something of a latecomer (also around 1925) in his "Futurist" insistence: "We need to convince Graça," he said repeatedly to Renato Almeida, "to rid himself of this Futurist nonsense. It creates an enormous confusion. The trouble is that he likes the word, and it no longer has the noble meaning he attributes to it; rather the meaning has been corrupted." [64] In his lecture on "As Bases da Arte Moderna," he tried specifically to mark the distances: "What is Modernism? Is the modern spirit perhaps confused with Cubism, Dadaism, and Surrealism? Or rather is it not that the modern spirit is, as we hear so often repeated, merely Futurism? I can tell you in advance that it is an uninformed error to make of Futurism the basis for the modern spirit. . . . Those who accuse the work of the modern Brazilian artist of being Futurist do not know what they are talking about." One year later Felippe d'Oliveira, in an interview granted to Jayme de Barros and published in the *O País* of Rio de Janeiro, also said: "This idea that is so hotly discussed now in Brazil which sees a premeditated Futurist trend set over against a traditionalist trend is absurd. There is no Futurism here. There are no Futurists."

The proof that the main line of Modernism rejected Futurism from the very start may be obscured in the echoes which the Futurist orientation inspired in the provinces. In the well-meaning but confused "literary letter" that Joaquim Inojosa sent from Recife to the young writers of Paraíba, a kind of Pauline epistle intended for the spread of Modernism in the Northeast, the following was one of the fundamental postulates:

> Today on the campgrounds of our intelligentsia there is, as there always has been in any age, a new generation which longs for new ideals. Above all, that generation has lifted up its eyes to the goal barely glimpsed in a dream in São Paulo, Rio, Recife, and Pará. Paraíba will not refuse the invitation I extend to accompany us in this herculean effort and truce-less struggle to be free of ancient artistic formulas in chivalric and, if necessary, heartless combat against the older generation. You youthful artists there will surely go with us in this requisite artistic renovation which some unjust critics have called "Futurism," a name that smacks of Marinetti and is, therefore, unacceptable in our circle and which is further a grenade in the hands of those who have no basis for argumentation.[65]

In November of 1927, in the third number of the review *Verde,* Martins de Oliveira still felt it necessary to clarify a certain confusion: "Many people will confuse *Modernism* with *Futurism.*

Now . . . it is necessary to make a distinction. *Modernism* is one
thing and *Futurism* is another. They differ in fundamental ways.
They are similar only in their desire to renovate. Modernism in
Brazil is a broad movement pregnant with new ideas. *Futurism*
was the ingenuous fantasy of the ingenuous Marinetti who, after
all, was lagging behind by a hundred years even in his own ideas,
and he ended up by forgetting the whole issue." We may well
assume that the question, at that point, had not been set to right,
not even in Cataguases, because in the fourth number (December,
1927) of the same review, Francisco Inácio Peixoto published an
impatient day letter which he had addressed to Martins de
Oliveira:

> When I met you around the middle of June or July, it seemed
> to me that you had attached yourself to certain stupid pre-
> conceptions in an effort to put on intellectual airs. And I
> was not wrong. . . . I also noted your mania for explaining
> and re-explaining what Modernism is and how it is different
> from Futurism. Now in the last number of *VERDE* you come
> out with all that rigmarole in a very long article titled
> "MODERNISMO." As you have everything confused I im-
> mediately compared you to those schoolboys who, early in
> their new studies, attempt to parade their profound compre-
> hension and usually make a mess of it. . . . Now I, who was
> born and reared within Modernist ideals, do not understand
> all the hubbub you mention. . . . Why go on explaining
> "our ideal is marvelous"? No one will ever understand. Nor
> do we need to understand. Therefore, your articles to explain
> modernizing tendencies are futile. Therefore, your witless
> article is totally futile.

It was also in 1927 that Eduardo Frieiro published his novel
O Clube dos Grafômanos, [66] a satire on intellectual circles in general, and not only on Modernism. At a certain point one of the
characters, Bento Pires, speaks: "And they've changed their name.
They're not Futurists, Dadaists, Simultaneists, or Surrealists any
more. Now they're just plain 'Modernists.' " As Mário Guastini
had written the year before, there had been a passage "from

Marinettian Futurism" to national *Modernism,* but it was a transition effected long before the novelist and the journalist thought. It was precisely with regard to Inojosa's book that Prudente de Morais Neto established the proper perspectives at the very time when *A Escrava Que Não É Isaura* was in circulation:

> But Pernambuco (and Senhor Inojosa is no exception) still is in the first phase of Modernism. A phase of rebellion, of destructive violence, of disorientation, in which one cultivates the absurd for the sake of the absurd, curiosity for the sake of curiosity, machines, styles, inventions, all the external paraphernalia of contemporary life for the appearance of the modernity of employing them as an artistic motif. It would be futile to deny that we went through that period, too, and that Italian Futurism could not surpass it. . . . Later a more profound comprehension of Modernism teaches us to establish some differences; each finds his own way and stops worrying about the latest inventions and the latest styles and recognizes with Senhor Tristan Derème that "the face of tragedy would not change if Corneille had ridden a bicycle."

But, to be precise, the face of tragedy would have changed. That is the essential esthetic truth which Prudente de Morais Neto, out of love for the *bon mot,* allowed to pass.

From Modernism to the Modern Spirit

In the natural dialectic of artistic movements, the passage from Futurism to Modernism might be considered a retrogression, a disguised return to the past; but that passage bore within it another opposing movement brought about as a second indispensable step: the move to the future, beyond Futurism, which in reality was the transition from Modernism to the modern spirit. Undeniably, Futurism was petrified by its own system of artistic ideas and consequently acquired the unexpected appearance of ridiculous traditionalism. Brazilian Modernism, on the contrary, which was much more flexible, will remain subject to the successive metamorphoses that characterize it: from the estheticism of the first phase to the *engagée* literature of the second phase; from poetry to the sociological novel; from the destructive spirit to creative criticism; from one genre to the other down to the organic coexistence of genres. It is precisely this polymorphism that has deceived so many specialists, causing them sometimes to antedate the disappearance of Modernism and at other times leading them to attribute to other influences that breath of creativity which derived indirectly, but unquestionably, from the Week of Modern Art.

To that oscillation in time corresponds an identical gravitation in space: at the conclusion of the aforementioned study for the *Panorama das Literaturas das Américas,* I had the occasion to remark in 1957 that modern Brazilian literature manifested two movements which were apparently contrary but which, in reality, worked toward the same end: on one hand, the literature became aware of itself and made an effort to resist foreign influences as it sought to assimilate them profitably and not merely to reflect them; on the other hand, this literature strove steadily toward the universal. Two fates—the fate of the earth and the fate of the world—bent over the cradle of Modernism and there cast their spell. Futurism reflected, in its beginnings, the fascinating lure of cosmopolitan Europe, which followed the war; Modernism was a remorseful reaction against denationalization; the modern spirit was an inevitable reintegration into an overpowering civilization.

Thus, when the last flame of Modernism was extinguished in 1945, it was blown out by one magic word: stylistics—once again the old estheticism and cosmopolitanism. Brazilian writers who wrote after the thirties within the Modernist process itself, and who went so far as to repudiate the Movement, never did deny their modern spirit; as the years passed, the same word came to define a literary and artistic movement which did not arrogate its own name.

So we see that Mário de Andrade had been aware of this transformation since 1924. In a letter to Manuel Bandeira, he viewed the problem as follows:

What I do—and perhaps you've noticed this—is make a distinction between moderns and Modernists. With regard to this fact, I have intentionally written about "the poet (like you) who is sincere and is not interested in founding schools and propagating novelties which are not his own. . . ." This is really a criticism of Z . . .[67] who wants to make us his disciples and also a criticism of all of us "Modernists" who were so concerned with novelties from France, Italy, and Germany. Especially myself: I nearly got lost. Every reaction has its own excesses. I had them because I rebelled against Symbolism. Today I am myself. I am no longer a Modernist. But I am modern, as you are. Today I can also say that I am a descendant of Symbolism. The modern spirit exists as evolution. In that regard, it is correct. This does not mean that the Modernists have not discovered their own thing; and had it not been for them, many of today's moderns would still be rigid traditionalists.[68]

Some months later (April 18, 1925), in correspondence which clarifies the origins of the famous "Open Letter" to Alberto de Oliveira, he returned to the same subject:

I'm going to work on a letter. And I'm going to try to find some way of answering Tristão in it. An ironic complaint and my definitive repudiation of the name of modern that they have given me. You understand, Manuel, I am today much too busy to be annoyed by that nonsense of Modernism and traditionalism. "I'm the one who's really modern." That is totally meaningless to me today. I have other things to do. I'm not joking, either. Modernism is a hundred miles from me today. What does it mean to be modern? The answer to that is either the most complicated thing in the world, or it's the simplest.[69]

Of course, it would be a gross error to imagine that, even if he did not admit it, Mário de Andrade was trying to substitute a more recent *-ism* for one that had exhausted itself. The importance that I see in these debates is precisely that they seem to bring to a close, in literature and art, the period of the *-isms,* a fact that not everyone, even today, seems to grasp. In May of the same year, another letter to Manuel Bandeira contained the main postulate of the problem: "I am not struggling between Modernism and anti-Modernism; I simply today do not find any more significance for the word Modernism. I have more important things to do and think." Nonetheless, with good or ill will, he lived and died a "Modernist," so tenaciously do the scholastic tags stick to writers. It is necessary to add that these priceless letters to Manuel Bandeira were not published until 1958. Many others, written to several personages and equally priceless, have still not been published.

At the far side of Modernism as a literary period, Otávio de Freitas, Jr., then considered one of the most significant talents of the new generation, answered Mário Neme: "The word 'modern' is very embarrassing. Today it seems to signify that whole generation of writers who followed the generation now between thirty and fifty years old: called the generation of 'Modernism.' " [70]

The -Isms

One of the greatest paradoxes of Modernism was that the Movement marched inexorably toward the abolition of all the *-isms* through the irruption and eruption of every variety of *-ism*. The *-isms* successively launched partial programs for Modernism, which is to say that from time to time the *-isms* placed varied emphases on different aspects of their implicit programs.

The first and most general of the programs which launched the Week of Modern Art, along with the adjective *modern,* seemed immediately to be surpassed by a great many others, even more radical, which followed in its wake. But it was that program, curiously enough, which bore hidden within it a secret capacity for permanence: the address by Graça Aranha, "A Emoção Estética na Arte Moderna," which should be read as an introduction to what Graça said two years later in the Academy. It is too often ignored that these two academic addresses, which did not *inaugurate* but *proposed* two revolutions—one of which was victorious—were published under the title *O Espírito Moderno* in a volume of essays which the publisher Monteiro Lobato did not hesitate to bring out. We should also not forget that this volume came off the press in 1925, that is, along with *A Escrava Que Não É Isaura.* The hostile but silent dispute between Mário de

Andrade and Graça Aranha was established, having been born of the seed which Mário sowed on the stage of the Municipal Theatre with his famous "no endorsement" hurled at the inaugural address.

The case of Graça Aranha will be studied later; for the moment it will suffice to emphasize that he defined modern art, in 1922, as an artistic movement characterized "by the freest and most fruitful subjectivism" resulting "from the extraordinary individualism which for almost two centuries has come through the void of time to reach our shores as the overwhelming feature of our age." The esthetic renovation of Brazil which, he alleged, "was initiated by Villa-Lobos's music, Brecheret's sculpture, the painting of Di Cavalcanti, Anita Malfatti, Vicente do Rêgo Monteiro, Zina Aita, and by the daring poetry of our youth, will be the liberation of art from the danger of inopportune arcadianism, academism and provincialism which threaten it." Graça Aranha also said: "Regionalism may well be the material for literature. It can never be the objective of a national literature which has universal aspirations."

Two years after this address, the Week of Modern Art had already assumed the form of the Modernist Movement. However, this occurred at the very moment when Graça Aranha sought (in a revolutionary rather than a diplomatic frame of mind) to scare away the phantom of academism which nibbled at his writer's liver rather than at Brazilian literature; and Oswald de Andrade had readied the first great heresy of Modernism which he unleashed, as it usually happens, in the name of restoration to orthodoxy. Paulo Prado's preface to Oswald de Andrade's book bears the date of May, 1924. Just one month later Graça Aranha addressed the Academy. Both were slightly behind the times: the academician with regard to living literature, the writer of the preface with regard to the Movement of which he had been one of the patrons and sympathizers.

After the address of 1924, Graça Aranha's literary career was characterized by an effort to regain his lost ground because he felt that he had been abandoned by both academicians and Modernists. It is sad to realize that he took a direction exactly opposite to the prevailing current, and the more vigorously he attempted to become more "Futurist" the more deeply he sank into academism. As for Paulo Prado, he saved two names from the poetry of the past: Casimiro de Abreu (whom Mário de Andrade later called "fatuous") and Catulo Cearense, "the backlands troubadour long since tainted by literary madness." [71] That was, however, not terribly serious. It was more serious to have indicated that Brazilwood poetry was "the first organized effort to liberate Brazilian poetry." One can sense perfectly well in Paulo Prado's tone and in his words a strange phenomenon we instinctively find difficult to accept: the lessened importance which, until late in the twenties, was attributed to Mário de Andrade. Modernism's true "leaders" at first were Menotti del Picchia and Oswald de Andrade. While more solid prospects were being established, Mário de Andrade's literary personality was strengthened and the personality of the other two writers was diminishing, although Oswald de Andrade preserved to the end of his days his role as the great anarchist of a movement which of necessity had to grow steadily more bourgeois.

Therefore, Paulo Prado saw in Oswald de Andrade's manifesto an impossible thing: a disciplining force which at the same time expected the new movement to crystallize the "new Brazilian language." As for the manifesto itself, it may be considered, first of all, as an attempt to recover lost innocence (in that regard, the Cannibal Manifesto which followed it was merely a step forward, primitivism being one of the two contradictory factors in Oswald's intellectual temper); secondly, as the proposal of a new regionalism; and finally, as Futurism's death certificate (although the author himself still lived as a Futurist). Moreover, one speaks of the Brazilwood *Manifesto,* when in reality there are two (with some differences in content): the document that was published under that title in the *Correio da Manhã* of Rio de Janeiro (reprinted in the *Revista do Brasil* of April, 1924, from which I now quote), and the "speech" which opens the volume *Pau Brasil,*[72] in which the first manifesto is reproduced with some modification. In so far as I can gather from this "speech," Oswald de Andrade was attempting to create a poetry that would be the expression of our history (that, at least, is the meaning of his paraphrases, or whatever they may be, inspired by our colonial chronicles), and this poetry was stripped of all "literary" artifice.

However, reacting to an acute literary instinct, he perceived that his primitivism was artificial, was a conquest of civilization: "Twentieth century. An explosion of knowledge. Men who used to know everything have become distorted like towers of rubber. They have exploded with encyclopedism. Poetry for the poets. The joy of ignorance which discovers. Pedr'Álvares."

Oswald de Andrade's poetic caravelle was thus contradictorily or anachronistically constructed of brazilwood. Although Paulo Prado did not understand it, the poet discovered a country that had already been discovered, a land so fertile that everything planted flourished there—even brazilwood, which in this case was a hothouse plant cultivated on that "navel of the world" (Paulo Prado *dixit*) Paris's Place Clichy. Oswald de Andrade was merely trying once again to recover the helm of Modernism, which had slipped from his grasp. But that pretext of literary politics was the least important; as a matter of fact it had no importance at all. What does matter is that he was reacting against the estheticism of the "Klaxist" manifesto, which was located at the opposite pole to primitivism and lauded art as a "deformer of nature."

Before the publication of the Brazilwood Manifesto, *Natalika*, the treatise on Modernist poetics signed by Guilherme de Almeida, was printed for Candeia Azul in January of 1924. The third "statement" in that treatise said: "If nature were beautiful, art would have no reason to exist." The first "statement" was an echo of Parnassian poetics: "Everything in nature passes away; everything in art endures. Nature is temporary; art is eternal. Because nature knows time as art does not." Guilherme de Almeida's -*ism*, which was not successful, was a kind of Parnassian-Symbolist code which was totally out of joint with the times. He was closer to the *fin-de-siècle* "pale-and-wan-withering-away" than to any branch, however vague, of the Modernist esthetic. His essential postulate stated: "In the beginning art was nature itself; then art became the copy of nature, next the interpretation, and finally the perfection. Now it is the negation of nature."

So many divergent trends served nonetheless to show that 1924 was the critical year, if not in the formulation of a definitive Modernist esthetics (there never has been such a thing!) at least in the choice of a specific course. Modernism preferred the nationalist course to cosmopolitanism, the course of primitivism to that of artifice, the sociological to the psychological, the folkloric to the literary, and (already!) the political to the nonpolitical. Between 1924, the year which saw the Brazilwood Manifestoes and the classicizing efforts of Guilherme de Almeida and Rubens Borba de Moraes, and 1926, when the Tapir, Greengiltist, and the Purple Land movements appeared, *A Escrava Que Não É Isaura* maintained itself as a fulcrum. Its esthetic principles had been immediately drowned, however, by a wave of primitivism to which Mário de Andrade himself paid consummate homage in 1928 with *Macunaíma*.

In reality, taking his symbols from indigenous mythology (which was a *conscious* way of antedating himself with relation to Oswald de Andrade), as early as 1926 Plínio Salgado had stated in his lecture "A Anta e o Curupira": "We are now in a position to create a native Brazilian art with exclusively Brazilian elements." In a text which readily revealed the mystical notes of the political options which were immediately integrated into the Modernist network, he stated that the Tupi "race," which descended from the Tapir, "the largest mammal in America," had contributed "enormously to the formation of our nationality," and seemed even "to predominate over all other races." His ethnology may not be the most orthodox, but by denying that it was attempting to create a new Indianism, the Tapir Manifesto in essence accepted all the Modernist propositions and was destined, through its "Brazilianism," to develop into the Greengiltist group and from there into a politico-literary or literary-political symbiosis that was totally foreign to the apolitical orientation of the first five years of the Movement. It was Plínio Salgado himself who claimed these ties:

It was on that Great Eve that I unleashed two preparatory movements for the decisive movement of 1932. The first was "Greengiltism." It was myself, Cassiano Ricardo, Menotti del Picchia, and Mota Filho. The second was called the "Tapir Revolution," a kind of left-wing manifestation of "Greengiltism," and it was fabricated by myself and Raul Bopp.

Exactly as I broke off relations with the so-called "Modernists" by way of the "Greengilts," because the "Modernists" diverged from the road of the necessary revolution, I also felt that "Greengiltism" was too deeply rooted in a form of nationalism that was excessively "external" and pictorial. What was wanting was an "internal" and intuitive nationalism. In manifestoes that filled the columns of newspapers in São Paulo, Pôrto Alegre, and Curitiba, I cried out such things as these: "Our generation needs to be convinced that it will be a sacrificed generation. It will not fulfill its purpose. It will not see the advent of the Poet, the Leader, the Initiate. Without creating the Consciousness of Nationality, it is impossible to launch the New Thought ("The Tapir Revolution").

That was in 1927. We had gone through a literary revolution (1922) and two political revolutions (1922 and 1924). The first as well as the latter two expressed the Nation's vague longings. Modernist literature, as well as painting, sculpture, and music, degenerated into groups and subgroups. Political idealism was still confused and vague.[73]

This National Chief (Salgado's title as leader of the rightist Partido Integralista) seems to juggle chronology a bit as well as currents—if they ever existed outside of sentimental historiography. At any rate, as Domingos Carvalho da Silva observed,[74] Greengiltism may be called "the first contradiction of Brazilian Modernism, the first reaction against that Modernism." This is obviously not the opinion of Cassiano Ricardo: "It was then that our group opposed Cubism, Futurism, Dadaism, Expressionism, and Surrealism and invented 'Greengiltism.' As the name itself implies, the campaign had found its true direction. It had acquired a Brazilian meaning—by joining primitivism to the modern —and a social and political meaning—the exchange of a contemplative, lunatic, lachrymose, and anarchic mentality for one that was vigorous and healthy and destined to solve Brazilian problems in a Brazilian way." [75] That vigorous and healthy mentality that was destined to solve Brazilian problems in a Brazilian way was Integralism, but let that pass. The fact that the Tapir and Greengiltism were attempts to bypass Oswald de Andrade on the left is the conclusion we reach after reading Cassiano Ricardo's words in that same article: "The 'brazilwood' of Oswald's theory was not right. 'Brazilwood' was a meddlesome wood, primitive and internationalist because it attracted many a Frenchman who came here to traffic in league with the Tamoyos. . . ."

We may leave aside, in this analysis of the *-isms,* the appearance of "Terra Roxa e Outras Terras," a vague and insipid page, which announced that it was obeying "a general line called the modern spirit" and confessed at the same time that "we do not really know what it is." [76] We should point out that four years after Brazilwood and two years after Tapir, Oswald de Andrade admitted that his primitivism had not borne fruit and, moreover, had been surpassed; he thereby delivered the final blow, Cannibalism, which was doomed to the same failure but which was really the ultimate outpost in the forest.

The Cannibal Manifesto was published in the first number of the *Revista de Antropofagia,* which circulated autonomously from May of 1928 to February of 1929 and flickered as a weekly page in the *Diário de São Paulo* from March to July of that same year. It was dated from Piratininga, the 374th year after the Deglution of Bishop Sardinha (who was devoured by Brazilian Indians), and it propounded as its basic postulate: "Only cannibalism unites us. . . . Tupy or not Tupy, that is the question." With a little more nerve, but also with a certain puffy prolixity, at heart Cannibalism proposed the same program as Brazilwood and had the tactical meaning of "answering" Tapir, just as Tapir and Greengiltism had been the polemical answer to Brazilwood. In the same preface mentioned earlier (see note 72), Plínio Salgado had written a clarification: "I spent many an evening with Raul Bopp studying the Tupi language. We preferably read Barbosa Rodrigues and Couto de Magalhães. . . . The extreme Modernists made fun of us and then imitated us by organizing a surrealist and dadaist Indianism which they called 'cannibalism.' " [77]

So ended the *-isms* of the Movement, since certain local manifestoes, like that of the Green group from Cataguases, added nothing to the successive avatars of the Modernist doctrine. The Revolution of 1930 came immediately afterward and, following intense political agitation, contributed an unexpected breaking point; it was the external *fact* of the scales inclining for some years in the direction of social preoccupation. It should be added that the Revolution was the unwitting result of the same leftist-rightist rupture that would sharply dominate the mind of the thirties until the outbreak of World War II. But at the same time, the Revolution of 1930 appeared at first to represent the political fulfillment of a revolutionary process in which Modernism itself was unwittingly inscribed: so many misunderstandings found only a false solution with the war, after having involved the Modernist generation and those following in fratricidal polemics.

We shall study the political face of Modernism, that is, its development into political, partisan, and ideological *-isms;* but first it may be necessary to express some warning against a tendency toward multiplying the *-isms* where they do not really exist or confusing even more the shadowy lines that separate them. Peregrino Júnior seems to fall into that error in a small book which—rashly—bears the same title as Mário de Andrade's 1942 lecture.[78] According to this author there were at least five groups clearly distinguishable from one another: the *dynamists* and the *spiritualists* from Rio, and the *hallucinists, primitivists,* and *nationalists* from São Paulo. All of these names are products of the fantasy, when they are not actually incorrect (as in the case of "hallucinism," a simple joke of Mário de Andrade's, who founded it and declared that his school had died at birth). Beyond that, the names have two serious defects: they are superimposed on the conventional names of the several groups (created and adopted by the groups), and they have no meaning with regard to the real content of each *-ism.* In the same way, if it is true that Brazilwood and Cannibalism (names which the author readopts after employing the imaginary names) contained the seeds of leftism, while Greengilt and Tapir tended to the right, it does not seem proper to regard the *Festa* group as representative of the center, along with Menotti del Picchia and Cassiano Ricardo. It was from the *Festa* group that Integralism recruited its outstanding intellectuals, which reveals the censurable nature of these distinctions.[79]

Saints and Heretics

It was Modernism's fate never to have found its place in the literary Vatican that was implicit in the Movement's ambitions. The image of bureaucracy or religious politics is not completely inappropriate when we consider that Modernism had a Pope, Mário de Andrade, just as it had a St. John Baptist invested by him in the person of Manuel Bandeira. But Mário de Andrade's papacy was one of the minority and was hotly contested, as the Pope was confined to the spiritual Avignon of Lopes Chaves Street, a chapel which was basically like all the others, where he practiced his ministry through correspondence, like St. Paul (and from São Paulo), or through encyclicals which from the "Extremely Interesting Preface" of the *Pauličéia Desvairada* to *Aspectos da Literatura Brasileira,* by way of the *Escrava Que Não É Isaura,* continually preached a kind of orthodoxy which the heretical trends of that esthetic protestantism could not tolerate.

Sérgio Milliet, testifying in the *Testamento de Uma Geração,* stressed the ganglionic nature which Modernism, like all the protestantisms, assumed from the very start:

> We were constituted into small groups, some oriented toward politics, others toward art, and still others toward philosophy.

Our anti-individualism was only philosophical; it had no
deep roots, because we continued to be terribly different
from one another. Our ideas and our common sentiments
were barely sufficient for the foundation of groups and schools.
Then great groups were formed: *Green and Yellow* with
Cassiano, Menotti, Plínio Salgado and Mota Filho; and
Klaxon with Mário de Andrade, Rubens de Moraes, Couto
de Barros, Camargo Aranha, Guilherme de Almeida, Oswald
de Andrade, etc. I joined the latter group. Later when the
Klaxon group dissolved, the Cannibalism group was formed
with Oswald de Andrade, Tarsila do Amaral, Raul Bopp,
Antônio de Alcântara Machado, etc. . . . ; but from the
standpoint of literature and art, the groups ceased to exist
after Cannibalism.[80]

There is some serious chronological and ideological confusion
in that panorama, because the "Klaxon group," like the journal
which lent its name to the group, had already ceased to exist when
Greengiltism came into being; they are two different ages separated
by the great schism of Brazilwood (which means that it is an
anachronistic error to place Oswald de Andrade in the "Klaxon
group" at the time of Greengiltism). Likewise, Raul Bopp was
Greengilt before he was a Cannibal——no, a "Cannibalist"; Plínio
Salgado had to excommunicate him, in *Despertemos a Nação!*,
when he mentioned that sub-heresy: "And there went Raul Bopp
with the 'Modernists' who were living here under a French pro-
tectorate."

Since the heroic and pious phase of Modernist historiography
has passed, it is indispensable to undo all these misty perspectives
and all this vague idealization. But it was true that Sérgio Milliet
underlined what at the time needed to be said: that multiplication
by schizogenesis was not only preordained but was in the very
nature of the Modernist Movement. In other parts of the country,
most of those spores were destined to increase the median orthodoxy of Modernism. This occurred with amazing rapidity: in
1924, as we have seen, the virus had spread to Pernambuco and
Paraíba, then to Amazonas; in 1925 to Rio Grande do Sul; in
1927 to Cataguases which, with regard to penetration on the spa-

tial if not on the temporal plane, was the symbol for territorial conquest. A little later in 1928, reviewing the several Modernist focuses, Carlos Chiacchio wrote, after mentioning the names of São Paulo and Rio:

> Minas, which had traditionally been receptive to liberal ideas, received the Movement with suspicion. One writer after another appeared to parade with the flags of the inaugural celebration. Emílio Moura, Carlos Drummond de Andrade, João Alphonsus, Martins de Almeida, Caio de Freitas, Rosário Fusco. . . . But the joyous thrill of renovation spread to the southern flanks. And Rio Grande heroically took up the banner of the rebellion, evoking in the ample meters of the pampa the infinite green of the land. Green, very green, one sings only in green. Augusto Meyer, Raul Bopp, Rui Cirne Lima, Pedro Vergara, Roque Calage, Paulo Arinos, João Pinto da Silva, Carlos Dante de Morais. . . . And the other states did not pale. Pernambuco: Joaquim Inojosa, João Vasconcelos, Gilberto Freyre, Ascenso Ferreira, Valdemar de Oliveira. . . . Ceará: Aldo Prado, Carlos Demétrio, Leite Maranhão, Júlio Maciel, Pereira Júnior, Lúcio Várzea. . . . And in Bahia? We must extinguish Aladdin's lamp in order to light that of Diogenes. . . .[81]

Jorge de Lima attributed this rapid expansion of Modernism to the fact that the times were ripe for anything new: "That there existed throughout the country a psychological preparation for the advent of a new esthetics is proved by the fact that Modernism had appeared practically at the same time in several places: in São Paulo, here in Belo Horizonte, in Pôrto Alegre, in Recife, etc. In Maceió we were also writing Modernist literature although we were certainly not bound to the leaders of Rio and São Paulo by any closer tie than that which unites writers through the same ideas."[82] Belo Horizonte published its first Modernist journal in 1925 (*Revista*), putting out three numbers in July and August of that year and in January of 1926; the famous *Verde* from Cataguases came out in September of 1927 and put out five numbers through January of 1928 and one more during a new truncated phase in May of the following year. It was also around 1928 that Modernism reached Manaus in the form of the "Flaminaçu" Manifesto, by Abguar Bastos.

> With that title I wanted to fuse the Latin and the Indian. Hence "flaminaçu" or "large flame." I ended the manifesto with these words: "Flaminaçu" is not an obstacle to the great riots of civilization. No. It admits evolutionary transformations. But its very special and intransigent objective is to superimpose a veneer of legend on the natural grandeur of Brazil, its people, its possibilities, and its "history." Immediately after that I delivered a lecture at the Ideal Club: "The Modern Phenomenon of Brazilianism." Many youths answered my call and Remígio Fernandez wrote a memorable letter. From that moment I outlined my first novel to be written within the literary program I had undertaken. This was the *Amazônia Que Ninguém Sabe* which was subsequently published in Rio under a new title: *Terra de Icamiaba.* That book, which was a novel, was also a platform.[83]

As to Pará, Peregrino Júnior testified that in 1920 he was already reading, with the restless *Efemeris* group, the names of Mallarmé, Rimbaud, Verlaine, Verhaeren, and Nietzsche. Thus, the "Efemeris" movement, which Rio was totally ignorant of, must have existed before the Week. Headed by Lucídio Freitas, Tito Franco, Dejard de Mendonça, and Alves de Sousa "it represented a daring and courageous provincial attempt at literary renovation. Whoever consults the collection of *Efemeris*—quite materially original, discreet, and different—will see that the 'group from Pará' deserved the attention of the critics and literary historians of our time. Moreover, the movement showed how the seeds of Modernism had been in the air for some time, merely waiting for the proper conditions in order to germinate and bear fruit. . . ." [84]

One city which up till then had not entered Modernist history was Paranaguá which, among its annals, can count the journal of old traditions, *O Itiberê*. It was from *O Itiberê* that the *Revista do Brasil* in 1924 transcribed "by way of a curiosity" the following poem by Correia Júnior:

FIREWORKS
(Impressions of a St. John's Eve)

Tátá . . . Sheee . . . Kaytá! . . .
Prráá . . . Boomboom!!! Booboo! . . .
Sheee . . . Tokee tá! Prrráá . . .
Teekee boom! Bambam . . . Bá . . .
Shóóó . . . Sheee . . . Vioot . . . oo . . .
Brra . . . Sheeen . . . papow!
Tatá! Prrr . . . Bóóó . . .
Tee boom! Crr . . . Fiów . . .
Crro óóó . Sheen . . . Bóbó! . . .
Prr . . . Brrrá . . . Sheee . . . Tibow!
—Lookit the balloon! Lookit the Santos Dumont
balloon! . . .[85]

So much for the vanguards; but there were also false vanguards.

False Vanguards

Within the false vanguards there were both traditionalists and ideological conservatives who were contradictorily attempting to build a Modernism on these foundations, both inspired by a spiteful hostility toward the "boys from São Paulo." One group operated in Recife in 1926 under the leadership of Gilberto Freyre, and until recently it maintained that it was directed by the Regionalist Manifesto. Another group existed in Rio in 1927 under the spiritual direction of Tasso da Silveira (1895–1968). It made every effort to create a "spiritual Modernism," that is to say, a Catholic movement. Chronology at this point means nothing; and the first group, even from the chronological point of view, is that of *Festa*, because it was not until the forties that we had any real knowledge of what is today called the "Regionalist Movement" of Recife, which had existed there only in the parochial and provincial sense. Moreover, this "movement" had ramifications considerably more modest than what usually is claimed for it, as we may see from the documents collected by Joaquim Inojosa in his book *O Movimento Modernista em Pernambuco* (1968).

It might be said that every modernism had its Graça Aranha. After 1923 Gilberto Freyre was the Graça Aranha of future regionalism in Recife; Tasso da Silveira was the Graça Aranha of *Festa* and literary spiritualism, which was much better represented in its authentic nature (let it be said in passing) by Jackson de Figueiredo. Both secretly wished to be not the Graça Aranha, as a matter of fact, but rather the Mário de Andrade of their respective groups; and to a large extent they were. However, in spite of so many bitter recriminations and resentful claims, they never succeeded in becoming the Mário de Andrade of all the modernisms. This is not strange, because neither did Mário de Andrade succeed in this role. On the other hand, he did not harbor such a high ambition.

One essential difference between *Festa* and the Recife Regionalists is that the former appeared from the very first moment as an intentional anti-Modernist force while the second group only tardily conceived of claiming their own importance, although both were equally opposed to the idea of faithfully recognizing the priority of São Paulo. At the heart of this quarrel, there is on the one hand the traditional rivalry of Rio and São Paulo, much more acute than today, and on the other hand the North-South rivalry which, on the contrary, although it was already steeped in resentment, seems singularly heightened today.

On the purely literary and ideological plane, each of these false vanguards contained an internal contradiction which admits of no solution. On the Catholic side it was a matter of structuring a "modernism," a word and a thing of which Church orthodoxy always manifested a quite justified mistrust; on the regionalist side it was a matter of articulating a more viable "traditionalist modernism." In other words, as they contested the Modernist legitimacy of the São Paulo Modernists, the two antagonistic groups attempted to create a new modernism which would be, curiously enough, anti-Modernist. Condemning the estheticism and the provincialism of the São Paulo group, they laid claim to older esthetic traditions (the *Festa* group) and to older regional traditions (the Recife group). Thus, not to mention their lag of an entire generation behind the São Paulo Modernists, the rival groups suffered from the beginning from their own polemical intent. The strategic positions of Recife Regionalism were enormously prejudiced and never saw effective fulfillment simply because there were never any repercussions outside regional confines.

An Ill-Humored Festa

Carlos Chiacchio, who fluctuated doctrinally like a weather vane as the winds blew, hailed the *Festa* group in 1928 as the longed-for bearer of the true message:

It is incumbent on us likewise to recognize in the intellectual nucleus of *Festa,* which has recently been founded under the guidance of Tasso da Silveira, Barreto Filho, Andrade Muricy and others who possess a clear understanding of the true road for Brazil to follow, that newborn spirit of reaction against the mental confusion of the hasty importers of literary schools unadapted and unadaptable to our taste and our temperament. It is indeed that current which, with some restrictions, may find a warm welcome by the intelligentsia of Bahia. Their dynamically traditionalist hearts beat with our own.[86]

At exactly the same time, in number 5 of *Verde* (January, 1928), Francisco I. Peixoto assumed the role of interpreter of the reactions which the ill humor of *Festa* was awakening among the Modernist youths:

MASTER:

In addressing you at this moment I do it not in the name of my 4528 colleagues who have been the target of your unspeakable drivel. I speak only for myself and at my own risk. It is necessary for me to accentuate from the start: I do not wish to arrogate to myself the role of professor. No, absolutely not. I do, however, desire to impress upon the underground galleries of your young critic's mind one idea, totally perfunctory, concerning the torrent of bombastic asininities which you, no doubt under the impact of deleterious influence, included in the columns of your article in number 4 of FESTA. It cannot be denied that, if you wrote that article, it was to put yourself in evidence by calling the attention of others to yourself in order to fill the followers of your group, of your literary clique, with encomium.

.   .   .   .   .

With all your dull-witted pedantry, you were bold enough to allow your illustrious name to appear on the list of collaborators of ELÉTRICA (the advertising organ for Osram-Mazda light bulbs), a review whose director is the pompous poet Heitor Alves, author of VIDA EM MOVIMENTO, a book that is a truly marvelous collection of baubles.

.   .   .   .   .

You see, MASTER, that business of making fun of the production of others is quite simple. Especially when we employ its indecent processes and, on top of that, we are fortunate enough to find heedless and ingenuous readers.

Now I have finished, my splendid young critic. I shall say no more of you. It is sufficient that I say only this: You are the T in FESTA. Look in the dictionary and see how many pretty words begin with that letter. For example: turgid, tedious, tacky, etc.[87]

As that was practically the last number of *Verde,* we can say that this Minas Gerais review ended its days in violent opposition to *Festa;* but the tone and the vocabulary of *Festa* were no milder, as can be readily seen from the volume in which Tasso da Silveira collected his "published articles, month by month, from January to

December of 1927, in the review FESTA, Rio de Janeiro, whose brief but efficient activities gave a new meaning to the movement of literary renovation which was taking place throughout Brazil in uncertain and dangerous directions." [88]

The importance of *Festa*, in spite of its undeniable tactical failure, resides in its having represented on the literary plane the spiritualist movement or current whose principal source was Jackson de Figueiredo; and it also exercised enormous influence on literature through Tristão de Athayde. Its most legitimate organ, still in existence, was the review *A Ordem* along with the intellectuals who flocked about it. The magazine represented, more than *Festa*, Jacksonian trends, that is, religious traditionalism and reactionary tendencies so thoroughly studied by Renato Rocha in the special number of the *Revista Branca* devoted to Modernism. The small biographical incident of Jackson de Figueiredo's having been the director of censorship in the Artur Bernardes government says more about his personality than long ideological disquisitions, and it will no doubt say more in the future than the hagiography that has grown up around his name. As to the trend called "spiritualist," the general attitude of Renato Rocha's study is negative:

In this way, spiritualist ideas led to a melancholy conclusion. That this was not the objective of the ideals of the Spirit was what we tried to show. Obviously we did not want the spiritualists of our modernism to form a group, which would be the very negation of their ideas; rather we wished that they should not connive together. What we see, however, is that they surrendered what they possessed that was most pure with their eyes fixed on temporal Power, and today one should see how they bemoan their not possessing the visible powers of this world. Even so they show in their quietism and in the dubious fame that some have acquired the very negation of the spiritualist vocation. [89]

It is curious that Tasso da Silveira's hostility to Modernism seems to grow more acute with the passage of time, as does that of Gilberto Freyre, instead of revealing a clearer historical perspective. In the same number of the *Revista Branca,* he proposes what can be considered his final view of the Movement and the role played by *Festa*:

> In itself, in its final substance, the Week of Modern Art was only an ideological coup. There was Mário de Andrade mixed up in the affair, a devout Catholic, but in whose temperament were fermenting all the germs of dissolution that slowly dragged him to the left. The rest were nearly all leftists. If they were not open Communists, they were at least opposed to God and Church. There is the true reason that the liberating gesture of the Week of Modern Art immediately degenerated into mere destructive activity. As late as 1924 the important thing was sarcasm, joking, blague. And also licentiousness to a large degree. Blague, jokery, licentiousness, sarcasm—not a clearing of the land to make room for new buildings—but for themselves, out of their sheer joy in degradation, and skepticism. To "enjoy life." That is why *Festa* appeared in 1927 as an attempted salvation from the genuine renovative anxiety which, having been initiated before the Week of Modern Art, was then smothered under a tremendous torrent.
>
> I have already explained elsewhere what *Festa* and the so-called Festa Group stood for. I say "so-called" because there was not, properly speaking, a Festa Group in the sense of literary chapel or a union for mutual praise. There was a review organized, directed, and supported by a few poets and writers of prose fiction of renovated sensitivity but whose pages attracted all those who at the moment, in one way or another, presented possibilities for authentic poetry which needed to be defended against the torrent.
>
> *Festa* totally changed the meaning which had been given to Modernism by the Week of Modern Art. In truth, it saved Modernism. Without *Festa* there would have been no ambience to foster the new poetry of a Drummond de Andrade, a Murilo Mendes, a Cecília Meireles, to cite only three names. I like to think that the impulse to return to authenticity and to discipline, unleashed by *Festa,* had its effect even on Mário de Andrade and on other leaders of the Week.[90]

It would be difficult to find a better example of delirious historiography. In the first place, there was *no* communist writer or even a sympathizer among those responsible for the Week of Modern Art. Oswald de Andrade himself, as is well known, years later regretted that for so long he had played the "bourgeois clown" and that on his first trip abroad he had discovered the wrong manifesto in Paris: Marinetti's instead of Karl Marx's. But that is not the worst: the reactionary impetus of Tasso da Silveira kept him from seeing that, in the last years of the twenties and throughout the thirties, the choices of "right" and "left" seemed imperative to the majority of intellectuals, to such an extent that he chose the right. There is a letter from Mário de Andrade to Carlos Lacerda recently published,[91] by which we can verify that the most intense personal anguish could lead to apparently irreversible gestures, without nobility's being an exclusive privilege of any faction.

Likewise it would seem to be a partisan illusion to assume that *Festa* could have exercised an influence capable of changing the direction of Modernism and of restoring a meaning to it. When the review and the group appeared, Modernism had already exhausted its first phase, precisely the phase against which the "spiritualists," with a curious lack of esthetic and ideological perception, had decided to react. In the same way the affiliation of the "klaxist" Carlos Drummond de Andrade with *Festa* is, at least, abusive, because since 1925 he had been collaborating on the *Revista* of Belo Horizonte and since 1927 on *Verde,* in the first number of which he published the eminently "drummondian" poem "Sinal de Apito." Not even Cecília Meireles, in spite of numerous affinities, could be monopolized by *Festa* because she was a poetess who lived on the edge of literary schools, and she had already published some of her most important books when the movement in Rio took shape.[92]

But what most eminently compromised *Festa's* campaign, and in particular Tasso da Silveira's anti-Modernist writings, was a lack of intellectual respect. To see Mário de Andrade, even in 1927, as a "talented fool" or to see all that was being done in São Paulo as a "torrent" passing through *Festa's* sewage disposal center revealed a poverty of literary sensitivity and a lack of liberality of spirit which, as a matter of fact, explains a great deal. Under these conditions it is not strange that certain unnoticed contradictions abounded: thus, for example, if it is true that the *Festa* group had been active since 1919 through publications like *América Latina, Árvore Nova,* and *Terra de Sol,* then it is demonstrable that it was not in the least Modernist and that, for that very reason, it could not aspire to the role of restorer of a current that the writers of São Paulo had destroyed. Along the same line of thought, the contrast between Mário de Andrade's first book and those that followed was only natural and a proof of Modernism, while the coherence and identity of all the work of Tasso da Silveira, which he claimed for himself, is precisely proof of the contrary.[93]

A Modern Longing for the Past

With reference to the year 1923 José Lins do Rêgo wrote:

There was at that time the Modernist Movement of São
Paulo. Gilberto [Freyre] criticized the campaign as if it belonged to another generation. The news of the Week of
Modern Art seemed to him to be a comic movement with
no real importance. Brazil did not need Graça Aranha's
dynamism nor the hullabaloo of the youthful writers from
the South; Brazil needed to take a clear look at itself, to
take stock of itself, to go to the fountain sources of its life,
to the depths of its conscience. Brazilian literature no longer
possessed men like Machado de Assis, Nabuco, Pompéia, men
who could extract from the wellsprings of their own being
what they possessed that was original and expressive. There
was land, there were people, there was a whole distinctive
Brazil in the Northeast, in Rio Grande do Sul, in São Paulo,
in Minas Gerais. So why tear out our roots which clung
so tenaciously to the earth and why disdain our native sentiments and values.[94]

There is no doubt that Gilberto Freyre had returned from
Europe in 1923, nor that the novelist above had met him in that

same year. It would seem to be tampering somewhat with the dates (and this occurred systematically in Recife's claims of Regionalism's autonomy over São Paulo's Modernism) to locate in 1923 either an effective understanding of what had happened at the Municipal Theatre some months before or, for a number of reasons, to locate in that year a pronounced feeling of antagonism to which José Lins do Rêgo as well as Gilberto Freyre refer in the introduction to the same volume. In all probability Recife's knowledge of Modernism came through Joaquim Inojosa, who maintained that he had asserted "at the end of 1922," that "we were doing nothing because everything we did was old-fashioned" —as far as literature was concerned, let it be clearly understood.[95] The meeting which he promoted in the lecture hall of the *Diário de Pernambuco,* probably in 1923, to hear the reading of a book by Paulo Tôrres offered a program that included old and new names.

There was, then, some sparse Modernist agitation promoted by Joaquim Inojosa who, in 1924, cited the name of Gilberto Freyre among the "vigorous intellects" who, although "they did not accept it in all its ramifications, at least did not reject Modern Art." It is quite natural that Gilberto Freyre could not for a long time accept the role of disciple of Joaquim Inojosa. We must point out that Freyre's singular preeminence at that time, as was intimated by José Lins do Rêgo, seems to be somewhat exaggerated. Moreover, he himself adds that he was "perhaps Gilberto Freyre's only friend" at that time, with the exception of the latter's brother Ulysses. A more objective view of the true intellectual atmosphere of Recife at that time (when the sociologist had not as yet claimed for the Regionalist Movement an importance at least as great as São Paulo Modernism) is provided us by Ascenso Ferreira:

The war had ended. Marinetti had visited Brazil. The so-called "modern movement" was on the move in the South. Joaquim Inojosa heralded the matter in Pernambuco; no one can hide that fact, in good faith. My first impulse was to resist, in spite of my ever-demonstrable desire for originality, even within the canons of the old poetry. At that time, Guilherme de Almeida came through here. A lecture at the Santa Isabel Theatre and the recitation of his poem "Raça" opened my eyes to the possibilities of a new esthetics. The *Revista do Norte* group had been formed. I approached its members more as a bohemian than as a poet. It was Benedito Monteiro who exercised the greatest influence on my transformation. Nonetheless, José Maria de Albuquerque Melo and Joaquim Cardoso should not be overlooked. Gilberto Freyre also belonged to the group; he had recently returned from the United States and his articles were evoking interest in our rural traditions, which were so vividly a part of my subconscious, and his writings took deep root in my spirit.[96]

As is the rule in Modernist memoirs, the poet reveals a noticeable confusion in his chronology; it is likewise true that Gilberto Freyre, who was "traditionalist" from the very beginning (reverence for tradition being the fundamental characteristic of his thought), could not have led a visible regionalist reaction against Modernist novelties. However, it is important to note that Ascenso Ferreira's "first impulse" was to resist Modernism. As a rule, that was the first impulse of all the intellectuals of the Northeast: José Lins do Rêgo, Jorge de Lima, later Jorge Amado, not to mention those who, like Graciliano Ramos, retained their distrust of it to the end of their lives. It was not until 1925 that the sociologist had conceived the mature idea of a regional "movement" similar to São Paulo's movement. However, because such a movement never had the slightest repercussions outside the sphere of influence of Recife, it was not until the forties that the campaign began to carve out for Freyre a niche of importance in the intellectual history of Brazil.

The first significant landmark of that campaign came in 1941 and was the volume *Região e Tradição*. As late as 1936, in writing an article entitled "Sociologia e Literatura" for number 4 of *Lanterna Verde*—a number all the more appropriate for the disputation of the question as it was, precisely, devoted to a "revision" of Modernism—he did not make the slightest mention of the matter. What he observed was that the generation of the thirties, which succeeded the *Modernists* of São Paulo and Rio, presented, "among its most salient characteristics," an interest in *sociology*. Although this sociological interest amounted in large part to regionalism, Gilberto Freyre did not raise the question probably because, as regionalism and sociology, it had no traditionalist traits. As for the real repercussion of regionalist and traditionalist ideas in the country (and no ideological movement, no matter how intrinsically important it may have been, acquires any meaning without repercussion), it could easily be judged from what Mário de Andrade wrote to Manuel Bandeira on June 26, 1925: "I don't know Gilberto Freyre and I don't think I sent my book to him." [97]

So, the São Paulo "Futurists" were as little known in the Northeast as the Recife Regionalists were unheard of in the South. Regarding Jorge de Lima's *Poemas* (1927), Otto Maria Carpeaux wrote: "It is true that Maceió was then a kind of literary hub; but the poet's friends, who supported him in his Modernist adventure, were all writers who were still unknown throughout the country. They were José Lins do Rêgo, Graciliano Ramos, Aurélio Buarque de Holanda, Valdemar Cavalcanti. No one as yet knew their names, nor were the 'renovators' from Recife (Gilberto Freyre, Olívio Montenegro, Sílvio Rabelo) known outside the Northeast. . . . Only vague rumors of the crazy carryings-on of the so-called 'Futurists' had reached us from the South." [98] The certain thing is that, even before it was properly understood, the Modernism of São Paulo was poorly received in the Northeast. Criticism and sarcasm ran rampant on pages by Olívio Montenegro and José Lins do Rêgo; and Jorge de Lima himself (who was converted late), writing a laudatory essay on the Movement in 1929, said nonetheless that it had miscarried.

Because in general the disciples were more daring than the masters, José Lins do Rêgo lent the tone to the objections when he wrote his critique of Jorge de Lima's volume of *Poemas*: "What some day will pass for Brazilian art must be attributed to our present-day indifference. It will no doubt not be attributed to Senhor Plínio Salgado's speeches to the stars nor to the very talented Oswald de Andrade's tightrope act." He noted that Jorge de Lima's regionalism was superior: "Because his regionalism does not hinder his emotion and moreover does not possess the character of a political party like that offered to the country by the boys from São Paulo with all the persistence of advertisements for patent medicine."

Words like these reveal a phenomenon rarely mentioned. Because it reached the Northeast as a *literary fact* (and not as a novelty known to a few initiates) after 1925, and more particularly around 1927, Modernism was identified with Greengiltism, that is, with the political tone that it was already beginning to assume. The poorly informed Northeasterners understood Greengiltism to represent all of Modernism, and thus in general they transferred all their hostility from the former to the latter. This notion is easily confirmed by other words by Lins do Rêgo in the same article: "Now, that counterrevolution (the counterrevolution to restore the integrity of Brazil) will not be effected through spectacular parrot-hunts and the other Parnassian pilfering of Senhores Menotti and Cassiano Ricardo."

After 1941, the retrospective notion that the Regionalist Manifesto of 1926 had been as important as the Week of Modern Art (and certainly more "Brazilian" than the Week) acquired the prestige of literary and historic doctrine. In 1947 Gilberto Freyre wrote in the preface to Jorge de Lima's *Poemas Negros*:

On one occasion I was so daring as to suggest this idea: the necessity of recognizing a distinctively Northeastern movement of renovation in letters, in the arts, in Brazilian culture. This movement of our own time, which has unfortunately been confused with the growth of the considerably more opulent "modernism" of São Paulo and Rio de Janeiro, nonetheless came into existence on its own terms. . . . It was mainly into this world that Jorge de Lima was introduced in 1922–23 as a poet of precocious formation, in no way stratified into a nineteenth-century sculptor of elegant sonnets avidly collected by pedagogues . . . but rather as a poet transformed by new stimuli from the South, from Europe, from the United States, into the supreme poet, the poet *par excellence*. The poet of *O Mundo do Menino Impossível*. The poet of *Essa Negra Fulô*.

It would indeed be splendid if Jorge de Lima's modernism dated from 1922–23. Unfortunately, *O Mundo do Menino Impossível*, the incontestable document of his adherence to the new esthetics, was composed in 1925 and *Essa Negra Fulô* in 1928.

This same chronological inaccuracy, which always tends to antedate the ideological movement called "Regionalist," inevitably occurs in historical references made to that movement by José Lins do Rêgo or Gilberto Freyre. The first lines of the *Manifesto Regionalista de 1926*, in the 1952 edition, state that "a movement of restoration of regional and traditional values" *had been outlined* in Recife two or three years before.[99] This takes us back, in the most favorable hypothesis, to 1923, the year of Gilberto Freyre's return from Europe. The very nature of things leads us to believe that no movement of importance could have been immediately unleashed by this illustrious intellectual; as a matter of fact, in 1924 he appeared simply as a spectator, with no special aura attached to his name, during at least one of the "Modernist" conclaves initiated by Joaquim Inojosa. It is obvious that only then did he conceive the notion of a regionalist and local campaign against the "importation" of São Paulo's Modernism. Moreover, Recife's Regionalism *at that time possessed no literary or specifically artistic traits*. The *Manifesto*, which appeared after all its attendant intellectualization had taken shape, referred only to the preservation of traditional *cultural* values, such as architecture, cuisine (on which Gilberto Freyre placed special emphasis), and popular crafts, with no reference at all to the novel, poetry, or the essay.

The notion that the "literature of the Northeast," after Jorge de Lima, was more a result of Recife's Regionalism than of São Paulo's Modernism rests quite simply on confusion of chronology: when the Northeastern poets and novelists began to appear in print, they did so in Modernist surroundings, because by that time (after 1925) Modernism had spread to the four corners of Brazil. On the contrary, Regionalism was always limited to Recife and never enjoyed the slightest repercussion outside its narrow confines. In the short introduction which prefaced the 1952 edition of the *Manifesto*, Gilberto Freyre recognized the facts: ". . . Recife's Regionalism—which was also Modernist in its way, but Modernist and traditionalist at the same time—in its heroic period lacked advertising and propagation in the metropolitan press, at that time indifferent, if not downright hostile, to anything that came out of the provinces . . . The real intellectuals of stature in those days paid scant attention to a movement so remote which, although provincial, pioneered considerable renovation and is today triumphant throughout the width and breadth of the land and has even gone beyond our seas." [100]

In actuality, the name of Gilberto Freyre did not reach Rio de Janeiro until 1926, the year he made the acquaintance of Prudente de Morais Neto and other luminaries of the old *Estética*. At that time, poets and novelists from the Northeast, published or silently preparing for publication, were already feeling the influence of Regionalism as well as Modernism itself. The simple truth is that if the two movements were contradictory, where ambitious rivalry was concerned, they nonetheless complemented one another because Regionalism was less alien to Modernism than Gilberto Freyre would lead us to believe. Only *traditionalism* was foreign to the Movement of São Paulo and Rio de Janeiro, and that name might better describe the intellectual trends of the second "Recife school."

Regionalism took the shape of doctrine only when it became a conscious reaction to Modernism. In this regard, Osman Lins has written: "The clamor of the Modernist Movement echoed in the intellectual circles of Brazil . . . Unattached to that Movement, and in many ways opposed to its policies, the Regionalist Movement appeared in Recife." [101]

Likewise, in a book in which he attempts to equate the importance and significance of the two movements, José Aderaldo Castello has observed:

In the Northeast, the Modernism of the Week of Modern Art had repercussions, attracted adherents, and was evident in the direct suggestions of Guilherme de Almeida and Mário de Andrade. But it is true that in the Northeast the majority of writers, under the guidance of Gilberto Freyre— with his articles and essays, the formation of groups and movements like the Regionalist Center and the Congress of

Northeastern Regionalists—took a position not only independent of but even contrary to what seemed to them to be least authentic and most Europeanizing, particularly from the point of view of the esthetic trends which dominated in São Paulo and Rio de Janeiro, which was taken as the center of contact and broadcast. . . . In turn, in contrast to Ascenso Ferreira, José Lins do Rêgo . . . figured among those who displayed some hostility to the attitudes of the promoters of the Week of Modern Art in his writings for the press or the review *Dom Casmurro,* which at the time he co-directed with Osório Borba. In any case, profoundly interested in the work that they were carrying out, he was able . . . to bring that Brazilian Modernism developing in the South to Gilberto Freyre's attention.[102]

Now, of course, the matter becomes clear and makes sense: on his arrival from Europe, Gilberto Freyre was informed by José Lins do Rêgo of the Brazilian literary movement which had been broadcast from São Paulo to all parts of Brazil and which had reached Recife through the offices of Joaquim Inojosa. So it was that the future novelist initiated the sociologist into Brazilian literary life, no matter how great the subsequent influence of the sociologist would be on the novelist. Supposing that José Lins do Rêgo was, from the first moment, hostile to Modernism, he would quite naturally have communicated his disfavor to the young traveler. Nonetheless, it is more likely that Gilberto Freyre, totally adverse to the acolyte's vocation, chilled any eventual enthusiasm on the part of his friend, immediately provoking in him the disparaging attitude which soon came to identify him.

So it was that Recife's Regionalism was, by and large, anti-Modernism: anti-Modernism which did not dare to utter its own name, in this way anticipating Augusto Frederico Schmidt's position, which was spiritually identical. Precisely because it was directed against Modernism, it could not be independent of Modernism, as Gilberto Freyre and those who share his view of literary history would have it. As it has been expressed, the great influence of regionalist ideas coincided with the period of the greatest expansion of Modernism which, since 1922, had long since set forth the program which the Northeastern novelists carried out in the thirties. As a consequence, it seems somewhat fanciful to attempt to place the importance and influence of the two movements on equal footing, as Gilberto Freyre does in this passage quoted by José Aderaldo Castello: "These two movements will doubtless go down in history as the most important in the revolutionizing of Brazilian letters and life in the sense not only of the authenticity but also of the spontaneity of intellectual or cultural creation; and they will mark a new era of self-confidence among Brazilians. In the sense of the intellectual and artistic liberation of Brazil from the excesses of colonial subordination to Europe and the United States." [103]

In the last analysis, if it is true that Gilberto Freyre, José Lins do Rêgo, and other intellectuals from Recife did not, at the time, understand the scope of the Week of Modern Art and the artistic movement that issued from it, we deal with a circumstance that does no honor to their sensitivity and intellectual acuity, both of which we have elsewhere noted as highly developed.

Tallies and Inventories

An error which grew up immediately after the heroic phase of the Movement ended (and an error which Mário de Andrade also seems to have made) was that of considering 1930 as the terminus of Modernist literature. After 1935, or beginning in 1935, literary investigations, evaluations, tallies, and inventories began to multiply. In all likelihood no literary school ever had so many death certificates as Modernism; still, because its presence continued to make itself felt, each of these certificates seemed, on the contrary, to revitalize the Movement. It would obviously be impossible to review here all the more or less personal declarations regarding Modernist chronology. It is sufficient to recall the four most important moments in that chronology, as presented in the special number of *Lanterna Verde* (1936) on "O Sentido Atual da Literatura no Brasil," in the great investigation which the *Revista do Brasil* initiated in the February number of 1940 in Mário de Andrade's lecture, *O Movimento Modernista* (1942); and, in 1945, Mário Neme's book, *Plataforma da Nova Geração*, composed of interviews with young writers originally published in *O Estado de São Paulo* after 1943.

If in 1936 all judgments which cast Modernism into the

limbo of the literary past were premature, in 1945 the Movement's demise was undeniable. The process of canonization lasted ten years, which served to demonstrate that during those last ten years, and to the contrary of what so many hardpressed scholars had affirmed, Modernism continued to live.

Leaving aside the purely emotional pronouncement which Octavio de Faria made in the *Lanterna Verde,* according to which "not only has the Modernist Movement ceased totally to exist: it never existed in the first place," the most pessimistic judgment was still that of Manoel de Abreu, which was published under the significant title "Acabou o modernismo no Brasil?" The author answered in the affirmative:

> Yes, it has come to an end. And the reason for this premature demise can be perfectly explained if we calmly read those pale pages which the storm of life is blowing away one by one. *Tôda a América* by Ronald de Carvalho, the American who forgets his own self in a fascination for virgin land and endless space. *Lanterna Verde* by Felippe d'Oliveira in which the rhythm of youth possesses the Universe. *Poemas* by Mário de Andrade and Jorge de Lima, the Brazilian and the Mandingan with their ancestral secret. *Cobra Norato* by Raul Bopp, a simple and distant legend, the beginning of our reality. . . . They are masterworks of Modernism which liberated our lyricism from hypocrisy and boredom. . . . In spite of its potential from the start, Modernism bore within it the germ of its weakness. It lacked seriousness. It lacked suffering. It lacked a sense of wholeness.[104]

It fell to Tristão de Athayde to synthesize the pronouncements of the writers then being heard: Afonso Arinos de Melo Franco, Gilberto Freyre, Jorge de Lima, Lúcia Miguel-Pereira, Manoel de Abreu, Murilo Mendes, Octavio de Faria, and Renato Almeida. He did so with his usual clarity.

1. Modernism not only existed but it lived.
2. Modernism died.

3. The literary heritage of Modernism was greater in spirit than in works.
4. Modernism prepared the way for a post-Modernist literary renaissance.

These, then, were the opinions on Modernism in 1936. At that time everyone more or less accepted the notion that a kind of "post-Modernism" had begun, this expression created by Tristão de Athayde who later likewise proposed the expression "pre-Modernism" to describe the period immediately prior to the Week of Modern Art. Precisely because neither of these expressions has any real meaning, it is easily concluded that they did not justly describe the literary situation at those two respective moments. Be that as it may, these are the coordinates designated by Tristão de Athayde for "post-Modernism" as the foundation of the investigation made by *Lanterna Verde*:

1. The post-Modernist literary phase has its own characteristics.
2. The tenor of present-day literature is more serious, more profound, more social, and more spiritual than that of Modernism.
3. Any definitive judgment of the quality of our present-day literary productions is premature.

But Modernism was not dead. This is proved by the fact that four years later the *Revista do Brasil* considered the Movement sufficiently alive to ask whether its spirit "still persevered." Here is the questionnaire set before the experts.

I (a) Did Modernism represent a critical or a creative movement?
   (b) Did it open new pathways for literature?
   (c) Does its spirit persevere?
II (a) Did political events of the last decade influence our literature?
   (b) In what way?

(c) Did these events put a more Brazilian stamp on our letters?

III (a) What are the present-day trends in Brazilian literature?

(b) Do they reflect literary movements prior to Modernism or do they reflect a new spirit?

(c) Which foreign influences prevail?

This questionnaire, with all its technical flaws, is significant because it reflected the predominance of political preoccupations over literary preoccupations in that first year of the war (1940). This engrossment with the political had existed for some time, practically from the first years of the thirties. It is the same *engagé* trend which was also found in the "Elegia de Abril," written by Mário de Andrade for the review *Clima* in 1941 and in his famous lecture of the following year, a true literary and personal testament.

This "turmoil of spirit" had astounding repercussions in the *Revista do Brasil*'s investigation. For example, Jorge de Lima said in answer to the third question of the first part: "No, and it would mean stagnation if it did persevere." On the contrary, Astrojildo Pereira answered: "It perseveres and it will continue to persevere as long as it does not expire on its own," a totally redundant way of thinking which, nonetheless, did indicate a feeling for the spiritual presence of Modernism. The answer which Álvaro Lins gave is a collection of errors: Modernism had not been a creative movement because it had not produced "any great representative work." At the same time, its victory "was absolute," although it had not opened "new roads for literature." Moreover, the Movement "does not have, nor did it ever have, a true 'spirit,' " it was a "transitory movement, a simple 'crisis' in our literary history," it was a "kind of interval between two eras."

Such was the substance of statements published in March of 1940. In the following month, Almir de Andrade expressed once again the conclusions that Álvaro Lins had reached: Modernism had produced nothing that was "either great or lasting." It had been "a moment of transition, a movement that had been ephemeral by nature," although Graciliano Ramos, for example, bore "the undeniable mark of Modernist influence—like José Lins do Rêgo, like José Américo de Almeida, like Jorge Amado, like many others." Mário de Andrade, as one might expect, revealed more lucidity and pointed to the two great characteristics of the Movement—its experimentalism and its revolutionary nature: "It identified with other revolutionary forces which, either openly or underhandedly, were developing in Brazil and throughout the world." Thus "the principal figures who had adhered to the Movement immediately showed their sympathies (if not their outright attachment) and this to an extreme degree."

In that particular number of the review, however, the most important reply (and the one which, perhaps, endured as the most important of the entire investigation) was that of Jorge Amado. As he himself emphasized from the start, his statement was that "of a post-Modernist, a writer who under no circumstances had the slightest connection with the Movement": "When the Movement appeared and began to grow, I was a mere lad in grade school and high school. And if the publication of *A Bagaceira* marks the end of the Movement in 1928 (the year in which Oswald de Andrade's *Serafim Ponte Grande* also was written, the novel which is a kind of inventory of the Movement), it will be clearly demonstrable that, with my first publication appearing in 1931 when I was eighteen, I could not possibly have had any connection whatever with Modernism."

Therein precisely, in his opinion, lay the greatest importance of his reply. Jorge Amado quite justly defined Modernist poetry as the expression "of a critical movement" at the same time that he indicated a circumstance which the pious historians of the Movement have taken such pains to conceal: that it was "necessary not to forget that perhaps no other movement had enjoyed such great support from the upper classes." Although he believed that the Movement had destroyed everything and created nothing, he added that "it had facilitated the appearance of a new Brazilian literature."

With the May number and the statements made by Jayme de Barros, Octavio Tarquínio de Sousa, and Guilherme Figueiredo, the investigation ended. To the first of these, the expression

"Modernist Movement" already seemed "almost meaningless." Nonetheless, the creative labor evidenced by the literature of the time was the result of the Movement: "The entire present generation of novelists, who have put the naturalist stamp and the objective character of investigation and research on their work, were born of the Movement." There was no doubt, therefore, that the Modernist spirit persevered. The other two writers added nothing of substance.

So, because of the incoherence of the replies as well as the fact that no one had been designated to interpret the lesson the replies might possibly have contained, the *Revista do Brasil*'s investigation reached no conclusion whatever. This was merely one more sign that the time of inventory was drawing near, the more so since to a great degree the political situation was muddling people's judgment. It is quite unnecessary to analyze in detail Mário de Andrade's lecture (1942), which the friends and enemies of Modernism know practically by heart. However, in the "Elegia de Abril" Mário de Andrade, with little clarity of vision, seemed to distinguish three literary generations: his own, the generation of the thirties, and the most recent one, symbolized by the "boring-boys" (as Oswald de Andrade called them) who wrote for the review *Clima*. The characteristics of this last generation were "a new realism, a greater interest in logical thought, which may be very clearly observed in the fact that the number of writers is growing who initiate their career in prose—and only prose—thus breaking the tradition of the little volume of first verses. Political opportunism." His own generation "had been quite worthy of its age, while the generation that is taking our place is considerably inferior to the historical moment in which it lives."

The fact is that, at that very moment, Mário de Andrade was suffering from his Modernist estheticism; the need was to produce a literature and create a "social" art as an instrument of partisan action and a quick road to political reform. Such was the theme of his lecture, which was spiritually torn between a reaffirmation and a condemnation of the Modernist Movement; somewhat later, in an interview granted to Homero Senna,[105] he described himself as a writer "concerned with participating

more directly in the political problems of our time, not hesitating
to recognize that my concept of *engagé* art and my artistic attitude, which was always directed by some kind of expediency, set
before me a poetry of combat and a circumstantial art; metrical
poetry and rhyme itself imposed their authority on my poetics
because they represented dynamic processes of greater social capacity." This is the same period during which he declared to
Francisco de Assis Barbosa, in an interview published by the
review *Diretrizes* on January 6, 1944:

> I do not create pure art. I never did. In this regard I feel
> that I am in disagreement with friends and dear comrades,
> friends and comrades whom I hold to be masters. I have
> always been opposed to disinterested art. In my opinion, art
> must serve. I may say that since the publication of my first
> book, I have been creating *engagé* art. At that time in 1917,
> if I had wanted to, I could have written a better book of
> verses for public consumption. . . . But I did not. I felt
> that it was expedient to publish my little book of pacifist
> poems written with my First-World-War emotions.

It is true that, at the height of his career, he declared that
he had written nothing that did not have a purpose; but it seems
that there is a certain distinction between his goal of literary
reform, which identified the entire Modernist phase, and the desire to transform literature into an instrument of political action.
Be that as it may, it was a lesson of compromised art that he gave
to the new generations in his lecture of 1942, which was truly a
sign of the times.

More expressive of that new state of mind were the statements
collected by Mário Neme. The tone once again was marked by
political preoccupations (one dared to cast the first barbs at the
Estado Nôvo), but the young writers still revealed that they were
quite close to the Movement. It might be said, in a general way,
that the upcoming generation agreed with the esthetic and artistic
postulate of Modernism but disagreed with the Movement spiritually and ideologically. Such was certainly the frame of reference of Mário de Andrade's lecture.

In that new series of testimonies, the great balance sheet—at one and the same time historical and critical—was proposed by Antônio Cândido:

The generation of the twenties should be regarded more as an explosion of *enfants-terribles*. It possesses a great deal of the show-off personalism of Oswald de Andrade, who described himself as a "bourgeois clown" at the beginning of a more functional phase of his career. The generation of the thirties is that of the great bourgeois historicism of Gilberto Freyre and also of the historical realism of Caio Prado Júnior. It is the decade of the "Série Brasiliana" and the foundation of the Graduate Schools, of the novels published by José Olympio and the schematization of Brazilian social problems. . . . Viewed in this functional light, it seems to me beyond a doubt that my generation is a critical generation. . . . "Your generation has been reading since it was three years old," Oswald de Andrade wrote in the fifth number of *Clima*. "By the time you are twenty you have Spengler in your guts. And the things you miss!" I assure you that this is not so, my dear Oswald. . . . The famous generation of the twenties, which here in São Paulo takes its place almost immediately before our own, also in their way formed a critical generation. And they did more: they criticized by creating, that is, by showing how things should be—which is quite natural when dealing with fiction, poetry, and art. It was a generation of artists, and it may be radically separated from our own in that regard. . . . But look at the matter clearly. "They have had little intellectual influence on us," for the very reason that above all they are artists. You will find practically no influence of Oswald, or of Mário, or of Menotti or of Guilherme de Almeida. According to the case, you will find a great deal of love for their work, a great deal of enthusiasm for the action they took. And nothing else. Their influence was all indirect and thus minimal. We are their continuators simply because of inevitable historical and cultural continuity.[106]

In Antônio Cândido's view, Sérgio Milliet represented the bridge between the first Modernists and his own generation. In a general way, Milliet and Mário de Andrade are the only two writers who were spared the repudiation of the young. While Edmundo Rossi, Jamil Almansur Haddad, and Edgard Cavalheiro considered that Modernism had fulfilled a useful function, Arnaldo Pedroso d'Horta relocated the problem within a politically *engagé* perspective: "The 'revolution' which they [the generation of 1922] created was all surface and form. It was all brilliance and little substance. The group which at that time took shape did not act as a group except on the strictly literary and formal plane." Thus he opposed the social and political struggle of the new generations to the "happy and heedless youths of 1922."

If there is a literary group of more or less uniform mind on essential questions, it is surely this one. Fernando Góes vehemently condemned the writers of 1922 as "true Pétains of literature and the arts." Rui Coelho repeated that "besides Mário de Andrade, Sérgio Milliet, and others who sought to deepen themselves in some branch of human knowledge, the members of that group lived on hunches." Paulo Emílio, having analyzed the apparent contradictions, said that the "young intellectuals acquired seriousness and efficacy of thought which immediately differentiates them from the bohemian tone of 1922." There is no doubt that Mário Neme's book may be considered one of the last landmarks of the Modernist era: those writers who were initiating their careers already *felt* Modernism as *history* and no longer as a *presence,* whatever may have been the permanence of such and such a predecessor individually considered. The review *Clima,* which did not immediately perceive the *political* character it embodied and generally confused it with the critical spirit, then represented for that generation what *Klaxon* had represented for the generation of 1922, particularly after number 11 with its political declaration (a little verbose and vague, but we must remember the existence of censorship) in which it declared itself both anti-fascist and anti-communist.

Other winds were blowing. And finally the Congress of Writers and the death of Mário de Andrade definitively brought the Modernist era to a close after so many tallies and inventories, many of them premature.

From Literary Politics to Political Literature

Ultimately the political problem involves a passage from literary politics to political literature, or from literary revolution to revolutionary literature. No one can deny that the first half of the century was lived out under the sign of revolution, not just of revolt and war. It would be difficult to decide whether the revolutionary climate conditioned literature or whether revolutionary literature led the intelligentsia to an attitude favorable to revolution, or to political and social revolutions. It would seem more sensible to admit that all of these are forms of the same mental process of transformation, and that it would be as unthinkable to perpetuate conservative regimes well into the twentieth century as it would be to have literature and the arts preserve the forms and formulas which had been instrumental in achieving their success in former centuries. The Chinese "intelligentsia" commanded at the beginning of the century that: "The revolution in literature should lead to the literature of revolution." Of course, this did not happen in China, but it did in Russia, in anticipation of the great schism and the great clashes of the sixties; fifty years before, the symbiosis of a part of Cubism and Surrealism with Communism was the symbol of an identity which, if not natural, was at least imposed by the face of the globe at that historical moment.

In Brazil the breaking point seems to have come with the Greengilt Group; it was at that moment, let us say in 1926, that one branch of Modernism accepted the Movement's political implications and bore to the Right with Plínio Salgado, Cassiano Ricardo, Cândido Motta Filho, and Menotti del Picchia, while the other branch admitted the same implications but bore to the Left with Oswald de Andrade at first and later with Jorge Amado and all the numberless followers who rallied around one or the other of those two flags. The curve went from the esthetic freedom of 1922 to the ideological compromise of the thirties, from the revolution in literature to the revolution in politics (which the revolutionary climate of the time favored and of which the revolts of the twenties were merely the more rudimentary and thwarted manifestations). Literary nationalism, or the nationalization of literature (which took the place of the regionalism in vogue in the two decades immediately prior to 1922), imperceptibly flowed into the political nationalism and intense patriotism that were represented by the books and political development of Plínio Salgado, the *República dos EE. UU. do Brasil* by Menotti del Picchia, pamphlet literature which for the most part was Communist preachment, and Jorge Amado's first novels. This was also the period of the ideological maturation of a unionist and corporative regime which developed into the *Estado Nôvo* and the books that form the second part of Oliveira Viana's career, not to mention the period of favor that surrounded the conception of *engagé* literature, which not even the greatest minds of the time escaped.

It is interesting to note that, having long since repudiated Futurism, first in its esthetic form and later in its political forms, Modernism nonetheless underwent the same evolution: "The heroic age of Futurism, 'l'età d'oro del movimento,' as Paolo Buzzi wrote, came before the War. At that time the entire world was viewed as the private domain of Futurism. After the War began, Futurism became more and more nationalistic; and after Marinetti's election to Mussolini's Academy, Futurism became practically an official movement professing an ideology and an art that were fascist." [107]

If Integralism had been victorious, it would likewise have indicated the direction taken by Brazilian Modernism; thus, as Bergman wrote, "Marinetti's little book entitled *Le Futurisme* (1911) would have been studied side by side with *Mein Kampf* and the writings of Lenin and Mussolini." In Brazil it was Plínio Salgado himself who time and again established correlations between his literary books and his political ideas, between the Greengilt Movement and the Sigma Movement. However, as a good Brazilian solution, Getúlio Vargas, who was elevated to power by a revolution that was equally nationalist and rightist, proposed in general a program undeniably leftist, which robbed all sides of their gains(?) and imposed the dialectical solution of the *Estado Nôvo—Estado Nôvo*, which Plínio Salgado was inclined to accept in 1937, and which Luís Carlos Prestes decided the Communists should accept in his famous campaign of "Constituent with Getúlio" (1945).

It may be somewhat unpleasant, but we must accept it: in the destiny and nature of Modernism there was not only political vocation but even totalitarian political vocation. Whether Right or Left, the truth is that the time was ripe for a spectacular repudiation of conventional democracy and for the temporary demoralization of liberal ideas. Speaking in the previously mentioned *Testamento de Uma Geração*, Abguar Bastos observed: "Nonetheless, it was impossible to keep the literary movement of 1922 from changing into a political movement. . . . After 1924 Modernism's 'nationalism' (the 'national' whole) was one thing and 'Brazilianness' (the 'Brazilian' synthesis) was something totally different."

It is expedient not to lose sight of the fact that the ideological options of the thirties began even before Getúlio's revolution. On May 11, 1929, Mário de Andrade wrote to Manuel Bandeira: "The problem of the contradiction between the intellectual that I am and the Communist that I am splits me in two, leaves me extenuated; my intellectual preoccupations of these last six months are so frightening that I have withdrawn totally from the world." But we can go even farther back than that. In the preface composed for *João Miramar*, Oswald de Andrade made patently clear his nostalgia for the "strong regimes": "After that [the 'glorious

Treaty of Versailles'], we witnessed the organic diffusion of every social convulsion. Poincaré, Artur Bernardes, Lenin, Mussolini and Kemal Pasha essayed unprecedented directives in the history of peoples' codes, in the face of Wilson's idealistic demise and the final bloody death rattle of unionism."

There was, then, after 1924 a vague tendency (which steadily grew less vague) toward any kind of totalitarianism; and this tendency was at first rationalized as a repudiation of all democratic forms of government. The problem was finally resolved almost indifferently (from the point of view of distribution of names) in the left-right bifurcation. Graça Aranha noted this with his extraordinary seismographic sensibility:

> If it was only an esthetic renovation which resulted in a few poems, a few musical compositions, a few plastic creations, then the Movement was very restricted and considerably short-winded. Its purpose was not to kill off the Academy, the academic spirit, the colonial deformities, and the bickering of the grammarians. All that was facile and required little effort. If Brazilian Modernism is truly a force, then let it go forward. Let it renovate the entire Brazilian mentality. Let its action extend to customs, to law, to the co-operation of social classes, to philosophy, to politics. New thought, new activity.
>
> The essence of this thought resides in the sense of the real. This is the lever for the destruction of everything that impedes the knowledge and efficiency of Brazilian reality and the lever for the rebuilding with new materials created or discovered by the modern spirit. Marinetti's Italian Futurism renovated Italian life and led to Fascism, its political expression. Mayakovsky's Russian Futurism collaborated and identified with Communism. The law of reality prevails in both cases. In Italy, Futurism is occidental and, therefore, patriotic, nationalistic, militaristic, and imperialistic. In Russia, it is oriental, communistic, universalist, mystical, pacifist and terrorist. In Brazil it will be neither Fascist nor Communist. It will be our own creation, a formula which corresponds to our spirituality, which is devoid of all terror, and to our supreme reality.[108]

It is somewhat amusing to recall that Ronald de Carvalho had called Graça Aranha's philosophy "Integralism" around 1924; in reply, Mário de Andrade suggested the name "Integrationism," which seemed more precise to him, a name in which a certain "stylist" of our own time did not fail to note some involuntary pun based on Graça's name itself. It was certainly as an unconscious reminiscence that the word later reappeared in Plínio Salgado's political movement. Thus the imperceptible plot which joined the political and literary fates of the Movement thickened.

Eduardo Frieiro's novel, *O Clube dos Grafômanos* (1927), lacks substantial value as a work of fiction, but it does hold enormous interest as an indication of the frame of mind of the moment. Besides reflecting the idiocies and incongruities of the provincial Modernists, it also contains pages that almost literally transcribe the general tenor of political thought. Here is one of the discussions of the members of a literary circle in which all the participants were intellectuals:

Porfírio Leiva continued:
"The so-called 'principles of '89,' which lent to civilization unquestionable services in the guise of the crumbling formulae of theocracy, once they had become mental idols, began to be eminently fatal to that very civilization.

Popular sovereignty is, in itself, nothing more than the formula of a crude fiction which consists, as Comte observed, of substituting in society the will of the individual—metaphysically armed with his ludicrous elective infallability—for the will of the monarch, theologically invested with divine right.

Liberty, considered as a *summum bonum,* has eaten away at democracy in a requisite evolution toward anarchy.

Reaction could not be long in coming. Once again the alternation of ebb and flow manifested itself as if it were the law of History.

Georges Valois, in the preface to the definitive edition of his prophetic work *L'Homme Qui Vient,* says that from now on it will be evident that the twentieth century will be known as the century of authority.

And so it is. Europe has rejected Democracy. Dictators appear on every side: Lenin, Mussolini, Primo de Rivera, Horthy, Mustafa Kemal, Pilsudzki, energetic leaders capable of re-establishing order and imposing a hierarchy of values, by co-ordinating resultant forces."

.   .   .   .   .

VITORIANO

The truth is that men always travel the same roads: when they hover on the brink of barbarism and anarchy, they understand the advantages of order and quickly accept harsh discipline and tutelary authority.

LEIVA

Take Italy. Italy was on the verge of being drawn into the Communist maelstrom. Class struggle threatened to sink the country into a horrible civil war. The people had become dissatisfied, envious, and covetous.

The middle class, self-indulgent and fearful, reacted defenselessly. . . . Some heroic solution was demanded. It was necessary to defend authority, property, and social peace against civil war and bolshevist insanity.

Salvation lay in fascist reaction. The Italian people were aware of the virtues—somewhat drastic—of the billy club and castor oil. . . .

.   .   .   .   .

Anti-liberal and anti-democratic, fascism eliminated the old ideas of universal suffrage and the metaphysical abstractions of the ideologists of '89.

Leiva answered an observation made by Vitoriano, according to which "bolshevism and fascism are the total negation of all democratic values": "Yes . . . Except that, as Georges Valois wrote, Lenin is the dictator of barbarism while Mussolini is the dictator of civilization." The *mystique,* the *spiritual exaltation* which Leiva found in the Italian regime, also fascinated numerous Brazilian intellectuals. If there was the irrepressible tendency toward any strong government, it seems that the majority preferred something along peninsular lines over anything taken from Soviet patterns. Prior to that dialogue, Leiva himself had said: "How could the fiction of democracy serve us, who above all else need a strong and respected 'central power'? Today, except for some laggard ideologist or other, no one is any longer a democrat in the sense of the old historical republicans."

This novel by Frieiro, contemporary with Greengiltism and the unconscious maturation of Integralist ideas, emphasized as a consequence the moment when the options became conscious options which were growing more and more antagonistic. It should not be forgotten that, at that exact moment, Oswald de Andrade was writing *Serafim Ponte Grande*. In 1932, year one of the Integralist Revolution, which would establish the Fourth Humanity (Plínio Salgado *dixit*) not only in Brazil but also throughout the world, Renato Almeida published *Velocidade,* one of the little books typical of Modernism to which I have already referred. The race for dictatorships seemed to him to be one of the consequences of the age of speed and efficiency:

But even far from these new forms of government [Bolshevism and Fascism], one can see around the world the daily increase of the strength of the State, which is justified by economic pressure even in countries like England whose traditionalism had always found the sacrifice of liberty repugnant. Mechanical speed has so distorted the socio-political problem, that all democratic ideology has crumbled beneath the weight of the new building atop it. . . . The socio-political phenomenon was altered by the power of the machine. Classes were undergoing change and that third estate which the Revolution had brought to the surface immediately enslaved the fourth estate, which was proletarian and was created by industrialism. And what do all modern doctrines seek to do? To bring society back into balance.

The following is his conclusion:

Speed has not upset human ingenuity. It merely gave it a new orientation, a new sensibility, broadened its view of things; but it did not lead its basic condition astray.

The fact that all the strong regimes of the twenties and thirties found their justification in technology and efficiency is something that we tend to forget all too easily. But at the heart of the problem lay a tremendous paradox: not only Modernism but all the military and institutional revolts down to 1932 were bourgeois revolutions, not only because in the last analysis the middle class stood to benefit from these revolutions but also because they had their origins in a bourgeois ideology, and they sought the consolidation of the bourgeois ideals of life. They were, therefore, revolts rather than revolutions but, nonetheless, revolts that were unwillingly and unwittingly inscribed within a general revolutionary process. Within the more solid traditions of Brazilian "revolutions" (literary or otherwise) it was form and not content that was debated; for that very reason, what is truly revolutionary in Modernism is form and style much more than substance. We have already seen that Gilberto Freyre saw no contradiction whatever in proposing a traditionalist Modernism for the same reason that the São Paulo Modernists returned to the Brazilian past, to the conventional structure of the novel. Jorge Amado, who in the forties had reached the height of his embittered political writing, in this regard observed in the previously mentioned inquest made by the *Revista do Brasil*:

> . . . the basic cause for the contradictions in Modernism: it was a movement that was brutally nonconformist in form while it was totally conformist in content. I say "almost" [109] because of "cannibalism," a small wing within the enormous movement, a wing that created a poetry and a prose which were not concerned only with destroying rhymes and omitting commas but also with renovating ideas. From that contradiction—nonconformity in form and conservatism in content—came all the limitations and contradictions of Modernism; from that contradiction also came the castration of the creative power of its artists. What did Modernism come from? From the rise in coffee prices, from the creation and enrichment of a São Paulo aristocracy based on the coffee economy, politically dominant in the country, an aristocracy polished by its European tours, which recognized on sight and sound literary movements of European origin, a class

which required a kind of literature that would satisfy its tastes that were formed somewhere between the plantation and Paris and as a consequence could not accept, like the rest of the country, the Coelho Netos, the Alberto de Oliveiras, who were products of another economy.

Seen in this perspective, the great novel of Modernism was, for Jorge Amado, *Serafim Ponte Grande,* that herald of the revolution which was in Brazil, in a literary and political sense, more than the revolution of 1924, a "melancholy revolution." However, from the angle at which we study these matters, the results are not so important as the frame of mind.

All of this was done, of course, on the Right and on the Left as a result of a tacit agreement: the systematic disrepute of the very idea of political party. Malraux, who was the great Communist novelist of the thirties and forties, already stood somewhat outside history when he placed this remark in the mouth of one of his characters: "We are entering the age of political parties." On the contrary, we were leaving that age behind, and leaving it for a long period of time. In Spain's particular case, down to the present, and in Brazil's case until 1945; that is, down to the end of Modernism itself. Thus, because of the exacerbation of politics, the Movement came to its own negation: the excess of ideologies ended by obliterating them all. In the twenties, life had taken on the task of proposing the perfect allegory for all these contradictions. We can see it magnificently depicted in the historical photograph "Eighteen from the Fort," a perfect symbol of romantic revolt: insubstantial, filled with beauty and heroism, but futile—the *beau geste* which preceded the sad years when the mystique dissolved into politics.

At any rate, to be a disinterested writer or artist after 1930 was a capital crime. In the "Elegia de Abril" Mário de Andrade gave a preview of the inescapable censure of his 1942 judgment: "We were abstentionists to a large degree. I cannot even say 'abstentionists' because that implies a conscious frame of mind: we were, rather, an unwitting group. Not even the nationalism that we practiced with somewhat greater latitude than our predecessors, the regionalists, could give us any clear definition of the consciousness of the intellectual's condition, his duties toward art and humanity, his relation to society and the state."

Nonetheless, the three Modernist decades were politically a time of great confusion rather than of great clarification and clear choice, beginning with the very idea of the "social function of art" and ending with political action viewed in concrete terms. In the *Plataforma da Nova Geração*, Paulo Emílio Salles Gomes, who may be considered one of the clearest and best-defined political minds of his generation, drew a detailed picture of the several lines of ideological orientation taken by Brazilian youth at that moment. It constituted a highly significant balance sheet, due to his political acumen, and revealed more ideological disorientation than orientation among the young Brazilians. At any rate, from those pages we may conclude:

(1) that the new generations, with a strong social and political consciousness, repudiated the gratuitous estheticism of 1922;
(2) that the several political possibilities of Modernism had already crystallized as
   (a) Right
   (b) Catholic
   (c) Left.

It is quite probable that the distinction between Right and Catholic was more the result of the desire to register all political shading than to take an objective look at reality, because the second group was subdivided into two groups: the Catholicism of a literary position and the Catholicism of those who saw in religion a substitute for a political mystique in which they could no longer believe. Between these two fell the ex-Integralists and the ex-Communists, both equally authentic. "The great figures of Brazilian Catholicism," Paulo Emílio added, "are found in neither of these groups. They are the young monks of our generation."

Reflecting one of the illusions of the moment, Paulo Emílio immediately said that these were nonetheless secondary sectors. What "really has meaning because of the number of its representatives and the high intellectual caliber of many of its members," he asserted, was the Left, whose comings and goings he recorded in great detail and whose point of reference was the Soviet Union, which he identified with every "renovative sentiment." If it is true that the Left—Communist and non-Communist—was at that time identified by the "high intellectual caliber of many of its members," it is debatable that it possessed great significance "because of the number of its representatives." This testimony was not published in the *O Estado de São Paulo* in obedience to the laws of censorship; and, when the *Plataforma da Nova Geração* (which did contain it) was published, the *Estado Nôvo* had already fallen. But we should not therefore think less of its moral courage and final suggestions: amnesty for political prisoners and freedom of political organization.

The Catholic Right, at that time, had Alceu Amoroso Lima as its great leader before it evolved into what was somewhat improperly called the Catholic Left. For that reason, Paulo Emílio Salles Gomes's stance in the face of this great adversary is significant:

In the presence of the importance of Senhor Alceu Amoroso Lima as a well-known director of a considerable number of the youths of the new generation, it is necessary to say from the start that he does not merit our confidence. Because a man of his responsibility and education could not have led, as he did, young Brazilian Catholics with a political vocation down the Integralist path.[110] But we must go even farther and ask whether Senhor Alceu Amoroso Lima can merit our respect. Because he quoted, approved, divulged, and continually developed the thought of Jackson de Figueiredo:—the worst legality is preferable to the best revolution—and he immediately took his place on the side of Franco's Fascist rebellion. Now, the uprising of the seditious generals, from Senhor Alceu Amoroso Lima's angle, perfectly fitted with Jackson's formula. It was the best of revolutions because it was reactionary and pro-clerical, against the worst of legalities, because it was Republican and Socialist.

Finally, in confirmation of what had been said previously, Paulo Emílio ended his analysis by certifying that "there is in the new generation no intellectual sector that is properly liberal, in the old sense of the word."

Between 1916 and 1945, Modernism, which had begun as a purely esthetic revolution, evolved into a type of art in which political concerns and interests ended up by superimposing themselves on the original esthetic problems. Later on the political current disappeared and gave up its place to the original estheticism. The graph which I have included here attempts to show

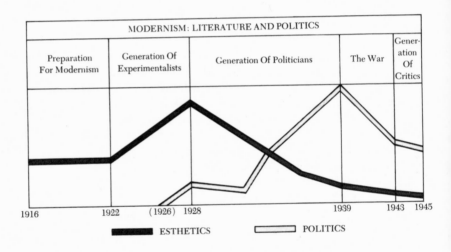

MODERNISM: LITERATURE AND POLITICS

| Preparation For Modernism | Generation Of Experimentalists | Generation Of Politicians | The War | Generation Of Critics |

1916   1922   (1926) 1928   1939   1943   1945

ESTHETICS   POLITICS

this play of alternations by placing them as strictly as possible in chronological series: estheticism defines the Modernist orientation down to around 1926, when the waves of political thought began to take on consistency and importance. Between 1928 and 1939, the political aspect clearly predominated over the esthetic. With the war, the situation continued more or less in the same vein, but the truly political frenzy subtly surrendered a part of its rights to the critical spirit and the essay. Through the door of literary criticism, estheticism once again entered the literary world to such a degree that, after 1945, all the emphasis of creation and criticism is placed on the esthetic nature of the work of art.

This was the general picture of the relations between politics and Modernism. With the end of the Movement, which also marked the end of the war and the *Estado Nôvo*, the democratic platform regained its prestige: the platform regained its prestige and so, above all, did the democratic vocabulary.

Nationalism and Regionalism

If ideologically Modernism went to extremes in its surrender to the trends of the time, psychologically its political vocation (in the neutral sense of the word) was contained in the two essential postulates of its spiritual configuration: Nationalism and Regionalism. With relation to these, the Modernists maintained an ambivalent—if not openly contradictory—position. Nonetheless, both Nationalism and Regionalism were part and parcel and the soul of the Movement.

In 1916, Júlio Mesquita made the following editorial comment by way of introducing the *Revista do Brasil:*

What underlies the title of this review and also the names of its sponsors is one simple and tremendous fact: the desire, the resolution, the unshakable will to create a nucleus of nationalist propaganda. We are not yet a nation with an acquaintance of itself, with self-esteem; or we might more accurately say that we are a nation which as yet has not had the spirit to advance alone toward a vigorous and resplendent projection of its own personality. We have existed since our birth as a nation, whether as Empire or Republic, under the direct or indirect tutelage (if not political, at least moral) of

Europe. We think with a foreign brain; we are dressed by foreign tailors; we eat a foreign diet; and to crown that act of collective servility, in our homeland we all too often stifle our mother tongue to speak a foreign language! . . . Our nationalism is not, however, and never will be, a form of hostility toward the foreigner. We do not wish to isolate Brazil from humanity, which would be sheer nonsense, nor can we deny the debt of civilization which we owe to Europe.

The nationalist consciousness affected all our intellectuals after 1916: it was the road of nationalism that Modernism followed after the Week of Modern Art once its cosmopolitan phase had passed. At heart, Greengiltism and Cannibalism were nothing more than purely esthetic manifestations of the nationalist sentiment, as some years before Brazilwood had been. The fact that such a state of mind was naturally reflected in artistic activities may be seen from the statements of the *Revista do Brasil* (from February, 1916) under the title heading of "Nacionalização da Arte":

The idea of nationalism is now shared by all our intellectuals. This very review, in its peaceful civilizing mission, is one fruit of that idea. One of the most interesting aspects of this idea may be seen with regard to literature. How far will it be permitted to a writer or an artist, who does not wish to fall prey to imitation or lose his nationalist stamp, how far will he be permitted to nourish himself on ideas, form, and style furnished by foreign literatures and arts? This is a difficult question to which Senhor Afonso Arinos (hiding under the pseudonym of Gil Cássio) supplied a brilliant answer some years back. . . . We are not an inferior people; neither are we decadent. We simply have not yet attained maturity as a nation, in the scientific sense of the word. That is to say, we have not yet attained a political and social integrity with thoughts, feelings, and actions which truly reflect the synthesis of our collective energies. Thus we should not allow Brazilian art, newborn from the unity of the autonomous spirit, to employ foreign forms. We should rather give to our art a flavor that is truly Brazilian.

If the editorial statement of the original number of the *Revista do Brasil* could be considered the first nationalist manifesto of Modernism, the second note firmly establishes the indispensable affiliation: ranging from Regionalism, represented by the work and deeds of Afonso Arinos, augmented by the work of Valdomiro Silveira, Coelho Neto, Bilac, Simões Lopes Neto, Monteiro Lobato—or rather, by all the unquestionably significant names of the Brazilian intelligentsia since the end of the nineteenth century, not to mention Sílvio Romero, Euclides da Cunha, or Rui Barbosa—to a form of Nationalism which was more ideological than political and more sociological than theoretical. Referring to the lecture by Afonso Arinos, "A Unidade da Pátria," delivered in 1915 in the city of Belo Horizonte, Olavo Bilac wrote:

In "A Unidade da Pátria," which truly constituted the first cry of alarm and the first fruitful gesture of the campaign of regeneration which involves us, Afonso Arinos summed up with cruel precision the ills which afflict and shame us: the attenuation of our nobler efforts; the distress of our backlanders, docile and resigned, preyed upon by epidemics and taxes; lack of education; administrative disorganization; economic incompetence; the insufficiency and often the criminal evasion of justice; the petulant and egotistical ignorance of those who govern this gigantic land, which does not yet exist as a nation. . . .[111]

It can be seen that it was not merely a figure of speech, nor even semantic confusion, to call the nationalism of 1916 the first incarnation of the "developmentism" into which the idea was transformed in the fifties. Nor did we lack, at that time, the excesses of nationalism represented by a kind of jingoism, particularly by attacks on the Portuguese. In his "Mensagem aos Moços," which concerned the Nationalist League, Júlio Mesquita found it necessary to define and delimit the idea of nationalism: "The nationalist ([sic] for 'nationalism') of the Nationalist League of São Paulo is extremely nationalism ([sic] for 'nationalist'); but with all its fervor, it is no more than that. We find in it not so much as a hint of jingoism. To the Nationalist League of˙ São

Paulo everything foreign, and especially everything Portuguese, is its friend and collaborator. . . ."

The Modernist attacks on Portuguese grammar and the purist tendencies and tyranny of the proprietors of language were not so gratuitous as they seemed at first: Rui Barbosa, if he had not yet "sold out to the Yankee dollar," seemed to be a spiritual traitor—because of his Lusitanist fetishism—to the nationalist idea (which, in a political way, he seemed to defend). In the history of intellectual movements, and particularly in the history of Modernism, one frequently misses the notion of integration, within the global atmosphere of the moment, in matters that are not directly literary or artistic but are nonetheless incalculably important for an understanding of the true nature of the movements. Thus was the Brazilwood of which Paulo Prado wrote in his famous preface: "Brazilwood poetry finds its most beautiful and fruitful inspiration in the affirmation of that nationalism which must break the ties which have bound us, from the moment of our birth, to old Europe, decadent and exhausted. . . . Let us free ourselves of the nefarious influences of the old decadent civilizations. Let us begin with language and grammar. . . ." Greengiltism or Cannibalism will seem to us better motivated and much more logical and natural if we understand that they were merely an attempt at the artistic and literary interpretation of a collective state of mind. For that reason, in a review of M. F. Pinto Pereira's book, *A Mulher no Brasil*, the *Revista do Brasil* said in June, 1916: "The nationalist concern is already passing from journalism and the public tribunal to the book. The fact is that it is beginning to crystallize quite naturally. The conviction is growing generally that it is necessary to do something to discover Brazil for the Brazilians and that nothing, or practically nothing, has thus far been done to make this discovery a reality."

In the same article, "O Êxodo," in which he contested, as we have seen, Catulo da Paixão Cearense's position as "supreme poet of the race" (the same Catulo whom Paulo Prado in 1925 had placed beside Casimiro de Abreu in his evocation of the only two poets who were truly national and "pure"), Alceu Amoroso Lima observed that "in our time literature has freed itself from those fripperies; the national aspect of our *letters* is today a heartfelt need of our intellect and not merely an effort of our sensibility." The Nationalist League, the League of National Defense, the "Beehive" movement, and Olavo Bilac's campaign on behalf of universal military service were all the offspring of this frame of mind within which Modernism itself was to a great degree inscribed. In a more restricted sense, in his famous address on the occasion of his repudiating the Academy, Graça Aranha suggested the "nationalization" of the Academy's work.

It is in this atmosphere that, as a necessary and natural consequence, we should locate literary Regionalism, which at first assumed the form of "backlands" literature—thus explaining Catulo's extraordinary success. On that same wave of nationalism and regionalism Jeca Tatu was born, destined to resounding success, and Mané Xiquexique, although less popular today, represented the "optimistic," proud, and compensatory answer to whatever was low-spirited and pessimistic in Jeca. In this way we can explain the image employed by the critic on the *Revista do Brasil* in his review (April, 1920) of *Sertão em Flor* by Catulo da Paixão Cearense: "The literature of the backlands is, evidently, the *xiquexique* [a cactus] of national literature. Hacked off here, uprooted there, everywhere burned down, it is futile to pile our criticism on it, with all its concepts and theories: backlands literature, slashed to the quick, will sprout anew with the first drizzle and put out leaves and blossoms. . . . Puny, disabled, wrinkled, deformed—but alive. It is a weed that cannot be driven out." It would not be too foolhardy to suggest that this note was written by Monteiro Lobato, as were many other reviews in the early numbers of the *Revista do Brasil* (that is, after he became owner of it in 1918). The allusion to the Northeastern cactus had been suggested by Ildefonso Albano in the volume *Jeca Tatu e Mané Xiquexique,* which was reviewed in the *Revista do Brasil* in April, 1920. The intention becomes quite clear from these elucidations:

The *xiquexique,* A. explains, is a cactus native to Mané's homeland. It is born and it prospers in any soil—good, bad, or indifferent; but abstemious, tough, stubborn and rough, it prefers over them all the bare stone, the hard rock . . .

According to A., the backlander who proliferates in the northeastern sector of our country zoologically plays the interesting role of that "shameless" plant. He also resists every meteorological calamity endemic to his *habitat*. Hence the nickname which, in this volume, introduces him to the admiration of the country: Mané Xiquexique. . . . As he is depicted there, Mané, whom A. considers the legitimate brother of Jeca Tatu, deserves from his fellows the greatest and most heartfelt sympathy. . . . And as, in spite of all his worthiness, Mané lies abandoned to oblivion while government after government sees fit to fill Jeca's lazy belly, that lucky parasite from the South, Senhor Ildefonso Albano, has written Mané's epic so that, by reading it, those who are all-powerful under the Southern Cross might decide to provide Mané with some trifling share of the public funds.

The political implications (this time in the narrow sense of the word) are obvious: Mané Xiquexique merely presages similar argumentation on the part of Gilberto Freyre and so many others. But to stay strictly in the literary domain, it was the regionalist, nationalist, and backlands climate that explained the late publication, in 1921, of the volume in which Valdomiro Silveira, giving the book a title which represented an entire program of action, collected his short stories. Indubitably in February of 1921, the *Revista do Brasil* was referring to this matter when it said that

the fathers of the present-day literary movement in São Paulo, which no one can ignore because it is a great *fait accompli*, are Cornélio Pires and Juó Bananére. Juó Bananére? Can that be? . . . The reader will ask this question, surely.

This serious matter, which is São Paulo's literature today, proceeds from the amusing dialect writer of the *Pirralho!* It is the offspring of the marriage of the jargon of "Abaixo o Piques" to the ally of the Chapel of Nossa Senhora da Ponte dos Remédios do Tietê! This statement may seem unusual, but it is nonetheless true. It was this minor backlands literature, in the manner of the Italo-Brazilian *pochade*, which invaded the market place of journalism and belles-lettres and broadcast the joys of reading; and, demonstrating the certain possibilities of a literary industry, suggested, encouraged, and promoted this lovely and powerful rebirth of letters . . . So, as a late-maturing fruit, the volume now appears—*Os Caboclos.* It is born out of time, but it arrives in the company of true and bountiful admiration. Twenty, thirty years late. . . .

These restrictions placed on Valdomiro Silveira's book, which did indeed arrive on the literary scene quite late, are understandable because by that time the future Modernists had unleashed their campaign against Regionalism, so well documented by Mário da Silva Brito.[112] When Modernism developed an awareness of itself and was preparing to be a movement, Regionalism, which came from Afonso Arinos and was made illustrious by Coelho Neto and Simões Lopes, had already begun to seem somewhat archaic and—what is worse—to be a kind of literature totally foreign to the esthetic values that had determined Regionalism in the first place. The paradox of literary history later wanted Modernism to reassume an even older tradition in the prehistoric territory of folklore and, by that path, return to Regionalism (which flourished in the thirties). That underground connection did not escape Ronald de Carvalho: "Because he was a 'son of the backlands' as well as one of the purest gentlemen of our race, Arinos succeeded in arousing an entire tribe of highly interesting writers. It is sufficient to mention, among the moderns, Monteiro Lobato or Senhor Peregrino Júnior with his profound and tragic *Pussanga,* to judge from its considerable influence." [113]

One of the most vigorous forms of Regionalism came from Rio Grande do Sul which, on one hand, seems not to have undergone any interruption of consequence (since the "Modernism" of 1925–26 was basically a continuation of Simões Lopes's work) and, on the other hand, seems to have felt little or no influence from the São Paulo Modernists. So the two books by Vargas Netto published in 1929, *Tropilha Crioula* and *Gado Xucro,* contain "gauchesque poetry" just as Simões Lopes's book had contained "gauchesque stories." In addition to that, the *Tropilha Crioula* was at least the pampa, dotted with Symbolism and Parnassianism certainly as much as Modernism. If there was some Modernist influence on Vargas Netto, it was rather that of Menotti del Picchia than of any other writer: I refer, of course, to the influence of *Juca Mulato*, the Menotti del Picchia of 1917. Such a presence was even more sensitively felt than that of Simões Lopes himself, as this portrait of the Gaucho attests. It is more Parnassian than epic, more Menottian than gauchesque:

> Perambulating o'er the pampa wide,
> To quell the vasty longings of his heart,
> This recluse lives his trusty steed astride,
> Like legendary pampa winds apart.
>
> This gaucho on the rugged countryside,
> Where yellow and the green their tones impart,
> Oft sleeps upon the prairie floor inside
> A poncho made of stars when day does part.
>
> A man to dominate and fear inspire,
> A man whose vibrant blood can nought excite
> Save thund'ring rifle shot or pistol fire:
>
> When blunderbuss the noose of death draws tight,
> He dies reliving all his past desire,
> Relives the Southern epic of the fight.[114]

Gado Xucro was more Modernist, as it abandoned regular verse, constant rhyme, but not Parnassian imagery. A typical poem is this "Dia de Verão Gaúcho":

DAWN

> Night has ripened the dawn
> and day will open the red lips of morn,
> to swallow the shadows
> in a great burst of sunny
> laughter.

I feel the green joy of morning on the Pampa!
The field is all bedecked with beads,
because night strung the white droplets of dew
on the slender shafts of needlegrass.

I go barefoot to the brook
and beneath my moistened feet I crush
the dewy designs on the gentle grass.[115]

Significantly the collision of the two trends, the regionalist and the modern, took place in Rio Grande do Sul as a result of the work of Alcides Maya. But in the polemic which took place between Paulo Arinos and Rubens de Barcellos [116] there is not a single allusion made to Modernism. The debate grew out of an article by Paulo Arinos entitled "O Papel da Nova Geração," published in 1925 in the *Correio do Povo* of Pôrto Alegre, in which he identified the writings of Alcides Maya as a kind of longing to return to the past (or *saudosismo,* as he called it). The young critic took umbrage at this statement and moreover proposed an extremely vague program for the new generations. It was rather an argument over content and frame of mind than over form and literary technique—or rather the contrary of what, up till then, had characterized Modernism.

It is interesting to recall that, ten years earlier in 1914, an identical polemic had taken place in São Paulo between the *saudosistas,* or defenders of the backlander, and Monteiro Lobato, author of the article "Velha Praga." It was in reply to the attacks it provoked that he wrote the article "Urupês," in which he created the character of Jeca Tatu. Here we find one more tragic— or grotesque—error which set Monteiro Lobato against the Modernists (and vice versa). Having been born as a realistic reply to the *saudosistas,* implicitly affirming a "modern" and enlightened program of recuperation, Jeca Tatu was involved by the youths of 1920–22 in the same unpardonable condemnation which they had hurled at "backlands" literature. In an article of October 3, 1921, cited by Mário da Silva Brito, Cândido Motta Milho unleashed an attack on Jeca, "the typical character in regional writing": "This comic monkey who goes through life squatting on his heels, indifferent to the world, a retarded example of the species and a hindrance to our country's progress, can never be the prototype of our national soul."

But that was precisely what Monteiro Lobato was saying! It is perfectly clear that, by natural inclination of spirit, the Modernists were optimists and super-enthusiasts. And this does not mention their patriotic pride, which in them is surprising but no less a fact for that reason. If they had been given a choice, they would rather have identified with Mané Xiquexique. . . .

In 1925 everything was ripe for nationalism to be confused with both the esthetic and political program of the Modernist generation: it was precisely because of the nationalism, so obvious in *Meu,* that Mário de Andrade initiated his observations on Guilherme de Almeida's volume with the following words:

Perhaps the most curious aspect of the creations of Brazilian Modernism is the violent longing for nationality observable in these authors. It is not, nor could it properly be, *nationalism* in the sense in which we usually employ the word. Even observing artistic nationalism, we note in it a political meaning and a movement of revendication which, if it from time to time appears also in the productions of Brazilian Modernism, is at the same time not exactly what sets the tone of the Movement. The tone is a result of a desire for nationality, but more than that: of a need for nationality which, because it is an almost generalized and, so to speak, unconscious phenomenon, should surely give the universalists considerable food for thought.

If we understand by "universalists" the pure esthetes of the first Modernism (1922–25), among whom figured Mário de Andrade himself, it is undeniable that after 1925 Nationalism and Regionalism were confused with Modernism. It was the necessary stage in the transformation of nationalist sentiment into thought or political ideology which had to lead to Greengiltism and Cannibalism (the nucleus of the future group of the literary Left in the thirties).

Even here we can see the importance of the year 1921, already emphasized by Mário da Silva Brito. In June, in the *Revista do Brasil*, Alceu Amoroso Lima observed in a panorama of the writing of 1920: "In that literary year one could observe the old conflict between nativism and cosmopolitanism, which is surely one of the fundamental aspects of our literature. It cannot be said that there is a concentrated and deliberate movement of creative nationalism. But unconsciously, owing to literary evolution itself, in the sense of a greater differentiation we can see a growing influence of the resources and spirit of the land." In September, in a review of Jackson de Figueiredo's book, *O Nacionalismo na Hora Presente*, the *Revista do Brasil* commented: "Nationalism is in vogue. It became popular with the nationalization of fishing, which created such a stir in the Brazilian press and also in Portugal's. Senhor Jackson de Figueiredo, the well-known philosopher and journalist, now enters the lists. *O Nacionalismo na Hora Presente* is a 'letter from a Catholic concerning the reasons for nationalism in Brazil and what it is possible to observe in such a movement, addressed to Francisco Bustamante by Jackson de Figueiredo.' "

Just as it happened in Europe, the war of 1914 cut short in Brazil the natural development of literary and political trends which had manifested themselves in embryonic form at the beginning of the century. In 1919, criticizing Nestor Victor's book, *Crítica de Ontem*, Tristão de Athayde wrote:

In 1906, in Nestor Victor's own words, the common preoccupation of the writers of the time was the national problem. Besides that, one could observe a certain libertarian and socialist current in the books of Fábio Luz, Curvello de Mendonça and Elysio de Carvalho. That two-fold character —nationalist and socialist—identifies our contemporary literary current. It was the War that determined the movement. The vision of Europe and the world in conflict brought us closer to ourselves. All wars produce a revision of values. This war made us consider our land with greater interest and affection. The action of the Center of Artistic Culture and the *Revista do Brasil* bears witness to this fact as also do, in São Paulo, the foundation of various nationalist centers and the national character of the latest books by Monteiro Lobato, Veiga Miranda, Godofredo Rangel, Alberto Deodato and Hugo Carvalho Ramos. The socialist trend, which was anti-anarchist but libertarian, also grew in importance. Antônio Tôrres, Lima Barreto, Miguel Melo, Assis Chateaubriand, Humberto Campos and José Oiticica prove this assertion.

In 1927, when the opposing groups had already broken apart, each group taking an aspect of Modernism with it (the "nationalists" being confused with the political right and picturesque regionalism and the "socialists" identifying with the left and social regionalism), Mário de Andrade gave vent to his feelings in a letter to Manuel Bandeira: "We have more stupid nationalism than we really require! They'll say that my book [Clã do Jaboti] is nationalist, that I, too, have jumped on the bandwagon with no one capable of grasping my intent, that I am who I am, not a nationalist but a Brazilian 'et pour cause' ever since Paulicéia, where I said that I wrote Brazilian and invented the speeches of My Madness and the Greengilt Youths."

At the center of all this confusion of ideas stood Alberto Tôrres with his 1917 book, rediscovered by the Modernists in general and by the Greengiltists in particular. O Problema Nacional Brasileiro is the manual of the perfect nationalist; later re-edited in the "Brasiliana" collection, it merely emphasized all those jumbled ideas which were, however, set in order around a common axis. From Alberto Tôrres to Oliveira Viana and Plínio Salgado the transition was natural; but it was equally so from the first two down to Gilberto Freyre, and from all of them down to an interest in so-called "Brazilian studies." Less than a monstrosity in the political history of Brazil, the Estado Nôvo, directly connected with the Revolution of 1930, was to a large degree the natural heir of that frame of mind. This explains why it was favorably received by Plínio Salgado and why it gained the collaboration of numerous Modernist intellectuals. The fact was that the Estado Nôvo needed to respond, simultaneously and contradictorily, to the aspirations of all, just as it had happened with the Revolution of 1930. Nationalism was the common value that united them to the essay literature which grew out of Modernism. It is not without reason that the splendid collections of Brazilian materials so greatly increased in number during the thirties and forties:

> The overriding interest in matters concerning Brazil's past, its social and historical formation, its cultural and ethnic characteristics, the psychology of its inhabitants, the identifying aspects of its family and social life, the outstanding traits of its institutions is steadily increasing and attracting the attention of an ever-growing number of scholars and researchers.
>
> The signs of this fertile labor are evident to even the least attentive observers; and if other proofs of this activity were not in existence, the collections inaugurated in the last few years by the leading publishing firms in Brazil would be quite sufficient.
>
> The "Brasiliana" collection, issued by the Companhia Editôra Nacional, has already reached number 200 in that series which contains some indispensable titles for anyone who wishes to have a more direct knowledge of the evolution of Brazilian affairs. We may say the same for the "Documentos Brasileiros" collection issued by the Livraria José Olympio Editôra.
>
> These two older and long-acclaimed collections are now joined by two more recent ones: the "Depoimentos Históricos," published by Irmãos Pongetti-Zelio Valverde Editôres, and the "Biblioteca Histórica Brasileira," issued by the Livraria Martins Editôra of São Paulo. This first collection opened with the reissue of the memoirs of Counsellor Francisco Gomes da Silva (the "Jester" [o Chalaça]), and the second collection lends valuable service to historical scholarship with the translation of the *Viagem Pitoresca Através do Brasil* by João Mauricio Rugendas.[117]

These collections represent the culmination of a movement that had begun in the mid-twenties, as it took up again the old lines of regionalism and nationalism from the preceding decade which had been sharply interrupted by the first manifestations of Modernist cosmopolitanism. However, throughout this entire process, from at least 1921, there was a dominant preoccupation with linguistic nationalization. Even in this area Modernism invented nothing; it inherited, rather than innovated, the trends that characterized it in this regard. Seen in the proper light, the Modernists systematized and consolidated the campaign for a Brazilian language, acting as they did in all intellectual and esthetic matters. A symbol of that procedure was the *Gramatiquinha da Fala Brasileira,* by Mário de Andrade, about which he spoke toward the end of his life to Francisco de Assis Barbosa: "I announced the book, but I never wrote it. I announced the book because I thought it necessary for the Modernist Movement. To lend more importance to the matters we sought to defend." [118]

Long before that, D. Xiquote (Bastos Tigre?) wrote a note with regard to the "Brazilian dictionary," which was transcribed by the *Revista do Brasil* of July, 1921: "For some time now we have exhibited a certain fondness for the nationalization of the Portuguese language as it is spoken in Brazil. The apostles of this crusade do not intend to fabricate an artificial language like Esperanto, Volapuk, *la langue bleu* [sic] and so many others that are no more than preserved languages, neatly canned."

In October the matter assumed a more serious tone: Peregrino Júnior had published an article in the *A Notícia* of Rio de Janeiro in which he lauded Monteiro Lobato. According to Peregrino Júnior, Brazilian literature was on the eve of proclaiming, along with the commemorations of its political independence, its mental independence as well. The living symbol of that independence seemed to him to be Monteiro Lobato for the steps he had taken against "grammatical jingoism." The fact that this disciple of Camilo and apostle of Lusitanian correctness should, at the time, be considered a reformer of language is a matter which we have now studied from three points of view: his role as a precursor of Modernism, his role within nationalism and, finally, within Regionalism. Thus, when in *Macunaíma* Mário de Andrade depicted his hero "perfecting his ability in the two languages of the land, spoken Brazilian and written Portuguese" (Chapter X), it is true that he represented the culmination of

one entire process of Modernism; but it is also true that he obscured the fact that the aspirations of linguistic nationalization
proceeded from former times and resided in the sources and not
in the consequences of Modernism.

At the close of the first Modernist decade, the process of
linguistic nationalization had been transformed into poetic license
and licentiousness. Reacting against this trend, which had become
quite pronounced, Mário de Andrade wrote to Manuel Bandeira
in 1929:

> I don't need that any more [excessive insistence on spoken
> Brazilian]. I even begin to sense that it wouldn't hurt to
> throw a little cold water into the boiling Brazilianistic pot.
> I'm much to blame for all that has happened; and if I had
> suspected that the matter would assume such outlandish
> proportions, I surely would have proceeded with more mod-
> eration. . . . But neither do I wish to force the issue in an
> anti-Brazilian way. And I note that all of you are tired of
> this harebrained Brazilianist nonsense of mine (mine and
> many others as well). It would take too long to analyze
> psychologically this weariness of yours at the moment. You
> people are the ones who are involved in a false antinational,
> individualist, and romantic reaction.

The thirties saw a generation of bad prose writers who mis-
took ignorance of language for linguistic nationalism and employed that crude instrument to create the "social novel" and the
political novel, which was directly copied from life and nearly
totally devoid of esthetic sensibility. This trend lasted practically
until the end of the Modernist era. It was not until after 1945
that the estheticist generations began anew to sense linguistic
virtuosity as an esthetic value.[119]

The Modernist "Hero"

All of these themes are related to another equally important one: that of the creation of a Modernist "hero." Every great literary movement has created a "hero" figure with whom it identifies: Classicism had the *honnête homme*; Encyclopedism had its *philosophe*; Romanticism had its foredoomed man; and Realism and Symbolism had their neurotics. Futurism and Modernism, both optimistic movements, at first proposed a renaissance type, athletic and strong, robust and vigorous, who represented joy (Graça Aranha) and the heroic life (Plínio Salgado). The distance which separates these two names in time and Modernist periods should not lead us into error, because the Integralist Chief, as we have seen, assumed many of the postulates of the Dynamist thinker. Mário de Andrade, as we might expect, questioned the national validity of this hero in 1925: "With Graça trying to make of the Brazilian a happy guy through . . . philosophical theory and integration into the Infinite All, with a total incomprehension of Brazilian man whom he never really observed, and flying in the face of the natural psychology of that man, making of joy a preconception to the point of seeing joy in my Dances, which are in reality so sad and doleful, Good Lord! I don't have time to read such rot: any stupid regionalist book has more documentary accuracy." [120]

In this same letter, he discusses at length the legitimacy of attributing the Modernist "leadership" to Graça Aranha, and he furnishes us with a document of inestimable psychological value: "You simply can't imagine the effort I have to make when my ideas coincide with Graça's—as, for example, concerning the Brazilianization of Brazil—not to be insincere with myself merely to show that I disagree with him. Fortunately I'm luckier than my friends and I tighten up on my vanity and remain sincere. . . . I despise Graça. That's the influence he exercises over me. But I will never show this because, in spite of everything, what he is presently preaching is good: he is nearly always right and should be heard."

Thus "despising" Graça Aranha for the inescapable influence which he exercised over him and, mysteriously, over the entire Modernist group, in spite of all the conscious disagreements (and trying to disguise this hostility, in his behavior and actions), it is possible that it may have appeared subconsciously and that Macunaíma, the "hero with no character," may have been the antithetical and somewhat tardy reply to the "happy guy"—the sport, robust, full of "character." Macunaíma, before he took shape as the "hero of our people," probably first existed as Johnny Boob [João Bôbo], the character whom Mário de Andrade had created in 1924 in a novel "thoroughly outlined, much of it already written even, but which I shall destroy," as he communicated in a letter to Manuel Bandeira. There was, indeed, a whole series of "heroes" floating in Mário de Andrade's mind, which indicates that he was making some conscious effort in that direction. Around the middle of 1929, after having solemnized the "hero with no character"—confirming the interpretation that I shall propose below for that word—he was considering the composition of an "Elegia do Caráter":

So that you may know, it is because of Ribeiro Couto's failure to understand me (which wounded me deeply) and Oswald's "judgments" that I have "conceived" the third volume of the "Elegia do Caráter," the "Demoralized." The first is Macunaíma, the ideal. The second is João Bôbo, the abnormal. The third will be the Demoralized, the real. My

only vengeance will be precisely that: out of misunderstandings, injustices, and insults I will make a real being. I have
already created most of his movements although I have
written nothing nor shall I for a long time. This in itself
seems to me eminently dramatic.[121]

None of this kept the weak and sickly Luís Aranha (his friend
and probably the first, in chronological order, of the many fervent
disciples he succeeded in attracting) from writing "athletic" poetry
by way of compensation:

> I am young and strong, I adore strength and valor,
> I abhor fear,
> I love hostile pride and savage evil . . .[122]

Appeal of athletics and animal "joy," preached by Graça
Aranha, and sports—which at that time were becoming popular
in Brazil along with the Boy Scouts and enthusiasm for outdoor
life—were themes directly and consciously connected with a concern for hygiene, public and private, and problems of national
defense. It is clearly evident that all of that was merely the other
facet of the political question, which was so lively in the twenties
and thirties. Renato Kehl was a household name in the twenties,
principally because of his books on hygiene and physical culture.
However, the great work of the period was Belisário Penna's
Saneamento do Brasil (1918), concerning which the *Revista do
Brasil* was saying even as late as September, 1923: "When Belisário
Penna's book, *Saneamento do Brasil,* appeared in 1918, we had
the feeling that we stood in the presence of a key book. And so it
was. That book closed off the Brazilian phase of the systematic
lie with regard to our health and opened up the fruitful period
of campaign against endemic illness."

Once again Monteiro Lobato's indictment of the situation,
symbolized by the character of Jeca Tatu (who was interpreted
by contemporaries and future generations quite contrary to the
author's intent), was the precursor of a vast change in public
opinion. It is in that atmosphere that we can best understand the

evolution of the symbol of which Oswald de Andrade said in the *Revista do Brasil* of December, 1923: "The symbol has been avenged. The popular imagination saw in it a tenacious Brazil, amply gifted with physical and moral fortitude, fated but not a fatalist, having adopted, because of the circumstances of his origins and his exile, this kind of vocation for wretchedness which ethnologists and novelists have unconsciously observed."

Because he believed that Monteiro Lobato had painted a pessimistic and sardonic portrait of the Brazilian—when in reality it was a well-intentioned and patriotic protest—Ildefonso Albano, as we have seen, created the character of Mané Xiquexique, the indomitable backlander of the Northeast. Rui Barbosa, nonetheless, was not deceived and saw in Jeca Tatu the "synthesis of the conception" which "men who exploit it have of our nationality."

It is interesting to observe that the conception of the Modernist "hero" oscillated regularly between pessimism and optimism in a kind of mechanical rotation. Immediately following Jeca Tatu, the symbol of nationality was Juca Mulato:

> . . . agile as a colt and strong as a bull:
> in the virile poise of his mighty limbs
> is the boldness of columns and the elegance of stately barks.[123]

Following this line of reasoning came the "handsome virile youths, gallant and intelligent," whom Homero Prates saw in Brazil after the nationalist campaign of Olavo Bilac,[124] and the young champion whom Graça Aranha depicted in his famous lecture, "O Espírito Moderno." Macunaíma, of course, appeared sardonically as an anticlimax. But then came those impetuous oarsmen, Oswald de Andrade and Plínio Salgado, together once again. The ideal of the "heroic life" was immediately suggested by Plínio Salgado; and soon afterward in the thirties, following the publication of *A Bagaceira*, came the man with neither will nor vigor who presaged the "failure" and dominated the Brazilian novel for so many years (and, in part, dominated poetry, if we think particularly of the early Carlos Drummond de Andrade).

The cult of sports and heroism was, as we know, one of the fundamental postulates of Futurism: Marinetti called it the "school of heroism" and understood that "man" and "fighter" were synonymous, thus defending the practice of violent sports. Even here an opening was made that was favorable to the growth of totalitarian and warlike regimes. On the purely psychological level, these trends were reacting against Symbolism's "neurotic." One of Menotti del Picchia's characters says in *Dente de Ouro*: "And when I received a letter from my old friends, weakened in the capital by alcohol and cocaine, I was almost ashamed that I had ever been one of them, rachitic and vice-ridden, a pale specimen of the wretched fauna of urban carousals. And I was proud to be the virile, thrilling type that I was. And the certainty that I was robust and strong lifted my head on high in a provocative but tranquil attitude. And in my sturdy arteries my blood sang the peerless glory of being 'a man'!" We can also find a reflection of this new frame of mind in the novel by Eduardo Frieiro, *O Clube dos Grafômanos* (1927): "What characterizes modern-day youth is their utilitarian and relativist notion of existence. Young men of today throw themselves into the struggle for life with a joy and a confidence unknown to previous generations. . . . Ethical and esthetic concerns are rarely found among young men today. They are caught up in a frenzy of sports, their only enthusiasm and passion. Reared with a taste and love for physical exercise, they face life with the confident and smiling impetuosity of one accustomed to the disputations of the most salutary verbal tilts." It is not surprising, then—nor is it an isolated case—that in the first number of *Estética* Graça Aranha proposed the figure of a "modern youth, intrepid and pure," rather than that of a pale, anemic intellectual absorbed in endless readings in his freezing garret. It seemed to him that the young Brazilians of the twenties belonged "to a sporting generation from whose athletic ruggedness they have brought forth a spirit that soars and attacks." And in number 2 of the same review, Prudente de Morais Neto devoted a long commentary to Dominique Braga's book, *5000*, which opened with these words: "It might be said that we have been present at the birth of a sporting civilization. Sport increases in variety, popularity, and importance. It spreads and predominates. Today either one is a sportsman or he is nothing, because he belongs to yesterday."

When Carlos S. de Mendonça, the son of Lúcio Mendonça, published a book in 1921 with the title *O Esporte Está Deseducando a Mocidade Brasileira* (Rio de Janeiro: E. Brasil Editôra), reaction was unfavorable and nearly indignant. *Guia Brasileiro de Escotismo* (1919) by Hilário Freire and, in the following year, Fernando Azevedo's volume, *Da Educação Física,* were considerably more successful. Before he abandoned his literary life, the athletic and fearless "hero" was incarnate in "Giant," the symbol of all the mythology of the Tapir group and Greengiltism. The mythification of *Martim Cererê* was opposed to the "anti-myth" of *Macunaíma:*

> And the village founded
> behind the wall of the Range
> (beginning with only three)
> became a den of Giants.[125]

In the thirties there was a noticeable trend toward "unheroization" of the literary character; this permits us a retrospective glance at the history of the hero, divided into two opposing parts separated by *Macunaíma.* Between Macunaíma and the "failure" who, as Mário de Andrade observed, would be the hero par excellence of our novel in the thirties and forties, the transition might be represented by the "fainthearted" (still a projection of Macunaíma). Flávio de Carvalho did not hesitate to embody this character in his novel *Os Ossos do Mundo,* with regard to which Gilberto Freyre wrote in the preface: "His courage to be afraid— which nowadays only children have—his courage to analyze his deepest sensations of fear is a kind of bravery which the conventional adult, who has been distorted by the preconceptions of valor Spanish-style, he-man American style, or 'modernism' Brazilian-style or Graça-Aranha-style, no longer possesses. Everyone knows that Graça Aranha has made fear taboo. He wanted no one to fear anything. The perfectly modern man would be afraid of nothing. At least, he should not even mention fear."

That is the tenuous, unexpected, and somewhat embarrassing bridge that led us to Ribeiro Couto and Sérgio Buarque de
Holanda's "affable man," whom Cassiano Ricardo, the creator of
giants, softened even more when he suggested replacing him with
the "kindly man." The fact is that, when *Raízes do Brasil* launched
the theme of "affable man" in 1936, "social" (and, therefore,
pessimistic and depressing) literature had long since imposed a
figure who was entirely different, and scarcely Modernist, in the
character of the "failure." Mário de Andrade was stressing this
fact in the "Elegia de Abril" when he wrote:

I forgot the human suffering created, or at least extensively
developed, in Brazil's contemporary fiction; that new hero,
that protagonist who is symptomatic of many of our best
present-day novelists: the failure. For about the last ten
years—without the slightest ambition to form a school, create
a literary fashion, or imitate—numerous national writers
have begun to sing (that is exactly the term!) the character
type of the failure . . . In our fiction—be it novel or short
story—we are not producing in abundance a failure who is
the product of two conflictive forces but we are rather depicting a being devoid of vigor, an individual totally lacking
moral fiber, unfit for life, who can bring to bear against the
world around him no personal element, no trace of character,
no brawn and no ideal. Rather, he surrenders to his own
long-suffering hopelessness. When I first detected this phenomenon and used practically these very words, I thought I
had discovered in it traditional sources. Today I am convinced that I was wrong. The phenomenon has no sources
other than contemporary ones and prolongs no kind of tradition at all.
    Perhaps the Carlos of the "Sugar Cane Cycle" is the
first typical example of this national failure.[126] Recall, too,
the dreary anti-hero of *Angústia*. . . . I have already written
a column about this subject where I mentioned another
hero created by Cordeiro de Andrade, no less than six others
in a novel by Cecílio Carneiro, and besides these cultivated
failures, another one who was a backlander created by Leão
Machado, and a Northeasterner of the lower classes, the main
character in the *Mundo Perdido* by Fran Martins. Some-

what later I ran onto the type again in the *Fragmentos de um Caderno de Memórias* by the short story writer Francisco Inácio Peixoto from the state of Minas Gerais. Then came the planter created by Luís Martins, and within the last few months I have been able to add three more illustrious portraits to this pestilential gallery: one, depicted with magnificent exactitude by Osvaldo Alves in his brilliant first novel (1940), *Um Homem Fora do Mundo*; [127] and the two main "innocents" created by Gilberto Amado in a book which is uneven but considerably important. One is Emílio and the other is that strange creation, a character truly exciting in his mystery, Faial, the youth who is gifted with all powers and yet renounces life and runs away to create a world of his own making in an unearthly *sertão*.

It was, then, really an ethical type that Mário de Andrade was describing, as he immediately clarified; and to explain the appearance of that type, he felt constrained to find a cause. Mário de Andrade omitted Belmiro the clerk, created in 1936 by Cyro dos Anjos, who was the source of numerous progeny. Brazilian fiction in the thirties identified ethically much more with *Macunaíma* (through the transposition offered by *A Bagaceira*) than with any other character created in the first decade of Modernism. Even Oswald de Andrade, who undeniably exercised considerable direct stylistic and esthetic influence over the prose writers of Modernism during the three decades of its existence, never succeeded in establishing his *João Miramar*, either as a novelesque character or as a character type. In compensation, we have seen that the sentimental and decadent characters in *Os Condenados* reappeared, after a space of time, as the "failures" of the subsequent period. We should remember that in *O Estrangeiro*, if Juvêncio de Ulhoa—the novelist's alter ego—finally presents a lesson of optimism and confidence, Ivã, "the most important character in the book," "the synthesis of all the characters," in Plínio Salgado's own opinion, is the perfect type of the "failure," both sentimentally and ideologically. By the same token, the *O Esperado* might be viewed as the novel that represented the failure of an entire generation.

Therefore, the unexpected paradox of the Symbolist "neu-rotic" reappeared in Modernism, although the character was less identifiable with the refined vices of civilization, let it be said in passing, than with lack of moral fiber and will power. The Bra-zilian "failure" was a "primitive neurotic," if such an incongruity could be imagined. He was not the man with a nervous disorder; he was the man who had no nerves. Moreover, if Modernist na-tionalism ended by being unfortunately identified with a sym-bolic character, like Macunaíma, the character inevitably passed on to the domain of abstraction and myth. If real society had little taste for this mythological vision of man, or for the mythification of man as giant and inviolate fighter, literature inevitably became a process of demythification, which was in large part also a process of demystification.

In the trajectory of the literary hero's evolution, it can easily be seen that Modernism progressively withdrew from Symbolism (in spite of the persistent vestiges of Symbolism in Oswald de Andrade's first novel) and Futurism. In the last analysis, the Brazilian intellectual did not welcome that rugged "sporting civilization" preached by Marinetti and Graça Aranha. It might be said that the profound inclination of the Brazilian intellec-tual's temperament led him more naturally to reverie and inactiv-ity, to a life that was both verbal and verbose, rather than to a life of activity and accomplishment. For that reason the modern Brazilian novel suffers from a chronic lack of action, which is, of course, extremely revealing.

Theory and Practice

These are the complex perspectives within which Brazilian Modernism developed as literary school and spiritual ambience. Next we shall observe how these matters were translated into the more critical domain of artistic creation. Each basic author imprinted his hallmark on the theoretical face of the Movement; each representative work was, dialectically, its own extension and also its own negation, however subtle. The fact that it broadened horizons beyond principles and postulates explains the enormous vitality of the school which, if it generally denied itself in its self-affirmations, nonetheless invariably affirmed itself in its self-negations. Aníbal Machado (1894–1964) said that the Modernists did not know what they wanted but that they had a very clear idea of what they did not want. Really, from 1916 to 1945, the several Modernist groups were identified by opposition and irony, by renovative instinct and independence of character (which, of course, does not exclude pastiche and servile imitation from the works of the Movement's descendents).

The following two parts of this volume develop Aníbal Machado's aphorism: the representative works tell what the Modernists wanted; the basic authors tell what they did not want. The credit balance goes to the latter, just as the debit goes to the former. Thereby, Modernism once again affirmed is dialectical nature (which also implies its critical nature), its intellectual perspicuity, and the transcendence of its own boundaries.

Part Two
Representative Works

All the representative works of Modernism were published in the first decade of the Movement and, in the strictest sense, were considerably less numerous than we might at first think. By representative works, it should be understood here that we mean those works which, in their conception and treatment, reflected the esthetic principles, postulates, and values of Modernism; those which were written with a predominantly vanguardist sensibility; those which preferred to be novel rather than great; those which were the product of a revolutionary rather than a creative frame of mind; those which marked the extreme limits of the school, not only its possibilities but also its realities; those which neither could be nor wished to be anything but Modernist, a word which in this instance should be stressed at the suffix; those which appear not only with the features and gestures of Modernism but also with its tics and grimaces; those which in one way or another accorded with the multiple esthetic semantics that Mário de Andrade seemed to sum up in the adjective *harlequinate*. Also we should include among the representative works those books that marked the end of the period properly called revolutionary and opened up new directions, until then hidden from both the literary man and the layman. For that reason it seems to me that the last representative work, in chronological order, would be *Casa Grande & Senzala*, the work of a man who throughout his life has disregarded Modernism, but who must nevertheless be included among the Movement's fundamental authors. Still it is possible that this landmark in Brazilian intellectual history might have been written without the advent of Modernism, but it would not have been read as it was had Modernism not occurred. Gilberto Freyre wrote that volume out of his own spiritual biography. However unconsciously, it was the "boys from São Paulo" who guaranteed the success of Gilberto Freyre's book, because with their own spiritual biography they empathized with it.

Representative works were not written after 1933—if we take as our point of reference the year in which *Casa Grande & Senzala* appeared. The novel of the thirties was Modernist beyond all doubt; but it was no longer revolutionary nor did it place great emphasis on esthetic novelty. There is, in fact, a considerable decline in artistic sensitivity during this entire period. After 1930 we find that Modernism has been consolidated; that is, it loses its renovating impetus and merely attempts to fulfill what already existed implicitly in its programs. In the same way one can say that, on the whole, genius, with all its lack of order, has been replaced by talent with all its efforts. Without any clear notion of what was taking place, one witnessed the "classicalization" of Modernism. All this means that Modernism was of necessity entering the era of its academism; the works created were no longer "representative" but rather "definitive," if we take that term with a large grain of salt. If it happens that in the thirties there were novels written that could not have been written in the previous ten years, an identical evolution might be observed in poetry, even if we leave aside all the external factors which imposed such a transformation. Not one of the great writers of the thirties and forties would have been what he was without the presence of Modernism. In reality many of them—Carlos Drummond de Andrade, José Lins do Rêgo, Jorge Amado, Graciliano Ramos, and Érico Veríssimo—may be numbered among the *fundamental authors* of the Movement, regardless of their individual attitudes toward Modernism. Here one can see quite clearly a fact which literary histories generally ignore: the representative work and the fundamental author are frequently on quite different levels. This is not always true, of course. Mário de Andrade, who contributes three representative works to the history of Modernism, is also one of its fundamental authors. The same is true of Oswald de Andrade and *Pau Brasil* and, for other reasons, with Gilberto Freyre and *Casa Grande & Senzala*. However, Plínio Salgado is a fundamental author without ever having written a representative work. It is surprising to note that this phenomenon also occurs with regard to Manuel Bandeira, Jorge de Lima, Oliveira Viana, and Antônio de Alcântara Machado. As a matter of fact, close analysis reveals that Jorge de Lima and Manuel Bandeira occupy important positions on pathways opened by others. They are not innovators but continuators, although on the level of quality and esthetic universalism the poetry of Manuel Bandeira, for example, may clearly be superior to that of Oswald de Andrade. But here it is not a question of the abstract level of literary creation but rather of its inclusion in a specific literary movement, within the picture of principles, values, concepts, and ideas which the *representative works* attempt to define, that is, to which they attempt to give reality in the form of a written text. In the "reactionary" phase which follows all revolutions, even literary ones, it is less a question of obeying the rules of the school than of surpassing them, of passing them by on the right, through obedience to a super-scholastic, esthetic ideal. In the revolutionary phase, on the contrary, the necessary rule is that of passing by on the left all existing literature, even that which is revolutionary.

I purposely have left for special mention the name of the writer who eliminates all doubts: Graça Aranha. Without ever having written a single representative work, not even including his discourses on Modernist academism or on academic Modernism, he is beyond a doubt a fundamental author in the history of the Movement: all of Mário de Andrade's denials of Graça Aranha's leadership cannot refute the more important fact of his *presence*. One cannot speak of Modernism and ignore Graça Aranha. The surprise is the greater, therefore, when we note that there is nothing Modernist anywhere in his work.

1922: Paulicéia Desvairada

In the letter to Alberto de Oliveira mentioned earlier—either for reasons of battle strategy or because of confused memory—Mário de Andrade stated that he had written the first version of *Paulicéia Desvairada* in December of 1919. The fact is of importance only for purposes of scholarship. The same is true of the fact that Oswald de Andrade's papers constantly prove that he had written the *Memórias Sentimentais de João Miramar* in 1916,[1] a notation which, we should say in passing, confirms the importance of that date in the history of Modernism. On the level of literary action, which is where the fate of literature is decided and, more often than not, the fate of innovative schools, what really counts is the date of publication.

Be that as it may, there is testimony from Mário de Andrade himself to confirm that the first Modernist book to be published was written in December of 1920[2] and not in December of 1919. "I had spent the year of 1920," he said in his famous lecture on the Modernist Movement, "without writing any more poetry. I had notebook after notebook filled with Parnassian stuff and some timidly Symbolist things, but the end result was always that it disgusted me. In my disoriented readings I had already made the acquaintance of the latest Futurists, but only of late had I

discovered Verhaeren. And I was dazzled. Mainly carried away
by the *Villes Tentaculaires,* I immediately took to heart the composition of a book of 'modern' poems, in free verse, about my
city. . . ." Thus "the first book of the Movement would sing
the praises of the native city." It is from the moment of its publication that we should date the rupture and challenge that ensued rather than employ the Week of Modern Art as our point
of departure. The vision of a Mário de Andrade, the born revolutionary, ferociously attacked by the Establishment from his very
beginnings belongs exclusively to the mythology of Modernism.
When in June of 1921 the *Revista do Brasil* published the first
article of the then unknown writer ("Debussy and Impressionism"), it thus justified the initiation of his columns: "The author
of these articles is one of those youths who are filled with rare
vigor and gallant independence and are revolutionizing ideas in
the field of literature and art in São Paulo. This study of his
should be read with pleasure and profit by all those who are less
than indifferent to questions dealing with the evolution of the
arts in these modern times." All of this points up once again
the fact that, without the incitement of the Week of Modern Art,
Modernism would have been evolutionist and not revolutionary;
however, it was precisely the nature of modern art to be exter-
nally revolutionary although it was intrinsically "evolutionist."
The first theoreticians of the Movement went to great pains to
make this point clear. At this stage of his career, Mário de
Andrade was a man who was respectable and respected by all
who knew him. Oswald de Andrade sought to give respectability
to Mário's Futurism when he wrote in his famous article of 1921:
"This tall, pale, and erudite Parsifal is well known for his critical
acumen. You will find him in the well-stocked stable of the
Revista do Brasil, he writes for the *Jornal de Debates,* he holds
an important post with *Papel e Tinta,* he lectures with the rare
honesty of his scholarship in our Conservatory." All of that was
thrown to the winds after the publication of *Paulicéia Desvairada.*
The *Revista do Brasil* itself thus received the book in 1922:
"Nonsense verse is not a new thing. The traditions of the Academy of São Paulo, related by Almeida Nogueira in a delightful
book which is our best history of customs, records a few which

are still repeated in our own day. They retain the same delicious flavor of the grotesque, the flavor that made them famous." A long disquisition on the nature of nonsense verse ended with the following words: "Thus we give to Senhor Mário de Andrade's book the label that it deserves, and deserves abundantly, in the field of poetry. If nonsense is rather the property of the orator, it does not totally exclude the poet, as this book proves. There is in the arts a universality through which the processes of one art may be transposed with ease to the other arts. This is the case at present. Senhor Andrade should not lose heart, then. His school belongs to . . . the future."

The difference in tone between the first critic and the second is shocking. Of more significance, however, is the fact that the *Revista do Brasil* unconsciously *refused* to criticize the book. In the November number of *Klaxon*, Carlos Alberto de Araújo (Tácito de Almeida) threw himself courageously and lucidly into that task. After observing that Brazilian criticism "abided within inviolate walls and sorely lacked the courage to admit or study a writer without drawing parallels"—and, he added, there can be no "criterium more pitiful"—he goes on to analyze the volume, pointing out its essential characteristics: the "strange, shocking, unexpected" temperament of the poet; his connection with the city, "the city-street, the public-city," the nature of this "book of crisis, of exaltation," its combative impulsiveness. He concluded with these words of rare critical acumen:

But it is not these defects of the book, *nor even the book itself,* which reveal to us the value of the artist. We discover that value veiled behind certain marvelous expressions, certain inflamed images, certain lines, certain words, a certain lightning-simultaneism. Mário de Andrade is an artist destined to open paths with the crimson of his artistry for the literature that Brazil is yet to have: civilized, serious, obedient to the present and to the needs of humanity. His influence is now making itself felt, although it is still underground, in this literary movement of São Paulo. Today no one any longer dares to exploit the passivity of our reading public with the sluggishness of Parnassianism. No matter how assiduously we seek, we find no perfect sonnet in our present-day literary magazines. The school which has for so long tormented São Paulo is now going through the painful crisis of silence. Its leaders are now suffering through that moving tragedy of losing faith even in themselves.

This is the outward value of Mário de Andrade. His personal inward value is found in his verses. They are ardent, vibrant, brimming with life, armed with penetrating irony, suggestive, modern. A powerful electric current shoots them through. One bristles on first contact with them, but one is captivated. He captivates so thoroughly that one ends up by losing his initial shock and discovering a joy, a voluptuous joy.

Once again, what a difference in tone! The *Revista do Brasil,* however, did not regain its equilibrium—except indirectly—until April of 1923 when Paulo Prado assumed its editorship and designated Mário de Andrade as art critic. It printed at that time a glowing article by Renato Almeida, published in Rio in *O País,* entitled "A Reação Moderna." In that article one reads such statements as these:

First of all I must say that in the author of the *Paulicéia Desvairada* what most interests me is his intelligence. That intelligence it was that awakened in him the craving for a new and personal mode of expression and caused him to abandon *metrical verses:* well-made, well-rounded, and well-polished, as so many others publish and he himself once composed. . . . His poetry represents a new esthetics which he went in search of and found. Therefore, Senhor Mário de Andrade represents among us the torture of a man who refused to sit down to a banquet where many others had already dined, and he has plucked a new fruit from a strange tree, a fruit bitter and different . . . The critical aspect of his intelligence is perhaps the most impressive. *Paulicéia Desvairada* is a violent and daring satire against fruitless and prosaic conventionalism, the affectations and preciosities which throng our letters and our customs . . . His satire is not the offspring of a refined and played-out sentimentalism. Rather is it crudely wrought out of a spirit that feels the obligatory duty to destroy what is useless in order to broaden horizons, to construct, to create. If at times he points only to the ridiculous aspect of things and laughs at them indifferently, as in the "Ode ao Burguês" or in the "Rebanho," in general his violence and his hatred are those of an intrepid knight, radiant in his faith, lavish with his might. "As Enfibraturas do Ipiranga," if it at once represents a great revolt, a grandiose violence, also contains gentle poetry, tenderness and hope, the tranquility of a faith which rises up against the confusion of the mediocre and the retrograde, but finally weeps in "repentence for the poet's delirium."

So great was the effect of the publication of *Paulicéia Desvairada,* and not of the Week of Modern Art, that it aroused the ire of the traditionalists who at that very moment in the *Fôlha da Noite* of São Paulo were being united under Aristeo Seixas. Seixas convoked a group of "knowledgeable and talented" youths to combat the Modernists in general and Mário de Andrade in particular. It was specifically in answer to that campaign that Mário wrote his column in the *Revista do Brasil* in April of 1923. Seixas, in a rancorous rejoinder, called the Week a "carnivalesque week" (an expression destined for brilliant and lasting success), and continued his vilification: "Bad enough that he should be a nighthawk-winged hack, a brat with his diaper still dripping excremental fluid, but he also comes out in his newspaper column, rather in his pseudo-literary criticism, to defecate undigested material, or material digested by others, to reproach the most respected figures of our national literature." Naturally, owing to such language, the traditionalists never really succeeded in gaining the respect of the reading public. This exchange did, however, set the tone of the polemic; and in the *A Tribuna* of Santos, Ângelo Guido, who had already seen his "essay on the *Estética da Vida* of Graça Aranha" [3] favorably reviewed in *Klaxon* (numbers 8–9, December 1922–January 1923), wrote: "We truly need a new art through which to express ourselves, not the sensations caused in us by the vendors of roasted yams in the Brás district, the namby-pamby girls and flitty boys on Avenida Rio Branco, the irritating horns of the automobiles, the guffaws of the clowns, the infernal din of the factories or the filth of cheap dives and brothels, but an art which better and more profoundly translates the unknown side of the human soul. . . ."

None of this today has the slightest importance except that it is picturesque. What is important is that Mário de Andrade was worth more than the *Paulicéia,* as in general he is worth more than any of his books considered one by one. However, without ignoring the historical significance of that slender volume, he also gave it a personal value. In a letter dated August 16, 1931, to Manuel Bandeira,[4] he commented:

> You say that my book of greatest magnitude and reputation was the *Paulicéia,* written in two weeks in an unleashing of rage and bitterness. I accept this in so far as it was my book of greatest reputation (noise made) and of greatest magnitude, with regard to a new esthetics in poetry. But I cannot accept your explication of the *Paulicéia*—with regard to its esthetics, its function, or at least its ideals—as the fruit of a simple unleashing. That unleashing was merely the bang of the hammer on the rifle . . . You forget the fact that I had been writing love poetry since I was twenty-one and had only found the courage to publish something in 1917, and that something was no longer individualistic: it was rather a state of the social being. You forget that I spent a year without writing a line before I undertook the *Paulicéia,* having written in June or July in the middle of that year a poem in semi-free verse, whose subject was São Paulo, and that I had Verhaeren as my bedside reading material at that time.

Many years before, in 1924, still in the heat of battle that had formed around the book, he revealed with an extraordinary sense of self-criticism that it was necessary to complete the *challenge* and the experimentalism of the *Paulicéia Desvairada* with a love poem on the "Paulicéia Reconquistada" (as he was to write in another letter of that same year):

> There are exaggerations in my work. That is a truth all my own. If I haven't told you up to this point, I tell you now

why I preserved them. It deals with a very special period in my life. *Paulicéia* is the crystallization of twenty months of doubt, suffering, anger. It's a bomb. It exploded. It had to explode or I would have wasted away like some dirty rotten Everyman, like X, like Y, like . . . (put here all the names of those wretches who are poets, no denying that, but don't know *how* to be poets). Fine: all bombs explode with noise and excesses of liberty. What I did wrong, if I did anything wrong, was not to correct in my book what it held of excessive noise and excessive liberty of construction.

In the nature of their particular atmosphere, the poems of the *Paulicéia* are "written to be bellowed, sung," Manuel Bandeira remarked in echo of what the author himself had already pointed out in the "Extremely Interesting Preface." There he wrote: "Besides, verses are not written to be read by mute eyes. Verses are meant to be sung, bellowed, wept. If you cannot sing, do not read 'Landscape 1.' If you cannot bellow, do not read 'Ode to the Bourgeois Gentleman.' If you cannot pray, do not read 'Religion.' Scorn: 'The Escalade.' Suffer: 'Colloque Sentimental.' Forgive: the lullaby, one of the solos of My Madness from 'The Moral Fibrature.' I will not go on. It disgusts me to hand over the key to my book." In *A Escrava Que Não É Isaura*, he condemned the oral quality of the book: "It is one of the greatest defects of the *Paulicéia Desvairada*. There is musical musicality and verbal musicality. I accomplished, or tried to accomplish, the first of these to the detriment of the clarity of the discourse."

As a document of literary history rather than as a book of poetry, *Paulicéia Desvairada* suffered the fate of setting not only the direction of Modernism, in its first phase, but also the direction of Mário de Andrade's literary career: experimentalism and individualism, which he in fact shared with all his contemporaries. That was to place him in a "stifling paradox," as he commented in 1942 in his famous lecture on the Movement: ". . . having deformed all my work by a willful and purposeful anti-individualism, the totality of my work is nothing more than a relentless hyper-individualism." At the same time a contradictory process took root in his spirit: the fact is that by following this direction he could never succeed in writing a great work, a great work which would justify him in his own eyes and compensate him for the inevitable desertion of his companions of 1922. "When it was for the purpose of destruction," he wrote in 1925 to Manuel Bandeira, "a time when *blague* and *esprit* meant more than knowledge, we all acted as one. But that time didn't last long. I, who made the greatest sacrifice, swore to myself that I had to prove that I was not the witless ham that they imagined and that our truth was just and propitious. My life and my labors have never amounted to more than this. . . ."

As a matter of fact, in that year of 1925, when he finally published a text that he had written in 1922—i.e., contemporary with the *Paulicéia*—he attempted to initiate the constructive phase of the revolutionary Movement; he tried to found, as the subtitle indicates, a Modernist esthetics. However, the evil fates watched over him, and it is precisely at that moment that the bogus dialogue between the "two Andrades" occurred, and all the critics, following in the wake of Tristão de Athayde, set about stifling the life of the Movement and thereby committed some of their greatest errors in appraising Mário's works. In truth, at the same time the *Escrava* proposed the inclusion of Modernist poetry in the universal current, *Pau Brasil*, created on the Place Clichy in Paris, threw Mário de Andrade off course in nationalist waters.

1925: A Escrava Que Não É Isaura
Pau Brasil

In a letter of May 19, 1928, to Alceu Amoroso Lima,[5] Mário de Andrade came to grips with the problem:

. . . as far as Oswald's manifestoes are concerned, I have a very personal bone to pick with them. They always come out at a time when *malgré moi* I get included in them. The first occasion came when Oswald was traveling in Europe and I had decided to *force the issue* of my Brazilianism, not only to get a closer attack on the problem but also to call attention to it (you will recall that in the *Paulicéia* I had stated that I spoke *Brazilian,* but no one paid any attention to that fact) and Oswald wrote me from Europe "come on over and find out what art is all about, over here is where it is really happening," etc. I, owing to my steadfast resolution, answered from here: "I am only interested in Brazil at the moment. I've explored virgin territory," etc. Oswald comes back from Europe, gets himself brazilwooded, and I'm just then bringing out my *Losango Cáqui,* because I was low on cash and I turned brazilwood like the very devil. . . .

With *Macunaíma,* as he had foreseen, the same thing happened; and since it was published immediately after the Cannibal Manifesto, it would be considered Mário's first act of vassalage to the new trend.

Oswald de Andrade was always behind by one book and ahead by one manifesto: that is how he gained a reputation as one of the leaders of the Movement, if not its undisputed leader. We have already seen, in the first part of this study, the postulates and the significance of Mário de Andrade's *A Escrava Que Não É Isaura.* We might say that, with this essay, Mário attempted to create in the "Brazilian" language for the specific purposes of Modernism the equivalent of Jean Epstein's *La Poésie d'Aujourd'hui* or, rather, a descriptive esthetic theory which departed in the Aristotelian fashion from existing works to propose platonically the model for works yet to be written. Oswald de Andrade, because of his literary temperament, his love for novelty, his lack of profound creative power, his instinct for the current fashion, his acuity in reading the compass, may be viewed as the Cocteau of Brazilian Modernism. The intellectual history of both men may be symbolized by the apologue from *Le Potomak* (1913): "Once upon a time there was a chameleon. In order to keep him warm, his master placed him on a gaudy Scotch plaid traveling-blanket. The chameleon died of fatigue."

One might apply to both men the aphorism from the same book: "Take care! He's not a revolutionary. He's a conserver of old anarchies." This fact was not properly understood in those early years either with regard to Cocteau or to Oswald de Andrade. At this very moment there is in process a reevaluation of Oswald de Andrade which grounds itself in that old error in perspective. Be that as it may, the simultaneous publication of Oswald's *Pau Brasil* and Mário's *A Escrava Que Não É Isaura* does not represent a moment of creative euphoria; rather it represents a moment of unperceived crisis, the crisis which revealed the "internal contradictions" of Modernism. For the individual, the gravest contradiction was to feel himself attracted by the universal or the theoretical, or in other words by literary erudition, while his profound nature called him to primitivism and the repudiation of "art." The Brazilwood Manifesto clearly distinguishes between the "philosophers making philosophy, the critics, criticism, housewives busy in their kitchens" and those poets making Poetry with the "joy of those who know and discover." With a certain exaggeration (but not much), one might conclude that Oswald de Andrade organized ignorance into a system: it was the repudiation of "literature," the period of the splendor of esthetic populism, which was clearly going to characterize the subsequent history of Modernism, particularly in the novels of the thirties, because at that time it was the novel that struck the literary keynote.

Significantly, while Mário de Andrade was returning to Rimbaud, Oswald proposed a division of the history of poetry into two phases—just as Victor Hugo, with the same secret intentions, divided the history of humanity into three: "Now, the revolution has made clear that art was returning to the elite. And the elite began by undoing. Two phases: first, deformation through impressionism, fragmentation, voluntary chaos. From Cézanne and Mallarmé, Rodin and Debussy down to the present; second, lyricism, presentation in the temple, materials, constructive innocence." Brazilwood would not have succeeded without the express repudiation of what had been done in 1922. One of the postulates of the Brazilwood Manifesto was cited earlier as an indication of the passage from Futurism to Modernism. However, another possible interpretation, no less pregnant with meaning, is one that sees in the expression *Futurist generation*—the name by which Oswald de Andrade designated the first Modernists—those who had taken part in the Week of Modern Art. Thus, the declaration of the Manifesto acquires a new meaning: "The labor of the Futurist generation was cyclopean. To set the Empire clock of our national literature. Once that stage has been passed, the problem changes. To be regional and pure in one's own time." One can see that, as in every genuine artist's manifesto, the meaning is derived not so much from the text as it is from the ornamental form of the text. One cannot simply read between the lines. The Brazilwood Manifesto is a polemic, indeed, but one directed less against the traditionalists than against Mário de Andrade. It is an event in the struggle for power, but it is also the charter that separated two irreconcilable personalities.

From the manifesto to the work of art proper or, in this case, the poem, the distance is less than we might suspect. *Losango Cáqui,* written before *Pau Brasil,* was published a year after it. However, as Mário de Andrade himself observed, the similarities between the two books are so great that they ended up by belonging to the same literary current. Thus, there is surprisingly more heterogeneity between *Losango Cáqui* and *A Escrava* than between *Pau Brasil* and *Losango Cáqui.* The reason is that since it was written in 1922 the volume of Modernist esthetics was already anachronistic in 1925; it no longer corresponded to the general state of mind. Literary justice would require that Mário and not Oswald should have been the author of the Brazilwood Manifesto, or something of its kind. The two Andrades must forever bear the burden of this *quid pro quo.*

Much more than the *Escrava,* it is *Pau Brasil* that set the tone and the manner of Modernist poetry until the middle of the following decade: Oswald de Andrade's poetry will always be anecdotal, wisecracking, seeking after simplicity, the picturesque, and the humorous. By its "angel child" or "brat" aspects, *Pau Brasil* awakened less antagonism than had the *Paulicéia* three years before. Still it is necessary to point out that the *Paulicéia,* and not *Pau Brasil,* was the book that was *truly new.* In 1922 everyone was more or less revolutionary. Oswald de Andrade perceived, however unconsciously, that it was less risky, and perhaps more expedient, to be what he himself would dub "the clown of the bourgeoisie."

Thus, for example, instead of violently combating the vices of the national temperament, he would say in the words of Gandavo's text:

> A certain animal can also be found in these parts
> Which they call Sloth
> It has a great lock of hair at the nape
> And moves with such slow pace
> That though it walk two weeks on end
> The merest stone's throw is all the distance trod [6]

While Mário de Andrade attacked the problem of language aggressively, Brazilwood stated the difficulty in terms of the wisecrack:

> May I have a cigarette please
> Says the proper language
> Of professor and student
> And the high-yaller putting on airs
>
> But the good black and the good whitey
> Of the Brazilian Nation
> Every day will say:
> Gotta smoke? [7]

These same wisecracking tendencies led him to recast the "Canção do Exílio," that enduring theme in Brazilian poetry:

> My land has palm groves
> Where warbles the sea
> Here the little birds
> Sing not so sweetly as there
>
> .   .   .   .   .
>
> God forbid that I should die
> And see São Paulo no more
> Nor Fifteenth of November Street
> Nor the progress of São Paulo [8]

A complete failure, as one can readily see. Later, in the *Primeiro Caderno*, he was somewhat more felicitous with the "Meus Oito Anos."

At any rate, 1925 is one of the crucial years of Modernism, not only because it produced two representative works, but because of what they represent. With 1925 came the end of the era of the barricades; from then on, Brazilian Modernism was to be a modernism of consolidation.

1928: Retrato do Brasil
Macunaíma
Martim Cererê

It is strange to note that the Movement has a ternary rhythm in its metamorphoses: three years separate the *Paulicéia Desvairada* from *Pau Brasil*; another three passed before the publication of *Macunaíma, Martim Cererê*, and the *Retrato do Brasil*; three more before the publication of *Cobra Norato*, and nearly three more before *Casa Grande & Senzala* came out. At the conclusion of each three-year period, the school subtly changed its spots without denying their origins but also without wholeheartedly accepting them, rather looking to the future than prolonging the past. It might happen—and did in the case of *Macunaíma* and *Martim Cererê*—that the representative work closed a cycle instead of heralding a new one. In that event it was not surprising to find that almost immediately a fundamental author would appear with a book of less moment and open new horizons. So it was that in the year of the publication of *Macunaíma, A Bagaceira* appeared; in poetry, the book which paralleled *Martim Cererê* did not appear until two years later. It was *Alguma Poesia* by Carlos Drummond de Andrade. However, it was the *Retrato* do *Brasil* that truly opened the royal road of "Brazilian studies," of which *Casa Grande & Senzala* was the decisive landmark. The *Retrato* created in the loftiest style a mode for the essay that was properly Modernist, or, perhaps more apt, properly modern.

No one ever defined the exact nature, the limitations and, at the same time, the great qualities and the unmistakable character of the *Retrato do Brasil* better than Paulo Prado himself: [9]

It was to flee from the influence of São Paulo's bovarysm, which is perhaps one of youth's pardonable sins, that the man who wrote these lines adopted the Goethean process for the creation of works of art, as if he were truly an artist: he withdrew. The provinces, lacking other attractions, can provide the man who lives and works there in the tranquility of involuntary solitude, the inestimable gifts of liberty and peace. Only there is it possible to picture the long study that Renan dreamed of, book-lined inside, and outside covered with roses and climbing vines, sequestered in the peace of a quiet neighborhood. . . .[10]

This was a book born of isolation, redolent of the province more than anything else: the book of an artist. The *Retrato do Brasil* is an essay, as that genre is best defined: these are the reflections—at once bitter, pessimistic, and moralizing—of a *grand seigneur,* of one of those "amateurs" in which Lanson saw an entire spiritual family in French literature. It would be a mistake to consider this a history book; it would be pure intellectual narrowness to fail to admire it as an extraordinary interpretive work. Bearing the stamp of a single man and only of that man, the *Retrato do Brasil* of necessity acquired its character as a unique work: unique in the bibliography of Paulo Prado *(Paulistica* is always instinctively viewed as a kind of intruder in the Pradian bookshelf) and unique also in Brazilian bibliography. It is impossible to formulate an exact idea of Brazil seeing it only as Paulo Prado conceived it, "as a work of art." However, it would be equally impossible to know the country without having read and reread the impressionist-pointillist portrait of this hybrid of Renoir and Sisley in Brazilian historiography.

This is an artist's book not only because it was written in solitude, that privileged hothouse of all the great works of art, not only because its style is spontaneous and eloquent (which is the usual style of true greatness), but because Paulo Prado saw Brazil and her history above all else as an intellectual creation, if not as an artistic creation. The characteristics which he attributes to the Brazilian people—melancholy, lasciviousness, greed —are, in one form or another, the psychological oddities of all artists of genius, which they pass on to a greater or lesser extent to their works of art. Paulo Prado conceived of Brazil as a passionate being, a classical being uprooted and anachronistic, that stifled within itself every passionate impulse. However, like every true classicist, this being surrendered itself joyfully to the brooding pleasures of auto-analysis, and of curiosity regarding mankind. The Brazil of Paulo Prado is less a country, a geographical and historical reality, than a human figure. Brazil, for him, is the Brazilian people, that sad people inhabiting a radiant land. What attracts him in Brazil is the population and its emotional growth, the action of man in moments of crisis, his typical behavior. For that very reason, in this regard he distinguished himself from those somber historians of archives and documents. He did not pretend to exhume lost documents nor meddle around in the dust of past centuries; he wrote a history as he saw it from a quiet, clean study, "book-lined inside, and outside covered with roses and climbing vines." His mission was to breathe new life into the body of that imaginary man, Brazil.

He himself defined the *Retrato do Brasil* as an impressionistic painting:

> The clear outlines of the design dissolved into the colors and the vagueness of the tints and, as one says in artist's jargon, into the "masses and volumes," which are—in the writing of history—the chronology and facts. Dates disappear almost entirely. Only aspects, emotions, and the mental representation of events remain, these the result more of speculative deduction than of the sequential concatenation of facts. In this way one seeks, in a never-ending exertion, to arrive at the essence of things, in which the solidity of particular cases is

not lost under the force of general ideas. I wish to consider history, not as a romantic resurrection, nor as a conjectural science in the German fashion, but as a composite of simple impressions, seeking in the mysterious heart of conscious or instinctive forces the influences which dominated, with the passage of time, individuals and collective man. In that way the painting—to uphold the image I have suggested—insists on certain smudges, more luminous or extensive, to create the better likeness.[11]

Moralists and lovers of art (Paulo Prado belongs to both of these spiritual families) know that a good portrait is the one that impresses us by its likeness to a model whose original we do not know personally. The *Retrato do Brasil* is, in the main, an artistic creation of that type, more like the country that inspired it than a mere photographic image would be. Others later wrote "X rays" or chromophotographs of Brazil because, whether it be a question of simplistic pride or reasonable optimism or disconsolate pessimism, Brazil is the great theme of our essays, whether of good or bad quality. This book of 1928, however, which is amazingly memorable, will remain not only as the source and inspiration of all other such books, but I am sure it will also remain the incomparable model which no other will ever equal.

The fact that Paulo Prado should find in "somber German erudition" and in the name of Martius the authority to despise bureaucratic documents and minute facts, "the scrupulous accumulation of quotations and legal documents which prove nothing," only points up the fact that historiographic and essayistic impressionism, if it is of a certainty less descriptive and precise, is beyond a doubt more faithful to the patterns of a fugitive and unstable reality, is sharper and more nearly complete as it captures the imponderables that make up the true character of men and nations. The truth is that a well-rounded social history of modern Brazil results from the work of Paulo Prado, even in so far as certain precise and objective ideas are concerned. Thus, for example, when Gilberto Freyre reveals that he got the real orientation for all his work when he perceived that it was not

miscegenation but rather slavery that held the key to an interpretation of the racial and social development of Brazil, he was
coinciding with these lines from the *Retrato do Brasil*: "The
Negro, in addition to being an ethnic element, represented in
our national formation another factor of considerable influence:
he was a slave. One of the horrors of slavery is that the slave, in
addition to losing dominion over his body, also loses dominion
over his soul. That weakness became a catalytic function in the
social organism: it reduced the illusory superiority of the white
slaveholder to the very moral and spiritual degradation of the
Negro." [12] Young pedants, well-versed in Marx or in his popular-
izers, later proposed the term "dialectics of slavery," suggesting
it as a proper description of the new and revolutionary methodol-
ogy for the study of the phenomenon. Paulo Prado, a typical
product of capitalist society and the capitalist class, as was also
Karl Marx, had long since written without the slightest am-
biguity: "In the promiscuity of this racial intimacy it could be
plainly seen that slavery always meant immorality, laziness, disdain of human dignity, ignorance, vice protected by law, laxity
in social customs, waste, heedlessness, subservience to the whip,
flattery of the powerful—all the faults that constituted what one
journalist called the philosophy of the slave-hut, to greater or
lesser extent latent in the unspeakable profundity of our national
character." [13]

The *Retrato do Brasil* is an attempted solution or one of
the possible answers to the enigma suggested by the term "national character." Paulo Prado was not ignorant of the fact that

in the psychological order, the problem is equally complex.
We draw attention in these pages to the importance of the
age-old impression left on the national psyche by the outrages
of lasciviousness and greed and later left on formally constituted society by the derangement of the illness of romanticism. These influences saw their development in the immod-
eration of the most disorderly and anarchic individualism
witnessed since the time of the isolated and free life of the
colonist, who also brought here the egotistical whining of
lovelorn poets. We lacked as reagents in our crisis of assimi-

lation the religious element, the Puritan endurance of New England, the social hierarchy of the old American pioneers, the instinct for collective collaboration. . . . The indolence and passivity of the population, however, facilitated the preservation of social and political unity in this vast territory. Portugal had the merest idea of the topography of her American domains and immediately drew up their limits as the Amazon and the Plate: natural, organic borders within which developed the vital attitude of the colony, thus ripping away the political barriers which the Treaty of Tordesilhas and those which followed attempted to regulate.[14]

The deficiencies of the "national character" are merely the reverse of its good qualities: those who sketched the word portraits of the Puritan pioneer world might well lament the absence of certain individualistic and anarchic "defects," of a certain element of passion that pervades the history of Brazil as it labels Paulo Prado's book like a watermark.

It is obvious that in the *Retrato do Brasil,* or in any portrait of Brazil, Romanticism is a factor, although this is not to say that Romanticism is a contributing factor in Brazilian psychology. This would of necessity result in a literature and in a temperament with strong romantic characteristics. Like every authentic gentleman, Paulo Prado's capacity for artistic appreciation was open and frequently scandalous for his time, his environment, his class: Mário de Andrade designated him as "the truest impetus of the Week of Modern Art," without otherwise ignoring, with his flawless acumen, that "the Modernist Movement was clearly aristocratic." Nonetheless, artistic and intellectual aristocracy rarely shows true empathy for the most characteristic and innovative aspects of the literary phenomenon it studies. Be that as it may, it is certain that an aristocratic and moralizing temperament, accepting with unexpected tolerance the phenomena of lasciviousness and greed, might have an aversion to romantic literature. Thus, Paulo Prado included Romanticism among the three great Brazilian evils, those which are the origin of all the rest, and which appear most irremediable. He was right in the sense that a romantic nature pervades all the manifestations of our social life, from politics to religion, and from domestic life to collective enterprises. To cite a single example, particularly linked to the *Retrato do Brasil,* the Revolution of 1930 was, in the history of the Republic, a romantic insurrection: the unrestrained aristocrat who praised himself for having foreseen it (the author's note to the fourth edition) exaggerated quite obviously the practical nature of his impressionist brush strokes. However, the Revolution of 1930 and the fact that he (Paulo Prado) had implicitly received and accepted it as a solution to all the political ills of the country indicate that he was partially right when he considered the *Retrato do Brasil* an optimistic book.

It is true that he immediately added that his was an "optimism of the physician or surgeon who wishes to effect a cure." It is an optimism that I would dare to call pessimistic and which can be expressed by the famous negative formula which concludes the *Retrato* and symmetrically answers, like an impressionistic "blot," the impressionistic "blot" which opens the book: "confidence in the future which cannot be worse than the past." Disdaining the pious and stupid patriotism with which so many Brazilians soothe themselves, he defined his pessimism as "the patriotic anxiety of one who loves his country and points out the errors and crimes of the money-changers in the temple." It was the "salutary optimism" which had so pleased him in João Ribeiro's observation that he was "the greatest mind in contemporary Brazil." In contradiction, lauding Action (with a capital A), lamenting the absence in our national character of those elements that contributed so much to the formation of New England, Paulo Prado, like another famous Prado (Eduardo, his uncle), denied the "American dream." And he necessarily fell back on the congenital pessimism from which he had just freed himself through great power of will and intelligence: "There are also pessimists in the United States," a true cry from his soul which, I think, signified that in his eyes that was the healthiest aspect of the American nation. Anti-Americanism—as is well known—before it took root among communist or communizing intellectuals, was an attitude peculiar to aristocratic spirits; one of its oldest exponents was that Eça de Queiroz whom Paulo

Prado held to be one of his closest friends. Paulo Prado lived, of course, in the spiritual atmosphere of the so-called "European traditions." And that is the other fundamental characteristic of the *Retrato*, the enrollment of itself in the traditional debates of the spirit, of the rational and intelligent interpretation of reality and of history. For that very reason, this book is above all a creation of style, and it is as a creation of style that it holds its place in the history of the Brazilian intelligence. One cannot disagree with a work of art; we have to accept it or reject it for what it is. In the case of the *Retrato do Brasil*, it seems to me that it behooves us to admire it as an extraordinary literary creation and as one of the possible fragmentary answers that the country has inspired to this date. Fragmentary and inflamed—but also inflaming.

That this book could have been published in 1928, that is, along with *Macunaíma*, is a less contradictory and surprising fact than it might seem to be at first sight. Mário de Andrade was also questing for the "national character," and he found in a splendidly Modernist paradox the portrait of a "hero with no character at all," as the subtitle states. *Macunaíma* is the Modernist book par excellence and—in spite of appearances—a book with no progeny for the simple reason that it could not possibly inspire imitators. However, owing to one singular fact that we must bear in mind, it fell to *Macunaíma* to broaden the horizon for creations that seem to us closer to other models, like the Northeastern novel, for example, or the work of Guimarães Rosa (well past the Modernist era).

Macunaíma, as I wrote in the *Panorama das Literaturas das Américas,*[15] is a bewildering book. It is rather a short story (a short story three hundred pages long) than a novel, rather a kind of oriental tale in which magic and logic are confused, in which there is no boundary between the natural and the supernatural. Basing himself on data gleaned from the author, Nestor Victor explained, in October of 1928, that Mário de Andrade

at first sought to create a symbol of the Brazilian, who seemed to him to have no specific character, not just from the moral point of view, but rather as a permanent psychic entity, which manifests itself in everything: in his customs, external action, sentiment, language, history, bearing, in his good points and bad. He sought to do something cyclical, in the Brazilian sense of the word. He disregarded geography on purpose as well as geographical flora and fauna. Then he decentralized his creation as much as possible, as he succeeded in conceiving Brazil as a homogeneous literary entity, a national ethnic and geographical unity.

Some critics of the day recalled Ulysses, others recalled Pedro Malasartes. The language is of such novelty and, at the same time, of such internal coherence and equilibrium that it marked the limits of linguistic "research" in prose for more than twenty years. Hailing it on its publication, Oswald de Andrade wrote that the author of *Macunaíma* had created the cyclical Brazilian hero and for fifty years the national poetic idiom. Nestor Victor himself thought that it was an Indianist novel turned inside out.

In a general way the true greatness of *Macunaíma,* which lies more in the daring of its conception and in the courage of its accomplishment than in any results it obtained, escaped its first critics. Precisely because it attempted to evade form and formula, *Macunaíma* cannot be judged by the standards common to the novel or the short story, as long as it is considered as literature. Taking it as folklore, the perspectives change utterly. It may perhaps be an epic in prose, but it is an epic that does not take itself too seriously and in which good humor is one of the constants. It is an epic after an ironic fashion, not in the usual epic mode. Moreover, it is a "simultaneist" epic, since it excludes time and, necessarily, historical succession. Macunaíma is not a character; he is a symbol. He cannot be compared with the "wily Ulysses," simply because he is a national replica of a folkloric type and not a literary type. He is at once in the past and the present; he is timeless and supergeographic; more American than Brazilian. We know today, through an unpublished preface,[16] that when Mário de Andrade wrote *Macunaíma,* he "did not want his hero to be a nationalist but rather a South American, and he therefore did well to replace his own conscience with that of a Hispano-American." Indeed, this fact did not escape the sharp critical eye of Ronald de Carvalho:

> Macunaíma is the hero of the American cycle. He is a pure force of the pre-Columbian cosmogony, higher, or perhaps better, than good and evil. Macunaíma transcends time and space. His dimensions are greater than reality. . . . Macunaíma is an aggregation of elements, a conjugation of energies which, in spite of his anthropomorphic wrapper, make of him an index of the species, a concentration of all the values of the species, human in his essential state. . . . Mário de Andrade projected Brazil in that figure. At least one of the Brazils which help to situate the different images of our national complex. Macunaíma could not have a character, simply because he is limitless and is not subject to normal contingencies. And it is precisely that absence of character which gives him a great superhuman character where, in the apparent tumult of indiscipline, are reflected the elemental energies.[17]

That super-reality led Macunaíma to unreality, and therein lies his frustration. The incalculable historic importance of the book, its immense value as an exemplar, should not prevent our recognizing that, in itself, *Macunaíma* was a failure, but in the same sense that we say that *Gargantua* was a failure, or in the same way that Virginia Woolf saw Joyce's *Ulysses* as a failure. Less important books will live longer: the modern social novel of Brazil descended from *A Bagaceira* (which alone for its implications can be considered as a Modernist book), not from *Macunaíma*. Mário de Andrade himself was aware that he had failed, when he observed in a letter to Manuel Bandeira: "I have begun and like very much a novel called *Café*, which will be eight hundred pages long . . . filled with psychology and intense life. But I feel that it is greater than my strength, and I more or less have the conviction that I'll fall short again, much as I fell short on *Macunaíma*—the masterpiece that didn't turn out to be a masterpiece." [18]

Nonetheless, *Macunaíma*, like *Ulysses*, like *Gargantua*, set the tone of its era and indirectly made possible all that followed.

Mário de Andrade attempted, in this book, to amalgamate a Brazilian language that was more genuine in its syntax than in its vocabulary: a Brazilian language of 1928, seen from the perspective of the São Paulo district of Barra Funda which, based on the Indian and the Negro, would not ignore the contributions of the immigrants, with a character destined to represent the "Brazilian" par excellence, that is, the offspring of an Indian. The book is, then, above all, as it was felicitously defined by Professor Roger Bastide, a "Discourse for the Defense and Illustration of the Brazilian Language." *Macunaíma* is, in so far as the linguistic aspect is concerned, the crowning glory and also the exasperation of a whole "quest" for the national language (as one speaks of a quest for the Holy Grail). The language of *Macunaíma* is spoken by no Brazilian, and it is not always totally understood by Brazilians. It could only be the language of some outlandish Brazilian who bore within him, in the exact proportions, the genes of all the Indians, all the Negroes, all the immigrants, and the recollection of all ages, all activities, all regions. But also, as Roger Bastide observed, it is not a question of understanding all the words but of "becoming joyfully lost in the torrent that carries us away." Probably no Brazilian will see himself in Macunaíma, as no Frenchman sees himself in Pantagruel. But are Macunaíma and Pantagruel less representative of their nationality for that reason?

One naturally wonders at this point to what degree this folkloric rhapsody by Mário de Andrade can be considered a "portrait of Brazil," parallel to and harmonious with that of Paulo Prado. Its subtitle has led to tongue-in-cheek interpretations which have no true relationship to its meaning. It is in the literary sense of the word that Macunaíma does not have a "character." To a degree this is true in the anthropological, ethnological, and sociological sense; considerably less in the moral sense. The moral extrapolation which is currently made (with a grin) is defensible, but everything indicates that it was not the author's intention. He rather sought to create an indefinite being, incoherent, made up of contradictions, quite the opposite of a "character" or of a "type," a being that would become a type solely because he was a composite. Here is what Mário de Andrade wrote to Manuel Bandeira in this regard:

> I took special pains to point out that Macunaíma, like the Brazilian he is, *has no character.* I spoke of that in the preface to the second version, and I'll show you here. Take note of this: Macunaíma is alternately courageous and cowardly. Nothing systematized into individual or ethnic psychology. He attacks and conquers the monster Capêi, but later he flees from a severed head. He rushes at the audience in the Stock Exchange scene and later is frightened because he is a captive and flees. Etc. etc. He had succeeded in deflowering Ci only with the aid of his brothers and he flees acting tough "Come at me and I'll kill you!," he's not brave enough to deflower another Indian maiden and he takes off like a lovesick calf. He ambles through the forest and comes across the waterfall of Naipi. Everything logical. He asks why she is crying. She tells him and he's furious with Capêi—the maiden has already said that he lives in the grotto—he sees her sex, maybe Naipi was trifled with. Macunaíma said that he would kill Capêi. Capêi listens and comes out of the grotto, he's a monster and he wants to kill Macunaíma. Then he, more rash than courageous, kills Capêi. And the severed head (tradition) becomes his slave and follows him. Macunaíma is afraid and runs away.

In November of 1927, before the book was published, Mário de Andrade revealed that he was totally aware of the fact that the "contradictions" in Macunaíma would serve to constitute his "character." However, since we always set up a certain resistance to any "character" made up of contradictions, the personage would of necessity be a hero. But let it be understood, a literary hero with no character. In another letter to Manuel Bandeira, Mário de Andrade wrote: "But the fact that the book is, properly speaking, logically and psychologically incoherent does not necessarily follow. . . . That is to say, the book has a logical and psychological coherence; who doesn't is Macunaíma himself and there exactly resides Macunaíma's logic: he had no logic. Don't think I'm quibbling. It's easy to prove that I've established from the very roots of the book that Macunaíma is a contradiction of himself. The character he exhibits in one chapter disappears in the next."

For that very reason—and this is one aspect which most analysts seem to ignore—Macunaíma cannot be, in absolute terms, a symbol of the Brazilian people, nor even in a larger sense a literary symbol in the basic sense of that word. Mário de Andrade made that fact clear: "Macunaíma is not a symbol of the Brazilian, in the way that Shylock symbolizes avarice. If I wrote that, I wrote it too hurriedly. Macunaíma lives for himself; however, his character precisely consists of having no character." [19]

It is enlightening to compare everything that has been said with what Mário de Andrade wrote in passing in his famous article "Poetry in 1930," now included in the *Aspectos da Literatura Brasileira*: ". . . the great macunaimatic impetus of the individual, . . . beings neither guilty nor innocent, neither happy nor sad, no longer gifted with that superb indifference which Plato saw as wisdom." However, the author himself agreed only once to the extrapolation from the technical plane to the ethical plane when he wrote in Chapter XIII: "Then they saw that Macunaíma was very immoral and had no character."

The irony of literary life decreed that *Macunaíma,* "written in December of 1926, all of a piece, in six days, corrected and lengthened in January of 1927," [20] should be published after the Cannibal Manifesto. Therefore, this placed Mário de Andrade, the super-erudite writer, among the "primitives." Even a critic of unarguable astuteness, like Tristão de Athayde, made that mistake, which Mário de Andrade protested in a letter dated December 23, 1927. The truth is that once more Mário de Andrade was not the rule but the exception of Modernism: alongside the *Macunaíma* and the Cannibal Manifesto, came Cassiano Ricardo's *Martim Cererê.*

Had it been written a century before, *Martim Cererê* would have been considered the Indianist epic attributable to the Romantic poets but which was only written fragmentarily by Gonçalves Dias. Appearing when it did in its own time, it was the Indianist epic that likewise lay in the destiny of the Modernist poets, of which *Macunaíma* was the prose version. *Martim Cererê* is not a book of poems: that is the first critical error to banish from our thoughts. It is rather a single poem, the song of literary nationalism, already colored at that stage by proper political nationalism. More than a simple document of Modernism, *Martim Cererê* is a document of Greengiltism, which restricts it yet at the same time characterizes its scope and meaning. In that light, it triumphs over the fragmentation of *Pau Brasil,* in which Oswald de Andrade three years before had shattered to bits the idea of "primitivism" and "Indianism" in Modernism. In a tardy correction the Cannibal Manifesto tried to regain the lost time, but it was already too late considering the fact that the Greengiltists had occupied the trenches which Mário de Andrade, in his turn, had not seemed eager to occupy.

Foreshadowing the political philosophy of Integralism, *Martim Cererê* is also a cosmogony of giants; in that regard it is more advanced than *Os Lusíadas,* which possessed giants only in restricted number and explained them away through mythology. In Cassiano Ricardo's Brazil, everyone is a giant, which seems to echo an unwritten law of the Greengiltists. In 1926 the library of the group included a volume by Alfred Ellis on the racial, anthroposocial, and psychological evolution of the *paulista* from the sixteenth through the nineteenth centuries. It bore the title: *Race of Giants.*[21]

A symbolic résumé of the book might be embodied in the poem "Brasil-Menino":

I

My father was a giant, subduer of leagues.
When one day he departed, on horseback
on his blue-downed dragon which was the Tietê River of the
    /pioneers
I well recall he said to me: see here, my son,
I'm going to wheel out through this door and one day I shall
    /return bringing some two hundred leagues of road
    /and tens of jaguars dragged by their tails dripping
    /blood from their snouts!
No sooner said than done! off he went pushing through the
    /ravined forest
through flanks of alligators and alban birds.

When Christmas came my father was far away,
fighting the wooly bugs, with the great cats with
/stripèd head and with the seven-headed mules that
/dwell in the heart of the densest trees.
On the tableland the tolling of a bell questioned: does he
/come?
Another bell with lower voice answered: no . . . and no,
/saying "nooo" and repeating "nooo" and no.

II

And it occurred to me to get a pair of boots
that my father wore and I put on the pair of boots
behind the door of the backland which mumbled ambushed
/in the grove.
How cold it was that night!
I was so filled with fright . . . A scurrying cat
went through the cracks in the loose roof tiles . . .
But morning came, lovely as a treasure!
and I went to find, with my heart skipping with joy,
  the two leather boots
  chock-full of gold!

III

Another year went by and my father did not come home.
I threw my clod-hoppers again behind the door
  and on the following day
I went to find my big shoes chock-full of emeralds!

My granny, a little old Portuguese lady with hair of mist and
/checkered blue shawl assured me:
"It was Santa Claus who brought them." Until one day
I pretended I did not see but I did; I awoke from my dream.
My father was a Giant, huntsman of leagues,
  a savage tamer of jaguars,
  terror of the forest, panic of the butterflies
but he had a great heart.

Finally I grew up. Today I am a big boy.
I am a coffee dealer. I possess enchanted viaducts.
My city is that many-splendored tumult that whirls past
holding factories by their black reins of smoke!

Fantastic din
of a world leaving the workshop.
Metallic cry of the American city.
Life rolling quivering beating hammers
    with muscles of steel.

And the Tietê River tells the story of the old Giants
who measured the boundaries of the homeland,
at a time when São Paulo was putting its boots behind the
    /door
And in the morning the boots were full of gold . . .

And in the morning the boots were full of emeralds . . .

And in the morning the boots were full of diamonds . . .[22]

1931: Cobra Norato

Just as *Macunaíma* was written in 1926 and published in 1928, so *Cobra Norato* was written in 1928 and published in 1931. These lags in time fill the history of Modernism. If they were studied more in detail they could reveal the hidden course of important themes and states of mind and also what we might perhaps call the Movement's ideological anxieties. Raul Bopp epitomizes in this book the mysterious attraction which the Amazon region and its legends exercised over the Modernist sensibility. *Macunaíma* is an obvious example of this phenomenon, not to mention other poetic creations by Mário de Andrade. At the same time, *Cobra Norato* is the finest of this entire current, taking its place between Greengiltism, where Raul Bopp saw his artistic origins, and Cannibalism, where his artistry terminated. Let it be understood through these distinctions that he soon repudiated the political garb which clothed such men as Cassiano Ricardo, Menotti del Picchia and Plínio Salgado and opted for the innocent dionysianism (at least for that time) of Oswald de Andrade.

To understand what Raul Bopp meant to the Modernism of 1927 (and which, with the exception of Greengiltism, he continued to mean to the Modernism of 1928) it is essential to know the famous "Greengilt Letter," by Plínio Salgado, addressed to Menotti del Picchia:

He is above all one of the most representative forces in the Brazilian mentality. He is an extremely well-traveled chap: he has already been up the Amazon, he has seen Acre, the Mato-Grosso, he has skirted the Brazilian coast by canoe as far as Oiapoque, he has been to Chile, Bolivia, and Peru, he painted walls in Cuiabá, worked in a bookstore in Buenos Aires, was a student in Pôrto Alegre, in Rio, in Recife, Bahia, Belém, he has gone on donkey-back, under the broiling sun, he has stuck a thorn through his foot, ridden horseback, rowed a boat, drunk *mate,* eaten jungle gruel, and done a thousand other exciting things.

.   .   .   .   .

Bopp represents roving Greengiltism. A half-breed of German descent and a backwoodsman: born in Rio Grande, he has lived in the Amazon jungle; he holds a degree and shuns the study; a poet and uses no rhymes; has a vast store of scientific and literary lore at his fingertips and is simple as a child; has read all the Modernists and keeps his own personality intact and profoundly disdains all "processes"; is a fellow with guts and is so surprising these days that you rub your eyes to make sure you're not seeing things out of an adventure story.[23]

The poet was at that time the very epitome of the Modernist writer. *Cobra Norato* also has the exemplary value of bringing the Indianist cycle in poetry within Modernism and marks the end of an epoch rather than the beginning of anything new. This is the meaning of the colophon which was used when the book was printed in 1931—an intimation of its vague anachronism, although *Cobra Norato* is the only Modernist creation which immediately gained a kind of mythological position in literary history, as had *Macunaíma.* Intrinsically, these two Modernist books were to be remembered as much for their failings as for their high caliber.

However, the proof that *Cobra Norato* surpasses these limitations to a certain degree lies in the fact that it permits mythical interpretation; in fact, it invites interpretation on several levels, some of them, or at least the mythical one, the broadest and most general possible. Such interpretations have already been undertaken, here and there, although not systematically. However, the marvelous journey of the *Cobra Norato:*

I go journeying   journeying
I mingle in the belly of the jungle biting roots [24]

has much more meaning, literary and Modernist, than the "marvelous journey" of Graça Aranha.

Let it be noted that the mythical journey in time and space
is the main theme of *Macunaíma, Martim Cererê,* and *Cobra
Norato*: Modernism was a roving and roaming school, fascinated
by geographical discovery and mesmerized by chronological discovery. In these artists so imbued with the sense of the *modern,*
contradiction is only apparent as we note the sense of the mythical
past represented by folklore. The fact is that behind all of this lay a
clear consciousness of time, as we have seen before.

It is perhaps here that we may find the first explanation for
the interest the Modernists had in the Amazon region: there alone,
as Euclides da Cunha had observed, the world was still in process
of formation; it was the Second Day of Creation; in other words,
it was the spot where one might live intimately with Time, where
one was a contemporary of his folklore:

Here is the subterranean jungle with fetid breath birthing
   /snakes

Lean rivers forced to labor.
The roots inflamed are chewing mud

In the thicket hammers beat
welding   sawing   sawing

They are manufacturing earth . . .
—Well   Here they are indeed manufacturing earth! [25]

It would require a more specialized analysis to determine
whether there are echoes of *Macunaíma* in *Cobra Norato* or vice
versa; what can be immediately affirmed is that the two books emit
absolutely identical sounds and correspond to a mythology (mythology proper and literary mythology) that is totally homogeneous.

The Amazon region continued, in the following years, to feed an entire current, whether Modernist or one similar to it. In 1929, Peregrino Júnior published *Pussanga,* a book republished, significantly, in 1931; the *Histórias da Amazônia* came out in 1936, both volumes already a bit past their literary prime. Gastão Cruls had authored *Amazônia Misteriosa,* published in 1925 and republished in 1929. Thus the climax of what we might call "Amazonian literature" within Modernism centered around the year 1930. This type of literature terminated, at least symbolically, with *Cobra Norato,* the book in which, much more than in *Macunaíma,* the secret voices of that enigmatic world speak, that world which well might hold the inexhaustible repository of Brazilian myths which Modernism so dearly loved to feed on.

1933: Casa Grande & Senzala

Gilberto Freyre, as we have seen, is not a Modernist, nor does he wish to be. *Casa Grande & Senzala* was not written from a Modernist point of view nor does it owe a thing, in so far as *conception* and *style* are concerned, to the São Paulo Movement. Why, then, do we consider it a representative work of the school? Because, as another example of what happened with the "Northeastern novel" and the poetry of the thirties, Gilberto Freyre's book accorded, without his knowing it, with the obscure program of Modernism just as it benefited from the spiritual climate created by the Movement. Although he worked independently and (why not say it?) with a certain hostility toward the Modernists, the truth is that Gilberto Freyre systematized in *Casa Grande & Senzala* an instinctive conception which they had of Brazil and to which they could not give expression, or which they could express only in imaginative literature and in poetry. At the same time, *Casa Grande & Senzala* revealed some contradictions in the tendencies and the nature of the Movement.

If the decade of the thirties represents a second phase in the history and evolution of Modernism, there is no error at all in supposing that such a phase had its beginnings in *Casa Grande & Senzala*. Even if we admit, as seems evident, that *A Bagaceira* inaugurates the cycle of the Northeastern novel, it is certain that from the ideological point of view, José Américo de Almeida's book meets the standard which was set by Gilberto Freyre's essay.

Add to that the fact that *Casa Grande & Senzala* was the first serious challenge to the ideas of Oliveira Viana, an author who also existed on the fringe of Modernism and was considered throughout the twenties to be Brazil's greatest thinker. Answering Oliveira Viana on the one hand and Paulo Prado on the other, *Casa Grande & Senzala* was an effective landmark in the history of our thought; however, it was so—at least in so far as its startling success was concerned—because the Brazilian mind had unconsciously been preparing itself for such an event during the years between 1922 and 1930 and, more particularly, after 1926. The Modernism-Regionalism controversy is highly exaggerated by Gilberto Freyre. Actually, to know Brazil thoroughly, to re-evaluate the Indian and the Negro, to stimulate regionalism and, because of all that, to perceive that Brazilian traditions belong to the very mental fabric of Modernism, were characteristics of Modernism as sensitive and fundamental as its "estheticism."

What has always distinguished Gilberto Freyre from the Modernists is neither regionalism nor traditionalism: it is a longing for the past (*saudosismo*). Around this sociological longing he constructed his entire social history, of which *Casa Grande & Senzala* remains the high point and the point of reference. The Modernists, on the contrary, shunned this longing and rather voiced a joy in living, more typical of the twenties and the schools of modern art than the nostalgia that appears to have been the characteristic feature of Gilberto Freyre's psychology from his earliest days.

The proof that his book can be included in the history of Modernism—if it is true that at the other extreme it escapes the Movement—is not found only in the chronological order. It rests mainly in its ambivalence. *Casa Grande & Senzala* was read not only for its scientific content but also for its literary form; and although some critics have commented on this adversely, the truth is that the two things complete one another on the lofty plane where masterworks are properly considered. It would not be difficult to prove that the sentimental attitude out of which this volume was born, and many of its themes, are also found scattered through the works of the Modernist poets and prose writers. Thus there existed a "climate" which presaged such a book, although obviously none of the Modernists could foresee it, and it was necessary that someone else should write it.

From the standpoint of literary history, the role of *Casa Grande & Senzala* is purely catalytic. However, if Gilberto Freyre claims for his book, as is proper, a significant influence in the development of the novel of the thirties, he confesses by the same token that his relationship to the literary climate of Modernism was equally important and profound.

Part Three
Basic Authors

From Graça Aranha to Érico Veríssimo, the basic authors of Modernism are obviously those writers whose names cannot properly be omitted from a history of the Movement. Just as a representative work may, in the long run, turn out to be less than a masterpiece (and vice versa), a basic author may be one who is not even a Modernist, as happens in the extreme case of Graça Aranha. He may be a modern poet but psychologically alien to the school, like Augusto Frederico Schmidt; he may be a writer whose career was cut short, like Alcântara Machado; he may be a writer who developed far from and outside of the Movement, like José Lins do Rêgo and Jorge Amado; he may be a Parnassian who became a Modernist only to abandon the Movement later, like Menotti del Picchia; or, finally, a man who only incidentally entered the literary arena, like Plínio Salgado.

Graça Aranha

Graça Aranha (1868–1931), as a follower of Tobias Barreto, descended from a "modernism" prior to the Movement of 1922: the intellectual debate which, in the words of José Veríssimo, "had become operative in Europe before the end of the first half of the nineteenth century with the positivism of Auguste Comte, Darwinian transformism, Spencerian evolutionism, the intellectualism of Taine and Renan and similar intellectual movements which, through their influence on literature, put an end to the exclusive domain of Romanticism." The effects of this intellectual debate were not felt in Brazil until nearly twenty years after the European activity. The writer who in 1924 attempted to modernize the Academy is the student who, while still in the provinces, had already rebelled against the "drowsy Academy of Recife": if the School of Law and the literary circle went by the same name of "academy," that is only an intellectual suggestion which the facts themselves present to us. The "Modernist" tendencies in Graça Aranha were not exactly a new thing in 1922. They were not incited by the São Paulo group, nor were they the result of a desire to "be in the main current of modern history." It is strange that while he was constitutionally hostile to Modernist esthetics Graça Aranha should have accepted it simply because Modernism represented something of a spiritual renovation. However, it is no less significant, as Nazareth Prado said, that he had never been "Modernist." As a matter of fact, the case is one of an academic spirit who held the Academy in horror, but not academic literature; who resisted, as far as he could, enlistment by the Academy and took the first opportunity which presented itself to break off relations with that body; who had fleetingly been an anarchist in his youth and had retained of that anarchism the urge toward literary protest.

In 1922, as he inaugurated the Week of Modern Art, he was a man from a spiritual world suddenly thrown in with barbaric youths. The words which he chose to describe the works of art on exhibit, even giving irony the freest rein possible, were "extravagant paintings" and "absurd sculpture." Politically, Graça Aranha seemed to proceed from Barrès and Maurras, that is, from two traditionalists (which brought about an unexpected liaison with Plínio Salgado to the undeniable extent that traditionalism is also political rightism). The mystical tendencies of his spirit, in particular nationalist mysticism, and the preaching of an optimistic credo contributed not a little to these last approaches. We might possibly think that he had always held to the modernism of ideas but that he lacked affinity for the Modernist idea. For that very reason he never acquired a Modernist style. He was a Symbolist (after Ibsen and Maeterlinck) in the time of Expressionism, in a generation of Expressionists. He was a student of Recife-style positivism who wrote a Symbolist novel, perhaps the only Symbolist novel of any merit in all of Brazilian literature. However, *Canaã* will also be for some time to come the nationalist breviary of a rhetorical generation. Graça Aranha was an open spirit, open not to novelty (like Oswald de Andrade) but to youth, to all that was young; the Modernist generation, ungrateful in the extreme, was nevertheless for him a fountain source of rejuvenation.

In the last analysis, Graça Aranha was a writer who produced no great work, which was the fate of many Modernists. However, we might ask whether he was truly a great writer or merely a man who sought in literature something new, but who eternally lacked the proper tools for the search. The fact that he was not, nor could he ever have been, the *leader* of the Modernists seems blindingly evident today. In this regard, there is no denying that Mário de Andrade and Manuel Bandeira were absolutely right. This was a well-known fact from the time of the *Estética*; literary histories have handed down the lie for years out of sheer mechanical repetition. Because he saw himself as "revolutionary by heredity," his natural place in 1922 was on the side of the Modernists. Besides, the first number of the *Estética* opened with an inaugural article by him, and he thereby dignified Modernism a second time. He put forth therein his favorite ideas, according to which a new esthetics would be born out of a civilization of iron and concrete, "the expression of all modern energy," an esthetics which is a philosophy of youth "because only youth can conquer Terror and transform everything into joy." At the same time, however, taking an anticipatory position against *Casa Grande & Senzala,* he condemned the "new man" identified with the mestizo: "the plague, scourge, and shame of Brazilian society."

In the pages of the same journal, Prudente de Morais Neto (in criticizing the book by Joaquim Inojosa) and Mário de Andrade (in his "Open Letter to Alberto de Oliveira") began to contest Graça Aranha's leadership. *Klaxon* did not proclaim him as the master, Rubens Borba de Moraes later wrote; and, by unhappy coincidence, *Klaxon* died precisely on the publication of the number in homage to Graça Aranha, more or less demanded by Graça, an event which led the Klaxonists to considerable squabbling among themselves. All of this has been confirmed by Renato Almeida in the article "Ronald de Carvalho and Modernism," mentioned earlier. Nonetheless, there is a small detail which demands our attention: the Week of Modern Art marks only the beginning of Modernism *as action* and Graça Aranha, who viewed literature more as action than as contemplation (so that he might be identified as the Philippe in the *Viagem Maravilhosa*), found a congenial atmosphere in literature.

We have already seen that he remained "Futurist," that is, he became imperceptibly traditionalist, while the youths of 1922 went from Futurism to Modernism and from Modernism to the modern. It is that separation which best places him within the Modernist perspective.

Jorge de Lima

First published in 1914, with his *XIV Alexandrinos*, Jorge de Lima (1895–1953) figures among the numerous Parnassians who appeared in the Modernist firmament like comets. Coming from different origins, they skirted the Movement for a brief moment and immediately departed. His Modernist period, properly speaking, runs from *O Mundo do Menino Impossível* (1925) to *Essa Negra Fulô* (1928). His Modernism was of shorter duration than we might think, because the *Novos Poemas* (1929) added nothing to his former work. From then until 1935, the date of his first metaphysical and religious poetry—which would later be hermetic and formalist—his books were mere inventories of all his former publications. Homero Senna once asked him about Modernism: "Didn't you take part in the Movement, then?" He answered: "No, despite the fact that I supported it from the start."

That reply does not coincide with the well-known and incontrovertible facts, according to which his conversion to Modernism was as tardy as his conversion to militant Catholicism; [1] at the same time this reply confirmed Gilberto Freyre's version of the story, which mentioned Jorge de Lima as a Modernist poet, and also contradicted Freyre because the poetry revealed a predominant influence of the São Paulo Modernists.

In reality Jorge de Lima seems to have succumbed to literary fashion when he passed from Parnassian Alexandrines to the free verse of the Modernists, and for that very reason he never burned his bridges. So he was able to take the long return voyage that brought him, no less, to the periplus of Vasco da Gama on the command ship of *Os Lusíadas*. Mário de Andrade, who rarely erred in his judgment of poets, wrote in 1939 in the critical note to *A Túnica Inconsútil*:

> From this point of view one might discover in the poet a kind of academician that is somewhat vague and masked. It is there to be sure. Jorge de Lima does not disdain academism nor has he made of it that bugaboo which has been the greatest disgrace, the greatest weakening of our contemporary artistic manifestations. . . . Another possible defect which Jorge de Lima has converted into one of the rarest qualities of his poetry is the lack of poetic invention. This book of his, called *A Túnica Inconsútil*, will be the best example that he has given us of this aspect of his work. . . . If Jorge de Lima had lived some centuries ago, he would certainly have been one of our great plagiarists, like Shakespeare or Camões. I do not think, however, that he would have possessed the same force of geniality . . . a book like *A Túnica Inconsútil* has an anthological flavor, in such a way does the poet compile in his pages all the thematics brought into focus by contemporary poetry . . . Franco-Brazilian poetry. The star appears, the angel appears, the sailor, guitarist, dancing girl, the circus, and the entire music hall appear.

Really, Jorge de Lima is a poet like Cassiano Ricardo, impregnated with literary reminiscences; he is, therefore, somewhat mimetic. Beside the "Northeastern novel," his work, along with *Catimbó* by Ascenso Ferreira (1927), could represent the "Northeastern poetry" of Modernism: on one hand a poetic Modernism of the second phase, on the other hand the expression of themes provided by the region. The Parnassian phase of Jorge de Lima, just prior to Modernism, is not so bad as critics would have it who wish to overrate his later poetry; nor is it as good as those would have it who wish to postulate the genius of the poet. The sonnet "Acendedor de Lampeões," justly famous, gives the measure of his Parnassianism, because it is beyond a doubt one of the best of that time. Nonetheless it belongs to a sententious Parnassus rather than to a poetic Parnassus, not to mention the fact that technically it is written in a facile and mechanical Parnassianism (the rhymes in -*mente*, and so on).

In his Modernist work, which is curiously reactionary, one finds "replies," sometimes polemical, to other poets, not to mention the "plagiarisms" which Mário de Andrade mentioned. The poem "A Minha América," for example, from *Poemas*, came to be titled "Não Tôda a América" in the *Poemas Escolhidos* (1932), proving what a reading of the work had already revealed: its imitation of Ronald de Carvalho.[2]

CITY OF CUZCO. HACE FRÍO.
Yonder comes the procession of the Lord of Earthquakes
Viva El Señor de los temblores! Viva el Perú!
There are *ñucho* flowers along the streets.
There are fat little girls on the balconies.
There are red flirtations on the corners.
There are drunks on brandy and *chicha!*
Suddenly the bells ring
carillons
of the Capilla del Triunfo. Bong! Bong! [3]
.   .   .   .   .
U. S. A.

Gigantic industries, colossal trusts,
Massachussetts [*sic*]
New Hampshire,
Rhode Island,
Connecticut,
Pensylvania [*sic*]
United States of America!
All the joyful and frightfully numerous rites:
Cults, lectures, the eucharistic congress
in Chicago handing out hosts to two million mouths:
The biggest record for the distribution of the Body of the
/Lord!
But above a supreme joy stamps the U. S. A.:

JORGE DE LIMA   215

—Love divorced 20 times and 20 times glorified,
always jovial and always new like the very
joyful soul of the United States
        of North America.[4]

There was more in the same vein. This was already Jorge de
Lima's second attempt at Modernism and an important effort to
achieve the cosmopolitan sensibility of Ronald de Carvalho. He
succeeded in imitating him, however, only on the outside ("Whitman!"). The Northeastern writers, even the well-traveled ones,
never lost a certain provincialism (which many confuse with the
theme of the province), and they cannot repress an instinctive
hostility toward the foreigner. Besides that, the entire poem is
based on the most conventional commonplaces and on an enu-
merative technique that has no meaning.

There is little doubt, however, that with "G. W. B. R."
(Great Western Brazilian Railway) and "Essa Negra Fulô!" he
composed the two poems most typical of lyrical Modernism in
the Northeast and thereby worthily balanced off all the weight
of the Northeastern novel. These are poems which deserve to remain, as they will surely, in the annals of our Modernist poetry.

G. W. B. R.

Through the window of my train I see
        the Sundays of the little towns,
            with little girls and young women,
    and well-starched traveling salesmen who come to see
the dusty passengers on the cars.

This Great Western Railway
    made to order for the Northeast
            is the most picturesque in the universe
    with its drowsy engines
    and its little Eye Brand match-box cars
            There was a time when the herds were frightened
by the whistle of those trains;
    today the little birds look on from the bordering telegraph
poles,
    at how picturesque it is,

its comings and goings, its fierceness,
endlessly creaking and squeaking.[5]

These are a few lines from a poem too long to include here
in its entirety; it reveals, however, that Jorge de Lima lacked the
capacity for expression that is properly poetic, no matter how surprising that may seem. In the Northeastern and Modernist poems,
as well as in the "restoration of poetry in Christ," which followed
in 1935, the prosaic rhythm is evident (although he attempted
to hide it by an arbitrary breaking of the lines) and also an editorializing and descriptive elocution. Coming from Parnassianism
(Parnassianism moreover limited in time and technique), Jorge
de Lima seems to have understood free verse as a simple and
capricious arrangement of the lines on the page or in the poem.
It is for that reason that his compositions with a more regular
rhythm are clearly superior.

In the third phase of his poetic career, which Tristão de
Athayde calls *mystical*,[6] also the last in the Modernist period,
Jorge de Lima initiated a curious kind of religious poetry (by
necessary definition, proselytizing): religious poetry linked with
poetic hermeticity (or, on the contrary, linked with simple prosaic
exposition in which exclamation and fervor take the place of
poetic rapture). In collaboration with Murilo Mendes, whose
book of *Poemas* was rated by Mário de Andrade among the four
most important of 1930 (the other three being *Alguma Poesia*
by Carlos Drummond de Andrade, *Libertinagem* by Manuel
Bandeira, and *Pássaro Cego* by Augusto Frederico Schmidt), he
tried to achieve in his works (beyond doctrinal preachments and
affirmations of principle) the famous "spiritualism" which Tristão
de Athayde and the *Festa* group had been preaching since the
end of the prior decade. But to be precise, at a time when Modernism—at least as far as verse technique is concerned—was going
to be hopelessly outclassed, its properly poetic possibilities gained
new dimensions in the work of Carlos Drummond de Andrade.
His work, and not that of Jorge de Lima, pointed to the royal
road of poetic development in the thirties. That line of development came along without any noticeable interruption through
the Modernist metamorphosis of Manuel Bandeira.

Manuel Bandeira

Since 1917, the date of publication of *A Cinza das Horas*, everything has been said and resaid about the poet Manuel Bandeira (1886–1968).[7] In collecting his complete works,[8] the Editôra José Aguilar has gathered much of the best and the worst that has been written about him in such a way as to preclude further criticism. What remains to be said of Manuel Bandeira after the analyses of Mário de Andrade, Sérgio Buarque de Hollanda, Alceu Amoroso Lima, João Ribeiro, Carlos Drummond de Andrade, Sérgio Milliet, Antônio Cândido, Otto Maria Carpeaux, Lêdo Ivo, Onestaldo de Pennafort, Octavio Tarquínio de Sousa, Murilo Mendes, and the biographical data furnished by Francisco de Assis Barbosa? Obviously, not all of this critical material which accompanies the complete works is of equal quality. So many fragmentary evaluations make us long for a definitive interpretation, which we do not find in the Aguilar edition even when we place all these diverse studies side by side. The complete interpretation has not yet been written. Nor indeed do the critics themselves, individually considered, always rise to their best from the beginning to the end of their analyses. Criticism of Manuel Bandeira in this regard reflects his own poetic work with its ups and downs, with its scales and vocalizing, with its unfortunate banalities.

Like every "easy" poet, Manuel Bandeira is very "difficult"
to criticize. One must resist the temptation to make him more
facile than he really is, just as one must not make him more difficult than God made him. We should not forget that we deal
here with one of the greatest poets of the Brazilian language, at
his best moments; however, it is sometimes difficult to hide the
sizable proportion of offal which exists in the totality of his work.
Not everything in Manuel Bandeira is Manuel Bandeira; often
he is merely the "well-behaved" poet of whom Mário de Andrade
spoke. There are as many levels in his poetry as there are landings—literary, human, technical, and social—where the poet successively stationed himself. Criticism that was apt in 1924 is not
so in 1958, nor in 1964 after the publication of *Estrêla da Tarde*.
Not only is it not apt but also it may be in error, materially in
error, as focus, as judgment of the poet.

This does not mean that historically these judgments have
lost their value, nor that they were unjust in the face of the
"avenues" which the poet offered with *A Cinza das Horas, Libertinagem,* and the *Poesias Completas*. Of course, ultimate judgment can be made only in the light of his total work. In literary
life generally, except in cases of bad faith on the part of the judge,
the estimation of a contribution is made from the high points and
not from the totality, from the great creations and not from
exercises which merely maintain the esthetic vigor. But a writer
is not only a creator, he is also a history and a biography. He is a
projector of influences and a prism which receives them and
breaks them up into their proper rays. If Manuel Bandeira can
compose his poems in his sleep or in a state of trance, it is quite
simply because while awake he succeeded in assimilating his
"literary thing" in reading, daily life, correspondence with friends,
conversations and contacts. Nothing is gratuitous in the life of
the spirit; and in the life of poets, Valéry observed, if the gods
often spontaneously supply the first line of a poem, it is so that
the artisan may—with great pains—be able to bring forth the remaining lines. In the history of Brazilian literature, that poet who
will make a name for himself as a great poet must produce hundreds of great lines, an anthology of great poems. To what degree

this ability will add, or has added, to his stature is a subject which critics up till now have avoided.

All the greatness and the secret of Manuel Bandeira reside in the fact that for forty years he has been the *uomo qualunque* of Brazilian poetry. I do not mean to disparage his poetic eminence or limit him in any way that might be critically untenable. He was a contemporary of the great and noisy street revolutions in the Republic of Letters, and he came from the aristocracy of Symbolism to the gladiatorial bouts and comic interludes of Modernism; he dwelt with the most outlandish revolutionary schools and expressed the most disproportionate demands for the reform of poetic language, inaugurating in our country free verse but keeping always in the most polished form all his Parnassian virtuosities. A spectator—perhaps smiling and amused—of all the generations that succeeded one another and which one by one "invented" poetry, he was content to be what he was: slowly evolving with the seasons, perfecting his instrument, enriching his sensibility, living his poetry daily and sincerely, without ever posing—either as the St. John Baptist of Modernism or as the St. John of the literary apocalypses. It is in that sense that I see him as a *uomo qualunque,* as the poet who was pleased to write his work modestly and in solitude, capable of being interested in the literary fair while he kept intact, with visible obstinacy, his unmistakable personality. As a septuagenarian, he yielded to the influence of the more puerile divertissements of "concrete poetry." And with all that, he gained popularity at a late date: until recently his books were published at his own expense.

Manuel Bandeira very early attained prestige, and with it the responsibilities of a great official poet. I employ that expression more or less as do the English, who made of the political leadership of the opposition and of their poetic leadership two public positions ordained by the Crown and financed by the Treasury. The idea is something more than a mere figure of speech. It is well known that the National Congress, in one of its most just and highly applauded honors, conferred on Manuel Bandeira by way of extraordinary title a full pension, recognizing in the work and name of the poet one of those collective and national values in which nations like to see their reflection and for whom sufficient gratitude can never be shown. Thus was Manuel Bandeira transformed from *uomo qualunque* to National Bard. But he did not sing the Empire nor did he command legions; and if he marched on Rio, it was only because at that time Rio de Janeiro was still the necessary capital of intellectual life in Brazil.

National poet he is, more than any other writer, beyond the official consecration and literary glory with which he was crowned while he yet lived. Above all else, because of the scholastic, or revolutionary, or technical marginalism that he succeeded in maintaining, he prolonged his romantic lyricism and his Parnassian technique throughout those years most intolerantly Modernist or hermetic, concretist or linguistic. Only recently, without thinking specifically of Manuel Bandeira, I had occasion to point out those constants in our poetry, but the example of Manuel Bandeira irrefutably sanctions that point of view. His poetry is an example of the uninterrupted enrichment that literary history can offer to writers capable of distinguishing the transitory from the permanent and the substantial from the accessorial. And here we come to a circumstance in the poet's life which has been regarded as an "accident"—however sad—which has no real connection with his poetry: his tuberculosis.

Everyone knows that because of this illness Manuel Bandeira withdrew from the Polytechnic School and this turned his life in another direction, eventually toward poetry. But there is something here more profound: that is, facing poetry, Manuel Bandeira always behaved like the sick man facing tuberculosis, as Francisco de Assis Barbosa takes note, with humility. I would derive all poetic interpretation of Manuel Bandeira from a single line, the last line of the delicious "Auto-Retrato": "a professional consumptive." A professional consumptive, a professional poet. In contrast to the "amateur" consumptives (like Raul de Leoni), and to "amateur" poets, in love with the glories of salon and café, of clubs and lecture halls, of the exhibitionism of theories and multisyllabled words, Manuel Bandeira is the professional poet, creating his poetry with superb craftsmanship, "without family, religion, or philosophy," not only in literature but also in life. It was that craftsmanship which allowed him to retain all his keenness and even his romantic virtuosity. But the lyrical raw material, that natural expression of our poetic sentiment, saved him from falling into mechanical and vacant exercise or into an "impassiveness" equally artificial and labored. If in a famous line he stated that he was "fed up with well-behaved lyricism," it was only to manifest his own lyricism with more liberty. A provincial in his own province, he was also the provincial of the Brazilian literary province, zealous of his way of being, accepting the world and things with good fellowship as long as the world and things accepted him likewise.

Beyond giving him a professional "attitude" toward poetry, his illness freed Manuel Bandeira from that inhibiting love for his own province which becomes irritating provincialism, and from the excessive satisfaction with self which stunts the growth of so many young poets. The trip to Switzerland for his health gave him contact with the ecumenical in many of its guises. While Manuel Bandeira inspired a love of poetry in a young man named Eugène Grindel—later metamorphosed into Paul Éluard—his own poetic vocation had already been stimulated by that spiritual awakening which often occurs on long voyages. In the sanatorium Manuel Bandeira consciously learned how to live with his illness and, without realizing it, how to become a professional poet. A professional poet, besides, who learned how to ward himself against internationalism or cosmopolitanism without disdaining the ways of the world. Probably it was Europe and that super-Europe that is Switzerland that shaped him into a professional poet as he worked in his shop like an artisan, creating a poem with his very hands. He was, then, a national poet, a Gonçalves Dias of that twentieth-century Romanticism which was Modernism. As a national poet his tools were the same as those of the Romantic poets: amorous and sentimental lyricism as the substance of poetry, the simplicity of a poetry without mysteries or pretensions, a "colonial" Brazilianism, balance and even a certain prosaic quality, the absence of the impetuous and of hair-raising sublimity, the sense of belonging to a historical moment. He is not a "difficult" poet, and if he were a bit more tearful, he would no doubt have won a wider public. In fact, the support of a broad public is still denied him, although his popularity is gradually increasing.

There is another side to Manuel Bandeira, however, which isolates him from the people: his skepticism, his restraint, his irony. This "unsuccessful architect" brings from his courses in design a nostalgia for the classical, profound demands for balance and sobriety, and extreme horror in the face of excess and loss of composure. As to his classical side, which is his Parnassian side, he reins in his emotions, his lyricism, his anguish of the "man alone," his longing for the grand passion, in an art that is all understatement, often unperceived or disdained by the common reader. In order to be, from the popular point of view, the great national poet, the Gonçalves Dias of his time, Manuel Bandeira would require a bit more melodrama, a bit more theatricality, even (why not say it?) theatricality of the commonest sort.

He is nonetheless the poet, more than any other in our time, who has been smiled upon by fame in his full maturity, a man of such great presence that it is common to consider him as the very expression of modern poetry in Brazil. He is the poet who merited, while he was still alive, the honor of an edition of the kind usually reserved for our great dead writers: that civic monument in which are collected complete works, critical studies, hurried praises, anecdotes, family photographs, annotations, and critical observations. By a curious coincidence, that edition does not synthesize Manuel Bandeira. Because of the abundance of commentators, and the fragmentation of the "preliminary notes," the edition does not do justice to this poet who requires a greater effort at condensation, a greater critical "simplification." Still, the pathway has been opened to a broader acceptance of this poet by the reading public and greater appreciation of him as the national poet, the only one that Modernism produced.

Menotti del Picchia

It was Menotti del Picchia (1892–   ), and not Mário or Oswald de Andrade, who directed the first phase of Modernism. He came late to Modernism,[9] after having violently rejected the Movement in the press; and he came in through the wrong door, the door of Futurism. But in a Movement with so many "Pauline conversions," as Tristão de Athayde would have said, the zeal of the new Christians is all the more intransigent:

> Everything that is rebellion, independence, sincerity; everything that wages war on literary hypocrisy, false idols, obscurantism; everything that is beautiful, new, strong and daring fits into the good and broad conception of Futurism. I who was a hardened persecutor of those rebels, if I merely heard the name of Marinetti, was overtaken by a desire to strangle; my hands grasped like tongs. The reader, like me, surely prejudged the new school for the madness of its initial programs and for the hailing of potatoes and catcalls which the apostles of the new creed received at each demonstration of force . . . Today I am not so angry. Without admitting its insanities, without applauding its aberrations, I have come to admire its beauties. . . .[10]

In two years of intense journalistic propaganda, he regained all his lost time, and in November of 1922, in a review of *O Homem e a Morte,* the *Revista do Brasil* gave some idea of the importance its author had acquired:

> . . . considering the role played by Menotti in the Futurist campaign and the vigor with which he bears the standard of the school, such a book was awaited as the "Cromwell's preface" of this revolutionary esthetics. Up till now Futurism has limited itself to destruction and . . . promises. It has put on exhibit a few sample swatches which left us dissatisfied. But they came from small factories—such were the excuses offered. The Crespis and Mattarazzos had still not advertised their products.
>
> At last they are on view. On view with *Os Condenados* by Oswald de Andrade and with this present novel by Menotti.
>
> Profound disappointment. Solid, traditional books devoid of extravagance, respectful of nature and man as they are, respectful of the common psychology of reader and of language. Only one element distinguishes them: the talent with which they are made and the vigorous personality of the authors which they exhibit.

The traditionalists' "disappointment" was justified, in the sense that the first Modernist books (at least in prose), including those by Oswald de Andrade, contained nothing that might be labeled technical innovation. The important matter, however, was the relative obscurity of Mário de Andrade until a couple of years after the Week of Modern Art. It is significant that in reporting in detail all of its *festivals,* the *O Estado de São Paulo* had not made the slightest mention of the speech offered by Mário de Andrade in the foyer of the Municipal Theatre. Likewise, in criticizing the *Paulicéia Desvairada* in the pages of *Klaxon,* in November of 1922, Carlos Alberto de Araújo wrote, as we have seen: "His influence is now making itself felt, although it is still underground, in this literary movement of São Paulo." In the same way Henrique de Resende, criticizing Murilo Araújo's *A Iluminação da Vida* in *Verde,* number 3 (November, 1927), observed in passing: "The moderns, always advancing, one fine day left Mr. Graça and Mr. Ronald by the wayside, two splendid examples among the great precursors. They went haywire for a spell without a leader, even newer, more distinct and different, if also more offbeat. Finally they found their true expression: Mário de Andrade . . ."

Mário himself, still in the pages of *Klaxon,* wrote the review of *O Homem e a Morte,* placing it in the harvest season of the "revolutionary artistic movement which was enunciated some two years past" (article of December 1922–January 1923). Along with *Os Condenados* by Oswald de Andrade and the *Epigramas Irônicos e Sentimentais* by Ronald de Carvalho, Menotti del Picchia's books seemed to him ample proof that Modernism was at last beginning to bear fruit. Although later Mário de Andrade had lamented the enthusiasm with which he wrote about a novel which had nothing to do with Modernism, nor was indeed even a good novel, the truth is that he indirectly confirms the idea that it just might be the "Cromwell's preface" of the new school. He probably did not mean to say that such books were at heart "traditionalist," but he did accentuate the fact that in all the literature produced up to that date, *Paulicéia Desvairada* occupied a position apart:

There may be some who think that out of modesty I did not cite *Paulicéia Desvairada.* . . . I did not cite it because I ought not to do so. *Paulicéia* (as I think, moreover, all my work will be) possesses a quality so special, so hallucinated, so extra, that it cannot have any plausible effect in working a renovation. Its savage character, proudly personal, robs it of that expression of humanity, of a universal and cosmic thing which permits development and assimilation. One can follow the orbit of the suns. It would be nonsense to attempt to accompany the trajectory of meteors.

There are signs in Mário de Andrade's letters to Manuel Bandeira that indicate that he had little faith in the sincerity of Menotti del Picchia's Modernism. That distrust, which an analysis of his work came to confirm, is explicit from the first moment in criticisms and evaluations of Menotti's books. The *Revista do Brasil* itself, in May of 1923, felt it necessary to return to *O Homem e a Morte,* and this time to state:

> This singular writer and poet is the leader of the new school which bears the name of Futurism, whose adepts have shown themselves to be in violent opposition to the *vieux jeux* literati whom they call traditionalists. But it was whispered about that Senhor Del Picchia was playing both ends against the middle: he remained traditionalist in his literature so he would not lose the readers that he had won by dint of hard work and talent, and in public he declared himself a Futurist in order to stay on good terms with the noisy group and merit their applause.

Menotti del Picchia himself, in a novel of 1931, *A Tormenta,* gave involuntary and indirect confirmation—and for that reason all the more significant—of that attitude: "He [Paul, the main character] along with his friends had undertaken a violent revolution in the arts; they had scandalized the city with the carnival prank of an exhibition of nonsense which had stimulated the theatrical exhibitionism of all those hams. His friends exploited that snobbish ambition with an honest and profound objective: to drag a vicious and unoriginal tradition through the mud and seek, in the spoils of that barbaric job, the esthetic and racial truths which he imagined had not yet been revealed." [11] It is in light of these statements that we should read what Mário de Andrade wrote to Manuel Bandeira:

> As for my opinions regarding *O Homem e a Morte,* they are opinions I no longer hold so forcefully, that is logical, and just so that I will not give rise to apparently greater proofs of immorality and cynicism, I must keep quiet. Are my proofs wrong? I don't think so. They're exaggerated. I was never blind where Menotti was concerned, and more than ever I support his intellectual and creative value. I have all my life been the systematic defender of Menotti as a literary value, and I have ample proof of my honorable conduct because

even now [after] what I wrote about him in *Terra Roxa,* the revolt, sincere and stronger than I, with which I have defended him against flippant and imperfect judgments which now surround me, doesn't come from any pretentions to spiritual elegance but is a profoundly honest judgment . . . The marvelous facility of intellectual adaptation which Menotti has, the wealth and vivacity of his intelligence, and the almost inevitable constant falsification of himself that this produces leads you people also to remain immune both to him and to his work . . . I was the great defender of Menotti on the occasion of the appearance of *O Homem e a Morte;* I had a furious and constant battle with his very friends who, incidentally, knew all about the conditions under which he writes, the fatal conditions of the need to sustain an inglorious battle against hunger in the home. And the result, in the face of the intensity of that battle I waged in defense of Menotti, resides in the exasperated exaggeration with which I stated, in my criticism in *Klaxon,* my admiration for him and for his work.[12]

More or less at the same period of that letter (on the occasion of the publication of *Chuva de Pedra*), Mário Guastini also wrote: "Menotti's literature, poetry, and journalism are not always sincere. Abusing his powerful talent, the sparkling columnist who wrote *Pão de Moloch* changes his ideas, his style, and his schools with amazing facility. . . . He is a traditionalist, when traditionalism is in style; he is a Futurist, when Futurism is in vogue . . . He will be an enthusiastic adept of the school of Silence, when silence becomes a literary school . . . Those sudden changes, considered by many to be the fruit of his artistic development, are on the contrary offspring of his insincerity." [13] The entire article demonstrates, by alluding to facts of literary history, the doctrinary vacillation of Menotti del Picchia. In reality he never ceased to be the Parnassian spirit who signed *Juca Mulato;* and, in an attempt to explain his vast variations at a time when a single volume of *Poesias* contained them all (1958), he wrote: "What one sees, then, in the succession of verses contained in this volume is unrest, irreverence, research, nonconformity, and a desire for constant renovation" (a note of 1947). The truth is that this "unrest" did not always project him forward; often it forced him to retreat. The old Futurist, when he wrote the novel of the Revolution of 1924, condemned warlike violence: it is clear to see that, for him, war was not "the sole hygiene of the world"; likewise, he never adopted the postulate of the First Futurist Manifesto: "we shall sing of the multi-colored and polyphonic tide of revolutions in modern capital cities"; and, to judge by the importance of moonlight in all of his work—in prose or in poetry—he obviously did not write with Marinetti: "let us kill the moonlight."

Even in *Chuva de Pedra,* a book of Modernist poetry, the moon and moonlight play an important role, always with Parnassian treatment. So, for example, "Festa Noturna":

> I think there is a Venetian *fête* in the mud puddle
> in honor of Our Lady New Moon.
>
> .   .   .   .   .
>
> And the phosphorine crescent sails
> in the dead water of the bog,
> dogal barge in a Venetian canal.[14]

In a wider perspective, Menotti del Picchia can be regarded only as a typical descendant: the descendant of all the schools in which he took part, including Parnassianism. *A República dos EE. UU. do Brasil* (1928) represents in Modernist poetry the invasion of a patriotism more directly political and certainly ingenuous—along the lines of Greengiltism which he then represented along with Plínio Salgado and Cassiano Ricardo. It is in that book that we encounter with surprise such lines as these:

> Lady, by all that's holy, be not mine
> for the good that I long for is an ill for us both.[15]

But we are less surprised when farther on we find a defense of the sonnet. That explains why, with *Poemas do Meu Amor,* in 1927 he returned to intimacy or poetic dimness, which constituted the semi-Parnassian form of Symbolism or the Symbolist form of

Brazilian Parnassianism, the tendency most congenial to Menotti's own spirit. His best poem of this type was "Piedosa Mentira," which is no doubt among the very best of the poetry produced by that kind of inspiration in Brazil.

His Modernist poems sometimes, though fragmentarily, reach heights like this selection from "Cenário":

> How I loved thee, picturesque America
> and tragic in your violent morn
> proclaimed by caravelles,
> roused by libertarian chiefs
> by cassocks and captains-general!

This was soon compromised by an unfortunate penchant for high-flown, banal, Lusitanian rhetoric:

> The Latin sun
> shone on the Lusitanian morn
> resounding with muskets and sobbing guitars
> and your sea-faring lover,
> son of the Bachelor and of Paraguaçu,
> with pioneer foot carved out the frontiers
> of the greatest American homeland.

This school-boy patriotism breaks its reins in an irrepressible form:

> I shall sing on my lyre [16]
> the millionaire wealth and the extraordinary beauty
> of my native land!

It is not surprising, then, that Bento Pires, a character in the novel by Eduardo Frieiro, *O Clube dos Grafômanos* (1927), summed up the matter in the following appraisal: "The writer Menotti del Picchia is a Modernist, notwithstanding the fact that his most avid readers number among the traditionalists."

Guilherme de Almeida

Literary history, which always handles matters in a proper fashion, deemed that in 1930 Guilherme de Almeida (1890–1969) should be the first poet of the Modernist group to be admitted to the Brazilian Academy. Thus the Academy reaffirmed, instead of disclaiming, the expulsion of Graça Aranha and Modernism because the *paulista* poet, as Mário de Andrade had been saying at least since the publication of *Meu* (1925), had never really belonged to the Movement. He was an Impressionist within the Expressionist generation, the continuator of an inspiration which, proceeding from Mário Pederneiras, found cultivators of the stamp of Raul de Leoni, Ribeiro Couto, Ronald de Carvalho, Manuel Bandeira, and even Carlos Drummond de Andrade. Although the problem still has not been sufficiently studied, the truth is that around 1925 Brazilian critics were fully aware of the existence of a "twilight school." Thus writing in *Estética,* number 2 (January–March, 1925), Rodrigo M. F. de Andrade stated:

Senhor Ribeiro Couto now constitutes a chapter in our literary history. Around his book, as around Constantinople, the first foreboding battles of the modern era were waged. If it cannot properly be said that he was the initiator of the abolitionist movement in our national poetry, it is at least certain that he inspired the first epithet with which the artists of the new generation were baptized. From his "twilight poetry," as Ronald de Carvalho called it, came the adjective *twilightist*, first applied to any poet who went elsewhere than to the rhyming dictionary to make his verses.

It is precisely these rhymes that burgeon like a force of nature in the poems of Guilherme de Almeida. However, before we go on to that part of the question, it might be well to recall that Carlos Drummond de Andrade published two "twilightist" or Impressionist poems in *Estética*, number 3 (April–June, 1925). One of them, "Construção":

A shout leaps in the air like a skyrocket.
It comes from the landscape of damp earth, debris and
/rigid scaffolding.
The sun falls on things like boiling metal.

An ice cream vendor cuts the street.

And the wind plays in the construction worker's moustaches.[17]

Of course, the Guilherme de Almeida of *Meu* is closer to Ronald de Carvalho than he is to Carlos Drummond de Andrade or to Mário Pederneiras; but it was precisely with regard to the *Epigramas Irônicos e Sentimentais* that Mário de Andrade, enthusiastic admirer of Guilherme de Almeida, wrote: "Since I have mentioned twilightism, let me mention the only drawback which I see in the book. Tinges of twilightism, true gray streaks in pink marble, here and there sully several pages in the *Epigramas*." [18]

Besides being an Impressionist in a generation of Expressionists, Guilherme de Almeida was a born, instinctive Parnassian in a generation of free-versifiers (many of whom wrote free verse purely and simply because they had no talent for regular verse). In that regard Mário de Andrade criticized *Meu*, noting that it had been an error on the part of the poet to employ free verse: the "intellectual lyricism" that it implied served only to show that he got along as badly in free verse as many others do in regular metrics: "In the face of that virtuosity and that perfectly admissible and free idea of metrical poetry, Guilherme did not need to abandon meter for free verse. It was an illusion of modernity which led him to that sacrifice of writing a kind of free verse that is positively wrong, in my opinion. Verse such as that contained in the *Canções Gregas* and the *Meu* is not absolutely free verse. It is an arbitrary verse totally devoid of meaning: psychological, phraseological, or rhythmical."

But is it possible to say that *Meu* did not contain one of the potential germs of Modernist poetry? The Movement, when it chose the path of revolutionary challenge and destructive tactics, may have truncated a more natural evolution, which would have passed from the addled Symbolism which we had to the Modernist poetry which we never got. As far as *poetry* was concerned, we were very rich in *modernist* poetic values. Our poetry passed over the gentle bridge prepared by the Ronald de Carvalhos and the Guilherme de Almeidas, who were immediately cast by the Modernists into the outer darkness where, incidentally, they found the shining palace of the Academy. Things probably would have followed that path had all depended exclusively on Mário de Andrade; but, at that point in time, Oswald de Andrade was already keeping an eye on the whole matter. We could observe them, the former as a *renovative* force and the latter as a *revolutionary* force, operating within Modernism. Probably Brazilwood poetry would have been like this, had Oswald de Andrade never existed:

> How beautiful is my land!
> Foreigner, see that palm tree how lovely it is:
> it's like a column straight straight straight
> like a great green peacock hovering on point
> his tail spread like a fan
>   And in the round shadow
> upon the warm earth . . .
>   (Silence!)
>   . . . there is a poet.[19]

Just as we can speculate that Ronald de Carvalho might have
been Modernism's best indoctrinator, the most able and capable
of making it acceptable to the general reading public, it is also
licit to suppose that Guilherme de Almeida possessed the necessary qualities to make him the model Modernist poet. All of this,
of course, had the Week of Modern Art not occurred as an event
in which both poets incidentally took part. They are writers of
an evolutionary spirit, more given to surprise than to challenge.
Meu is one possible example of a classicism that is both Modernist and successful. But obviously all of this would be so only if we
could accept the paradox of a "conservative and academic Modernism" like "As Danças" in which one does not know whether
to prefer the "Maxixe":

> The rattle of the toads croaks
> like a scraped *caracaxá*. Everything moves.

or the "Cateretê":

> hoedown
>> shindig
>>> hoochy-kooch.
> Whopping drops leap through the brown roof tiles

or the "Samba":

>>> And the samba booms
>> bursts
>>> rumbles
>>> bombards.[20]

Still, nothing pointed up the true antagonism, or at least the
alienation, existing between Guilherme de Almeida and Modernism as did the pages of doctrine collected in *Natalika*. It is quite
enough to say that he invoked his "beloved Wilde," his "lovely

Wilde," whom two years before in one of the inaugural addresses of the Week of Modern Art Menotti del Picchia, in his convert's zeal, wished specifically to kill: Let's kill Verlaine, that despondent Wilde, that psychopath Zola, that butcher Farrère, that frock-coated Ohnet, that milksop Géraldy . . .

   Géraldy, indeed!

Ronald de Carvalho

Mário de Andrade was displeased with the cosmopolitan estheticism of Ronald de Carvalho (1893–1935), with his tendencies to popularize, with the touch of Graça Aranha he had within him—perhaps without wanting it. "Ronald needs to stop being the man-who-delivers-lectures," Mário wrote to Manuel Bandeira with regard to one of the volumes of *Estudos Brasileiros*. But it was precisely because he was "delivering lectures" that he would have made the ideal apostle *ad gentiles* of Modernism, had his relationships with the revolutionaries not been so distant and cold from the very beginning.

It is not without reason that he was attracted to the diplomatic career: Ronald de Carvalho was of an aristocratic temperament and—without being captious—a bit "salonesque." Besides that, his critical sensibility would have kept him from accepting without some mental reservations the carnival-like contingencies of Modernism. In addition, it so happens that at the time of the Week of Modern Art he was already a writer of some renown, something like a literary dictator. At least, this is how Tasso da Silveira sees him in retrospect in an article on Modernism written for a special edition of the *Revista Branca*: "A diplomat who employs Itamarati as a backdrop, a man of high civilization, a writer and poet of breeding, Ronald has long since caused the prestige and renown of other poets to pale." [21] In the budding company of unknown youths who were responsible for the Week of Modern Art, he was, along with Graça Aranha, the respected writer attempting to tutor his younger companions, exerting himself to enlist Modernism in the eternal ranks of Western literature.

But it is precisely because of his abilities as a popularizer, his universal culture, his sensitive balance, that he might have been (and was, to a certain degree) the best theoretician of the Movement, the man who immediately inspired confidence. It was during the Week of Modern Art, as we have seen, that the *O Estado de São Paulo* could not conceal its surprise when it learned through Ronald de Carvalho's lecture that Modernism was not intellectual bolshevism. In fact, of all the manifestoes, the best synthesis, the one that forecast concretely all that Modernism would come to be, was his article "A Revolta dos Anjos":

The evil angels are rebelling against:

(a) crabbed grammatical pedants, incapable of understanding the true scope of philology, of that profound metaphysics of language, who give themselves over to futile squabbles and are ignorant of the fact that language is an instrument constantly changing and jeering at the efforts of all those who labor uselessly to rob it of its virile impetus;

(b) the survivors of Parnassianism and Arcadianism who have reduced our literature to a puzzle by S. Prudhomme. Heredia, Petrarch, Sá de Miranda, etc. Poetry was reduced to formula and weak-kneed poetics. With no *rime riche,* no rhymes for support, no acutes or graves, no golden key, poetry had no recourse to law, it was devaluated coin. Only the fops with their sonnets got the goodies . . .

(c) superficial, shy virtuosity, collector of busts (especially of Dante, Plato, Eça de Queiroz, and Camilo the notorious), that virtuosity that is wild about Bataille and calls Anatole France just plain Anatole, as if one were beckoning to a hotel porter, that makes versions of the Latins and Greeks translated by Leconte de Lisle;

(d) borrowed regionalism, the companion in bookstore profits of cheap pornography, proper and admirable when it is spontaneous but pernicious when it is elevated to a literary system because it would end up by lowering Brazil to the rudimentary level of plantations and slave huts;

(e) the precocious old-age of despondent youths and the sly obstinacy of retrograde old men who, with their little rules and tics which they picked up abroad, would like to direct and orient the spirit of men who, on reaching the age of reason, were amazed at having been their own masters.[22]

As a poet, and therein reflecting one of the profound tendencies of Modernism which was immediately stifled, he takes his place on the American plane rather than on the Brazilian plane. And here we find a particular semantic misunderstanding: Ronald de Carvalho encountered in Whitman, as is well known, the great master of telluric poetry; therefore, he also wanted *to sing America*. But the truth is that when Whitman sang America, he sang his own country, or rather he did something very like what the "Brazilianists" in Modernism were doing. On his part, when Ronald de Carvalho "sang America" he fled the geographical and spiritual borders of his country to create a kind of continental poetry which the North American poet had never even vaguely conceived and which, as a matter of fact, was alien to him. Be that as it may, the document which reflects that tendency was *Tôda a América* (1926) in which, as in the last chapter of the *Pequena História da Literatura Brasileira* (composed for the 1925 edition), he opposed not Brazil but America to Europe:

> European!
> On the chessboards of your village,
> in your wooden house, tiny, ivy-covered,
>
> .   .   .   .   .
>
> you cannot know what it is to be American! [23]

The first poem in the book is "Brasil," frankly Whitmanesque in tone; the others are American "portraits" which correspond

frankly and felicitously to the title of the volume. He was the first
to introduce into Brazilian poetry certain themes heavy with feeling through the simple invocation of place names: Trinidad, the
Antilles, Barbados, Broadway, Tonalá, the *pampas*. However, what
lies behind that far-ranging geography is a new world stirring and
evolving. The poem "Tôda a América" expresses such a sentiment:

> America of coffee plantations, of rubber forests, and of
> /cane brakes,
> America of locomotives and oxcarts, of elevators
> and cranes, of peroba gates and the floodgates
> of Pittsburgh chrome steel
>
> .   .   .   .   .
>
> Where are your poets, America?
> Where are they who do not understand your voluptuous
> /noons,
> your hammocks heavy with eurythmic bodies, which
> sway in the damp shadows.[24]

The *Pequena História da Literatura Brasileira*, which possessed a pre-Modernist and cosmopolitanizing balance, is suddenly
transformed, through the last chapter written for the third edition,
into the first history of Brazilian literature to reflect the Modernist idea. Ronald de Carvalho ended his history with the following
words:

> The modern man of Brazil, in order to create a literature
> of his own, ought to avoid every kind of preconception. He
> has before his eyes a great virgin world filled with exciting
> promises. To organize that material, give it stability, reduce
> it to its true human expression: these should be his basic
> preoccupations. An art direct and pure, deeply rooted in our
> national structure, an art which will secure the tumult of
> our people in gestation, that is what the modern man of
> Brazil ought to seek. To that end, it is meet that he should
> study not only Brazilian problems but also the grand Amer-
> ican problem. The primordial error of our elite up till

now has been their insistence on applying artificially the European lesson to Brazil. We have reached the hour of our American lesson. We have at last come into our own time.

Tôda a América and this chapter of literary history were in the end Ronald de Carvalho's Modernist will and testament. Because he died in 1935, he never saw the "second Modernism" which to a large extent came to fulfill, unintentionally and unwittingly, a part of his program.

Oliveira Viana

In the first of a series of six articles, I wrote in the *O Estado de São Paulo* of July 16, 1949, that Oliveira Viana (1883–1951) indisputedly marked with his work twenty fertile and productive years of Brazilian intellectual life. To him we owe not all the modern orientation of our sociological studies or of our social psychology, but at least the impulse that transformed that area of our researches, stamping it with the vitality that today identifies it. Since the publication of *Populações Meridionais do Brasil* in 1920, his books have always epitomized a state of mind which was perhaps only embryonic in our scholars of other periods. His studies have always marked the face of Brazilian culture at any given moment. If we leave aside *O Idealismo na Evolução Política do Império e da República* (1920), which is today included in *O Idealismo da Constituição* (1938), his writings are titled: *Pequenos Estudos de Psicologia Social* (1921), *Evolução do Povo Brasileiro* (1923), *O Ocaso do Império* (1925), *Problemas de Política Objetiva* (1930), and *Raça e Assimilação* (1932). This cites only those that adhere most closely to matters of social and political history (which in his mind amounted to the same thing). Well out of the "Modernist era," he published *Instituições Políticas Brasileiras* in 1949. In this, he explained, all his researches were completed and rounded off, in so far as what he called "the deep strata of history and also the proto-history of our institutions of public law" were concerned.

It is generally admitted that *Populações Meridionais do Brasil, Evolução do Povo Brasileiro,* and *Raça e Assimilação* are his outstanding books, those in which his fundamental ideas appear, and also those which best show him off as a writer. This is not the proper place to analyze his thought on the scientific level; it is more important to attempt to characterize him and measure his influence on the intellectual climate of Modernism.

In the twenties, Oliveira Viana was considered in intellectual circles to be our greatest thinker. His name appeared and reappeared for all purposes in our articles on criticism and doctrine. It is unnecessary to recall the immense success that immediately surrounded the *Populações Meridionais do Brasil* or the *Evolução do Povo Brasileiro.* The fact of the matter was that he had the longed-for answer to the two most profound problems of the national mind at that time: in the first place, the affirmation of our social aristocracy concealed beneath the appearance of a miscegenation which, at that time, constituted our national shame (recall the words of Graça Aranha with regard to the mestizo); in the second place, the doctrinaire bases for the political inclinations—if not exclusively rightist, at least undeniably totalitarian—which matured after 1927 and blossomed into Integralism in 1932 and the Estado Nôvo in 1937. It is well known that, like Farias Brito on the philosophical plane, Oliveira Viana was considered along with Alberto Tôrres, on the political and institutional plane, the great precursor of the nationalist and corporative ideas which lay at the base of those two conservative movements, one successful, the other unsuccessful. It was precisely as a kind of Giovanni Gentile of the 1937 regime that he lived out his last years of intellectual and scientific decline (but years of considerable political esteem) in the area of ideas as well as in the bureaucratic sphere.

On one level or another, the secret of his success lies in the fact that he considered all problems from an idealizing perspective in which the Brazilian seems to be able to re-discover himself. Just as nature abhors a vacuum, the Brazilian abhors realism of

the spirit and objective analysis. For that very reason, in defending his Aryanizing and aristocratic theses, the mestizo Oliveira
Viana probably surmounted intimate problems which it is not
our place to analyze; but at the same time he was certain to interpret not Brazilian reality, but Brazilians as they would like to be,
as they like to be seen. In that regard *Casa Grande & Senzala* was
directly and indirectly a reply to Oliveira Viana; and, along these
lines we verify once again, as we have already observed, that this
was a matter of a representative work of the Modernist era. By
reinstating miscegenation and the mestizo, Gilberto Freyre reflected a new intellectual climate in force in the thirties, resulting
from the realistic anguish of the twenties. As was natural, Freyre's
books served to justify and, therefore, to fortify the anti-Aryaniz-
ing and anti-aristocratic reaction which stamps the vision of Brazil
in the second Modernist period.

In 1958, on the occasion of the issue of unpublished writings,
which family sentiment or his friends had collected under the title
of *Introdução à História Social da Economia Pré-Capitalista no
Brasil,* and in which Oliveira Viana openly devoted himself to
the defense of the aristocratic thesis, I had the opportunity of syn-
thesizing his global orientation:

> But, if there still remained a great deal to say about the
> luxuriousness and refinement of the Portuguese *fidalgos* who
> moved to Brazil (at least in the first century of colonization—
> and here I establish a question of chronology to which I
> shall later refer), much more serious is the error in vision
> committed by Oliveira Viana as he studies the history of our
> aristocracy. That mistake can be summarized in a single
> word which, moreover, defines his entire work: *idealization.*
> More than a sociologist, more than a social historian, Oliveira
> Viana was the "essayist" of Sociology, of Social History in a
> sense more or less parallel and extensive than is proper to
> attribute to that word: he saw facts through the prism of
> special values and he is, *par excellence,* a thesis writer. It
> would not be fair to say that his work did not make a posi-
> tive contribution to the study and interpretation of our
> past: on the contrary, his observations were acute and stimu-
> lating and, in many cases, they felicitously revealed essential

aspects of Brazilian social history, and they have always served—even when they lacked foundation and were inexact —to provoke a search for the proper view of the problems. Most especially his observations stimulated study of the problems. If his basic theses seem unacceptable to me (even in his most significant books), I do not conclude from that fact that his labors were futile. On the whole, I grant him the inestimable value of having committed the "useful error," the "constructive error," of such great importance in the history of ideas. In the realm of thought every book is a thesis book: it happens merely that certain theses reveal greater vitality or more visible agreement with the facts; they reveal, in a word, greater objectivity. Oliveira Viana's theses, in general, are characterized by their ideal quality, by their detachment from fact: he does not write; for the most part he re-makes social history. Like every bourgeois, like every petit-bourgeois, he nurtured an iron-clad vision of the aristocracy and he desired for his country an aristocratic past. He is the writer of the grandeur of the daily, of imaginary grandeur, without the complement of misery. He is the observer who, because he suffers from an incurable ocular disease, could see only the "essence" and could not see the "existence." [25]

Nonetheless, it is undeniable that all the "idealism" of the twenties—expressed in successive military rebellions, in a renewed interest in Brazil, in the multiple proposition of the so-called "necessary reforms," in short, in what we might call by a recent word, "developmentism"—found in Oliveira Viana its prophet and its most stimulating indoctrinator. Even the Modernists, who were by definition Oliveira's enemies, could not resist his fascination: through the gateway of *Populações Meridionais* or of *Evolução do Povo Brasileiro* there passed into Brazil all the ambitious sociological studies which we know from the thirties.

Mário de Andrade

The complex literary personality of Mário de Andrade (1893–1945)[26] has still not shared with us all its secrets. Quite the contrary. In spite of the numerous partial studies which have been devoted to him—and, to a degree, because of them—it would not be difficult to support the apparent paradox that in the annals of Brazilian literature he continues to be the great unknown. A careful sorting of these studies would show that the greater part of them are repetitious; a great many others, expressly destined to praise the incomparable master, have little critical value. Thus the writer who has probably inspired the most admiration as well as the greatest sarcasm, who has prompted the most laudatory pages or the most furious attacks, remains in our literature virtually an enigma. And so much the better.

We might add to this the fact that his polymorphism has contributed no little to the difficulties that he presents as a literary theme, much to the bewilderment of critical studies. Essayist and fiction writer, critic of literature and music, treatise writer and researcher in folklore, poet and theoretician of art, withdrawn and studious in his creations and vigorous in literary battle,[27] Mário de Andrade is a writer who, in his multiple fragmentation, nonetheless resists mutilation. It might well be that the secret of a proper critical analysis of him rests in accepting his complexity, or it may lie in a serious effort to apprehend at once all the facets of his personality which are not mutually exclusive but rather complementary to one another. Criticism of him up till now has strayed little from the idea that it is not only possible but essential to distinguish his *faculté maîtresse*. Now, from all indications Mário de Andrade might well give the lie to Taine and show himself to be a writer without *faculté maîtresse*.[28] His main *faculté* would be himself, having the greatest freedom within himself. His critical essays are "constructed" like pages of fiction, but this does not keep him from giving them here and there a poetic vision of things. In his poetry the critical and political contingent is worthy of consideration.

If he wrote criticism like an artist—not in the usual meaning of the expression, which seems unacceptable to me, but rather because he felt himself more integrated in the art that he criticized than in the criticism that he practiced like a work of art—it is no less certain that rarely do his artistic creations appear without some hint or other of critical intention. The proof is that only his relatively less important pages are "gratuitous"—and even at that I should not like to risk the statement that this occurs in all cases. At any rate, pressed by the incomparable lucidity of his self-criticism, he himself observed on a certain occasion: "In the midst of my writing, always so filled with intention, the newspaper column was only a brief moment of repose, the true escape valve through which I took a good rest from myself. Also, it is true that I never gave to this more importance than the brief moment, during which I played at writing it, seemed to merit."

That inextricable interpenetration of genres, which harmonize finally to constitute his admirable personality, cannot be torn apart if we wish to understand him in his authenticity and in his true greatness. In my opinion, those who take pains to show that in him the poet was greater than the critic or the critic more interesting than the fiction writer are in error. Although he himself, as we shall see, has fallen into that trap, it is not possible to consider his protean qualities as other than an indissoluble unity. So thoroughly is this true that we find him in all his spontaneity in each of the genres that he practiced, and his qualities as a writer and artisan are always the same. Even more: in a general way, all his several qualities are balanced when seen as a whole. It is impossible and evidently wrong to see in Mário de Andrade a poet who by accident practiced the other genres or a critic gnawed by the ambition to write creative literature. In such cases the difference in quality between the "vocationed" pages and the others immediately tells the truth about a writer. With Mário de Andrade, that difference simply does not appear. He is always the same: in his short stories, in his criticism, in his poetry. He is not a Victor Hugo attempting to write a novel, nor a Sainte-Beuve trying his hand at poetry, nor a Balzac attempting criticism. His creative impulse—whatever his limitations may be—is genuinely the same in all his books and on all his pages. Whatever his limitations may be . . . In effect, we know nothing definite about Mário de Andrade. His human presence is still too strong, too moving, for us to approach him with the cold instruments of critical analysis. There is no Brazilian writer of these last forty years who has not felt his human presence outside of literature. And here we pinpoint a fact that is essential for the proper comprehension of his historical role. It is that Mário de Andrade was also, more than any other Brazilian writer of any period, a *presence*. The presence of a man identified by his warmth, by his winning laughter, by that kind of angelic innocence which was observed in him on one occasion. A presence that, without the slightest intention of indulging in literary "politics," sacrificed to this end an enormous amount of time that might better have been spent on personal tasks, prompted by a sensibility which led him to write long letters to obscure or unknown beginners; or to discuss with his companions in literary adventure, in letters no less extensive, the crucial problems at that time heatedly debated.[29]

The problems. Here is the key word for the comprehension of Mário de Andrade. Literary and artistic matters were always that and only that to him: a problem. A problem that he did not approach with the usual dilettantish detachment, but a problem that he felt within himself, that filled him with personal anguish and dragged him along against his own best interests, against his dearest friendships. That is why this shy man was able to meet head-on all the "storms of ridicule"; that is why this sensitive and affectionate man faced the painful condemnation of his family, of his friends, in behalf of an idea, of *his* idea, I mean, of his personal authenticity. That is why, at heart, the totality of his work is after all an immense question, a question that overflowed in him, that demanded an answer, and that he often transferred to the common ground of collective debates. Even here we can invoke his own testimony: "The other day in an article I wrote down, as I frequently do, some half-extravagant ideas, ideas that I'm not too certain of, just to see the reactions they would awaken and the fate they would suffer in their struggle for life." Or again in the foreword to *Losango Cáqui*:

> However, I ask that this book be taken as a question, not even as a solution that I think is transitory. I have dedicated this entire admirable life that I lead to a quest. God grant that I shall never reach my goal. That would mean finding rest in this life, a stoppage more odious than death. All my works, with their true meaning, I don't even show as possible passing solutions. They are quests. They consecrate and perpetrate this delicious anguish of searching. This is and, I imagine, always will be my work: curiosity on the way to satisfaction.

This attitude, in a concrete way, gives unity to his work and demonstrates the truth of what I said about his structural "totality," about the difficulty of separating his several parts into hierarchies. Thus, regarding his *Poesias Completas*,[30] it can be argued that in the "fertile expansion of creative individualities," as the publisher states, that of a poet stands out above the rest. That, however, was not the opinion of Mário de Andrade himself (and here we draw attention to the "error" I mentioned earlier). In the melancholy evaluation of Modernism, which he pronounced in 1942, he spoke of having horribly deformed his life: "I abandoned—a conscious treachery—fiction in favor of the role of a man-of-studies which, fundamentally, I am not." In his work as a whole it was the fiction writer that he isolated as the most genuine expression of himself. We must admit, in the broadest possible acceptance of the word, that we may include the role of poet

within the other role. We hold, then, that he believed himself to
be more "creator" than "critic," although in practice he may
have been more "critic" than "creator." Not only because he
practiced the several criticisms throughout his career as a writer,
but also because his own fiction, his own poetry—as we have established—are filled with criticism. Mário de Andrade created by
criticizing and criticized by creating, whether in the practice of
objective criticism—directed against circumstances external to himself—or whether in the exercise of subjective criticism—in in-
cessant research on virtualities and on the techniques of their
means of expression. Craftsmanship was as important to him
as imagination; craftsmanship is, after all, in large part a critical
task applied to a creative work.

So, in the poet Mário de Andrade, the critic of the future
must necessarily distinguish between the creator and the experimenter, the sensitive man and the artist curious to know the
exact limits of his artistry. As those limits are deceptive and elastic
and correspond in art to the line of the horizon—which cannot be
located anywhere—it may be concluded that that fruitful existence
never interrupted his researches and that many of his "creations"
were the direct result of his study. All of this, of course, does not
in the least prejudice the essence of his "poetic idea." Those who
require concrete examples to understand him may read, among
other pieces, poems XXXIII and XXXIII No. 2 in *Losango
Cáqui*.[31] The first, published in *Klaxon,* had inspired hilarious
laughter:

> My profound delight before the morning Sun
>   carnival life . . .
>   Friends
>   Loves
>   Laughter
> Little immigrant children surround me begging for pictures
> of movie stars, the ones that come on cigarette packs.
> I feel like the Assumption of Murillo!
>
> I'm free now of the pain . . .
> But I'm all atremble with the joy of living
>   That is why my soul is still impure.

Then the poet, as a joke, garbed his ideas and sensations in the dress of this sonnet:

Plato! I'd have my wish and follow thee,
Of joy and pain my soul I'd liberate
And like Chimera's gods all pure I'd be
Which she beyond this life did fabricate!

But how shall I reject this blissful state
Beneath this golden morn of spring be free
When carnal woman does so irritate
This madding love of joy I feel in me!

Oh lovely life! Oh theories dreamed in vain!
Then let my body shine a thousandfold
Beneath the mantle of my austere brain!

'Twixt concord and perfumes I walk the lane,
I bless, while cursing loud the sage of old,
The divine lewdness of my soul, my bane.[32]

It is the same poem, except that the second one was written "as a joke." Mário de Andrade tried to show to those who identify poetry with verse that the one has nothing to do with the other and that, therefore, the sincere admirers of the sonnet were obligated likewise to admire the composition in free verse. In a way he was teaching his readers how to read poetry. Obviously, an "experiment" like this can only be made with poems that really contain poetry; unfortunately, not all of the "modern" poets could pass such a test and come out unscathed. Against such "poets" the critic Mário de Andrade never ceased writing.[33]

It is impossible to deny in the face of that example and so many others that Mário de Andrade sacrificed in part, in his poetic work, the creator for the experimenter. His preoccupation with innovation, and that attitude of defiance, which was educed by Modernism and corresponded in no way to his deepest nature, took root in him like a habit or vice and in many cases worked to the detriment of his poetic expression. Here is the most delicate and at the same time the most important point in a study of the poet. It will not always be possible, evidently, to distinguish the poet from the artisan and the creator from the revolutionary, but there are sufficient examples in his work to attempt an analysis of that type. Its importance lies in the obvious necessity of knowing the exact nature of his poetry and in the additional proof it will afford us of the correctness of the ideas expounded at the beginning of this outline study.

Among his books we would choose *Paulicéia Desvairada* as a document of Modernism; *Losango Cáqui* as an example of research into craft; and *Lira Paulistana* (published posthumously, after the Modernist era) as an example of an exclusively poetic creation, as that work in which the writer surrendered most openly, most "innocently" to the yearnings of his sensibility. As a creator of poetry, Mário de Andrade will be remembered above all as a lyricist (the *Meditação Sôbre o Tietê* and *Café*, owing to the failure of their epic intentions, could serve as a counterproof of that affirmative) and above all as the poet of São Paulo. *Lira Paulistana* contains his most moving poems, the most spontaneous, the most poetically "mature." There the poet assumed his eternal expression after the tortuous adventures in the area of simple technique. *Lira Paulistana* is the final point on an arc whose opposite extreme was the *Paulicéia Desvairada*—because the "first book of the Modernist Movement also sang regionally of the mother city."

Thus it is all finally made clear, and the profound unity of Mário de Andrade is re-established. He was three hundred, three hundred and fifty—as he wrote in a well-known sonnet—and was never fragmented. On the contrary, he ceaselessly completed himself. In his multiplicity, he had a "vocation for unity," that vocation that once inspired in him the wonderful opening poem of *Remate de Males*.

Oswald de Andrade

Both Mário and Oswald de Andrade (1890–1954) were greater than their works, but for different—even opposite—reasons. While the work of the first was characterized by a certain diversification, the work of the second might be defined by dispersion and lack of the unifying principle we found in Mário. What separated them, as Oswald said in one of his frequent jokes, was a question of "morals"—literary morals more than anything else.[34] It is possible to view them as representatives of the serious and the frivolous sides of Modernism, for while Mário lived the scandal of artistic research, Oswald lived the scandal out of sheer joy in scandalizing (and he succeeded in it, if we can judge from the bristling pages by Tasso da Silveira which seem to have issued still warm from a reading of *Serafim Ponte Grande*). Mário de Andrade had true literary sincerity: he is the mystic of literature. Oswald de Andrade, on the other hand, was more than the "clown of the bourgeoisie," as he defined himself in the opening note to *Serafim Ponte Grande*; he was the literary clown. He was not the mystic, but the mystifier. One of them lacked the flair for mystification, the other the flair for sincerity. But it was Oswald, by way of paradox, who gave his son the name of Rudá, "the god whose mission it was to inspire tenderness in the hearts of men in order to effect their return to the tribe." Brazilwood and anthropophagy thus returned to the reality of daily life by unsuspected pathways; and, with all his apparent aggressiveness, did not Oswald de Andrade have the subconscious desire to "inspire tenderness in the hearts of men"?

Between them they express the two faces of Modernism—that is, all of Modernism; but Oswald was fulfilled to a much lesser degree and fulfilled much less the programs of the Movement. His life is an uneasy search for the masterpiece that he knew he was incapable of producing. If Diaghilev said to Cocteau: "Shock me," Oswald de Andrade, the Cocteau of our Modernism, seemed constantly to say: "I'll shock you" and moreover "I'll shock myself, into the bargain." To delineate him as the Cocteau of our Modernism, as a plump and plebeian Cocteau, whereas the other one was lean and aristocratic, is more than just a figure of speech: between the two—beyond a common thematic tendency—exists the bond of a similar attitude vis-à-vis literature and the reading public. They have in common the theme of the Horse on the stage, which created for them an unpleasant recollection of failure in the theatre; the theme of the work of art as orphic fulfillment and of a kind of orphism as a modern and lay substitute for religious sentiment. Oswald de Andrade wrote in his memoirs: ". . . even though I had the worst possible notion of the Church, I still held within myself a deep religious sentiment which I never attempted to get free of. That is what today I call the orphic sentiment." [35]

It is strange that, citing so many names of foreign writers who had an influence on him, Oswald de Andrade, with the single exception of the preface to *Serafim Ponte Grande,* mentioned the name of Cocteau only to justify his own Catholicism. Cocteau was, and could not help being, bedside reading for all the Modernists: Mário de Andrade cited *La Noce Massacrée* in the preface to the *Paulicéia Desvairada,* and Oswald could hardly pretend to be ignorant of him. The French writer, as well as the Brazilian, insisted on the absolute and decisive importance of what he was doing. As for the proportion of mystification, he found the magnificent formula for that in the words of the photographer,[36] which might well serve as the key to Oswald de Andrade's work: "Since

these mysteries lie beyond our comprehension, let us pretend to
be the originator of them."

Oswald de Andrade came into contact with Futurism and, as
a consequence, with Cocteau during his first trip to Europe in
1912:

> Of the two manifestoes which announced the transformation
> of the world, in Paris I knew the less important, that of the
> Futurist Marinetti.
>
> .   .   .   .   .
>
> But Paris—one aspect of the second front was initiated there
> —had provided me with the spectacle of the election of Paul
> Fort, a free poet, as prince of French poets at a soirée at the
> "Lapin Agile," where I perchanced to be. Only in that way
> did I come to know that it was, after all, a matter of banish-
> ing meter and rhyme from verse, both obsolete tools of the
> past . . . A whiff of Modernism had reached me, the result
> of the spread in Europe of Marinetti's "Futurist Manifesto."
> I tried my hand at free verse. I still keep its title. It was called
> "O último passeio de um tuberculoso, pela cidade, de
> bonde." [37]

He came to free verse rather tardily, let it be said in passing,
and it allowed him to conquer the inborn incapacity for rhyme
to which he confessed in his book of memoirs: we have already
taken note of the nature of "Brazilwood" poetry. In the *Primeiro
Caderno do Aluno de Poesia Oswald de Andrade,* he continued
to cultivate the kind of poem which became the model for the
entire first phase of Modernism:

> I want to write a poem
> Erotic and sentimental
> Like the little bands
> Of my native land
>
> I want to write a poem
> Of all the love I feel
> For the palms and banners
> Of my musical land [38]

We must add at once that the rest of the poem degenerates considerably. All of Oswald's work, in prose or poetry, is made up of flashes of genius lost in a heavy mass of halting composition. Of course, I am omitting his drama, the would-be importance of which some modern critics would like us to see. In that regard, I think the definitive judgment has been passed by Samuel Rawet: "Oswald de Andrade, in addition to the formal changes, wished to attack a question which has always been absent from our national drama: class struggle. His theatre, like it or not, is eminently political in intention. But just how far do his acts and ideas go? [His characters] meld and combine to produce a gigantic farce which an excess of cerebralism and individualistic and amoral hallucination robbed of what, precisely, it might have been: drama." [39]

As for his novels, no study has yet surpassed the essay which Antônio Cândido devoted to him in *Brigada Ligeira*. The São Paulo critic observed that Oswald de Andrade's fiction presents three distinct faces: the *Trilogia do Exílio,* the pair *Miramar-Serafim,* and the *Marco Zero.* He might have said three stages, because they are really three phases of a dynamic and frequently contradictory evolution in the process of which we nonetheless can see a coherent development. The reader who attempts an explicative analysis based on the chronology of the editions, however, will be thrown off course. *Os Condenados* dates from 1922, *João Miramar* from 1924, *A Estrêla de Absinto* from 1927, *Serafim* from 1933, *A Escada Vermelha* from 1934, and *A Revolução Melancólica* from 1943.

The same critic revealed that Oswald de Andrade kept his original manuscripts for a long time (he wrote with considerable difficulty, as we can observe from the papers which he left), and published them without heed to the date of composition (in 1933, for example, he gave out the *Serafim Ponte Grande,* which he had completed in 1928, and indicated that he was publishing it in its original form). Thus the *João Miramar,* completed in 1916 (published in 1924), and the *Serafim Ponte Grande* served to prove that Oswald de Andrade lived the internal drama of being ahead of his time while he was writing and the drama of being *passé* as soon as he was published. Such irregularities may explain, at least in part, the feeling of perpetual anachronism which his work inevitably transmits.

In an attempt to order Oswald's fiction ideologically and spiritually, Antônio Cândido has proposed the following:

. . . Senhor Oswald de Andrade's novels may be grouped according to three moments in his evolution, the first stage of which is the *Trilogia*, the second is the pair of novels *Miramar-Serafim*, and *Marco Zero* represents the synthesis of the foregoing two stages. The first moment corresponds to the Catholic and post-Parnassian attitude assumed by the author before 1922 and accords with a fixation so strong that its characteristics vigorously burst forth in the *Escada Vermelha* years later and will still color many pages in his *Revolução Melancólica*. In the second stage everything has changed, from language—naked and incisive, all concentrated in social satire—to the unpretentiousness of his literary attitude, nonchalant about making life beautiful. . . . These two phases find their synthesis in *Marco Zero*. . . .[40]

All of Oswald de Andrade's prose fiction can be considered autobiographical: In the *Trilogia do Exílio* we find long passages that are almost literal anticipations of *Um Homem Sem Profissão*; João Miramar, or more correctly Miramar, is the *nom de guerre* he used at the time of the famous *garçonnière* mentioned in *Ponta de Lança*. Thus in the title of that first novel (novel?), the word "memoirs" should be taken in the strict sense. Prudente de Morais Neto and Sérgio Buarque de Holanda, reviewing the volume for *Estética*, number 2 (January–March, 1925), observed: "It befits us—and the author's silence gives us full authority for this—to place his verbal process in the story of João Miramar, or rather, his impressions, among books of indeterminate genre." As to knowing whether it was really a "modern" or "modernist" book, that is another matter. Under the name of Machado Penumbra he wrote in the preface to *João Miramar*: "Let us calmly await the fruit of this new revolution which offers us for the first time a telegraphic style and a stabbing metaphor." Read and reread today, these novels (?) justify the paradoxical disappointment of his contemporaries who always thought Oswald de Andrade's books considerably less Modernist than their author.

As exceptional documents for the spiritual biography of Oswald de Andrade, and even for the history of Brazilian thought at a given time, we cannot deny that all of his novels are artistic failures, not simply because he inevitably stopped short of his own intentions. Thus we find in *João Miramar*, as well as in *Serafim Ponte Grande*, a "telegraphic style" but more rarely a "stabbing metaphor." The novel which was to be "extremely interesting, extremely modern, exaggeratedly partisan"—as Mário de Andrade had overheard and subsequently announced to Manuel Bandeira—turned out to be a book that did not come up to its author's reputation and, beyond a doubt, fell short of his ambitions.

In 1933, on the publication of *Serafim Ponte Grande*, he disowned his former works; with these Modernism was also disowned because, once again sensitive to the way the wind was blowing, Oswald de Andrade passed from unwarranted clowning to political literature which was decidedly Communistic in tone. In that regard, we would need to know up to what point— since he kept his originals in the desk drawer for an indefinite period of time—he modified them prior to publication. For example, between the first and last volume of *Os Condenados* there is such a substantial difference (his initial esthetics, which had somewhat of a Symbolist turn, taking on a position of lucid political conscience) that the first idea to occur to us is that he brought the book up to date although he preserved the original date of composition.

Seen in that light, the preface to *Serafim Ponte Grande* is another "Modernist manifesto" written by Oswald de Andrade: the manifesto which interpreted the state of mind of the political generation that followed the esthetical generation of the twenties. If this latter was, in the political overlapping, a "lost generation," the generation of the following decade was no less so with its ultimately fruitless gesticulation and verbal rebellions. It is precisely the verbal rebellion that, after *Serafim Ponte Grande*, Oswald de Andrade expressed in his work (novel and drama) and to which his declaration of 1933 gave the definitive tone: "The 'revolutionary' situation of this South American mental dung looked something like this: the opposite of bourgeois was not proletariat—it was bohemian! The masses, unknown here and, like today, living under the complete economic debauchery of the politicians and the rich. The intellectuals playing games on the sidelines. From time to time, they took a potshot in rhyme. . . . With little money, but outside the revolutionary axis of the world, ignorant of the Communist Manifesto, and not wishing to be bourgeois, naturally I became a bohemian." At that time the Cannibal movement and not Greengiltism seemed to him to herald the revolution. At any rate, he felt it necessary to repudiate Modernism also: "The Modernist Movement, culminating in anthropophagous measles, seemed to indicate an advanced phenomenon. . . . The pricing of coffee was an imperialist operation. Brazilwood poetry idem. That had to crumble with the herald trumpets of crisis. As nearly all Brazilian vanguardist literature crumbled, provincial and suspect, if it was not downright depleted and reactionary."

And there is the problem: Oswald de Andrade's revolutionary literature found its deep roots in the resentment of the now adult little rich boy who was wiped out by the incomprehensible machinations of "capitalism"; a name, naturally, that covered everything from his parents' lamentable real estate operations to the wild dissipation of the son. *Chão* was the document of that state of mind: "[The Saxes] going periodically from Luz Station to the Gare St. Lazaire, with effusive send-offs, sensational landings. Leaving behind substitutes who died for them in the banks they controlled, in brokerage firms where they maintained gentle monopolies on the coffee market, supporting violent and active tenants on their peerless plantations. Finding servile, unctuous ambassadors eager to take them to 'the girls' and to the politicians of the time." Or also (Jango speaks here):

I have no vocation at all [political vocation], Bruno. As a matter of fact, my life and my vocation can't hide my country-gentleman origins. The Wall Street crash wiped my family out as it did all of São Paulo labor and made me feel that we were all victims of the imperialists. Up till now it's been imperialism that has hindered the free development of our economic power. Up till now it's been imperialism that, through our lackey government, has maintained the ignorance of the masses and has kept property in the hands of the few in the pay of foreign capital. The Internationale supports the nationalist policies of any native bourgeoisie.

Oswald de Andrade or Oswald de Vengeance . . . against Wall Street. . . . Thus once again Modernism missed the chance to write the great social novel which was implicit in its program. *Marco Zero* was the unsuccessful attempt to show the great racial mixture of São Paulo, with the social betterment of the immigrant (Syrian, Italian . . .) and the concomitant decay of the old aristocracy. There are along those lines two parallel resentments in the novelist's mind—complementary and contradictory: on one hand, against the illiterate immigrant who grows rich while the good landed gentry crumbles in economic and moral ruin; on the other hand, against the aristocracy because of its unjustified and ridiculous pretensions, if not for the downright incompetence that has brought it to the abyss. In addition, there is his resentment of the bourgeoisie, in so far as it is a social class; of the world, in so far as it is a force outside him that he could not understand; against the coffee crash, in so far as it represents the injustice of fate. Only the idyllic vision of the "proletariat" is left over. The writer, who from his first year at the university felt he was an anarchist, found in the verbal Communism of the thirties and forties the fodder of anarchy he so sorely needed.

A man of a satirical but not dramatic mind, Oswald de Andrade had to fail in the novel. *Marco Zero* is a proto-novel, a novel yet to be written by someone who might be a combination of Thomas Mann and Marcel Proust, a two-headed monster which destiny did not give Modernism the power to create.

Plínio Salgado

Plínio Salgado (1901–   ), the creator of Integralism, is of double interest to Modernist history: first, because he represents one of the political currents deriving from the Movement; second, because he wrote the earliest, and moreover the best, political novels of the first phase. He is completely revealed in his little book of verses, *Thabor,* published in 1919. In that volume we find the mystical tendencies and the vague Symbolism which were embodied in his fiction as well as in his political tracts. As to literature, it is a kind of second Symbolist broth in which are revealed "thuribles of silver swaying" and St. Theresa swooning in the delight of human pleasure.

With Salgado, politics is mystical and mysticism is political. Thus the unquestionable nobility of the one is obliterated by the inevitable sordidness of the other. As for his philosophy of history, which he attempted to carry out first in the novel, then in militant politics, its only shortcoming was that it was not original, in spite of the fact that he wore himself out in numerous volumes of political doctrine to affirm the uniqueness of his ideas. Catholicism and Totalitarianism are practiced with a greater or lesser degree of success in various countries throughout the world, whether in their conservative forms (assumed, as we have seen in Greengiltism) or in their leftist forms. It is significant that Plínio Salgado combatted Communism not because it was totalitarian but because it was "atheistic": "The disgrace of the modern world, the greatest of all, is represented by this shocking fact: it is the confessed materialists, the ostensible atheists, in a word: the communists. . . ." [41] For that very reason, he understood that "democratic liberalism" was "the most precious ally" of Nazism and Communism, when he applauded Pius IX for having condemned "liberal Catholics." [42] In his books the readers who look for mysticism will find politics; those who seek politics will find mysticism.

But in the years around 1926, when *O Estrangeiro* [43] appeared, his political thought had not yet crystallized, and he was mixed up with the more or less polemical "nationalism" of the Greengilt group, which was also more or less nebulous and poetic. Nonetheless, it is not true, as he states in the preface to *O Esperado*, [44] that that novel had been "the first statement . . . of the modern spirit in style and form after the literary revolution of 1922. . . . All subsequent Brazilian novels (with the exception, up to a certain point, of *A Bagaceira* and the most recent and courageous efforts of Senhor José Américo de Almeida) preferred to take up the old rhythms. . . ." It is obvious that in 1927 Plínio Salgado could not possibly allude to *A Bagaceira* and to the subsequent works of José Américo de Almeida; that preface was composed at a later date for the publication of his *Obras Completas* and represents, for that very reason, a distortion, conscious or otherwise, of literary history. At least *João Miramar* had already been written and published; and whatever reservations we may have about it in other regards, it was considerably more modern in style and form than all the books of Plínio Salgado.

However, it is certain that *O Estrangeiro*, as well as *O Esperado*, are the best novelesque achievements of the twenties. With the same Expressionist style that Oswald de Andrade had employed clumsily, Plínio Salgado created the sketch of what would be the "social" and "political" novels of the following decade. Their tardy utilization, on the part of the author and his readers, as documents of a partisan ideology removed them from the literary arena; and, moreover, *O Cavaleiro de Itararé,* in 1933, finished off the series lamentably. That is why in 1928 *A Bagaceira* became the initiator of the "Northeastern cycle," which was destined to dominate our prose fiction throughout the thirties. The main difference was that Plínio Salgado surrendered to his deep-seated desire to create a totally symbolic form of fiction, while the Modernists of the first phase were interested only in purely esthetic matters and those writers of the following decade were realists. Both were closer to the intellectual atmosphere of the moment. Oswald de Andrade, who in the history of Modernism can be taken successively as the reagent of his contemporaries, wrote in this regard: "Among us, only Modernism could alter narrative technique, giving to it the jerky quality of animated cartoons, the lyrical waves of the unconscious and the heights of intellectual invention. While I was laboring hard on *Serafim Ponte Grande,* Plínio Salgado reproduced in *O Estrangeiro* the technique of my *Memórias Sentimentais,* and two great workers in the creative arts gifted Brazil with *Macunaíma* and *João Ternura.*" [45]

Besides, where style is concerned, Plínio Salgado's work shows steady degeneration. From *O Estrangeiro* to the *Cavaleiro de Itararé,* to call to mind only his fiction and books published over a seven-year period, his stylistic degeneration is obvious and alarming. The explanation for this lies certainly in the fact that he immediately surrendered to theoretical tendencies and abandoned esthetic preoccupations which were purely external to him; they were acquired and were, therefore, transitory. From the preface of the first edition of *O Estrangeiro* we can see that his nationalist "theses" took precedence over his Modernist "theses":

This book seeks to establish certain aspects of São Paulo life in the last ten years. Rural life, provincial life, and life in the great metropolis. Ascending cycle of the colonist (the Mondolfis); descending cycle of the ancient races (the Pantojos). March of the half-breed to the backlands and neo-pioneerism (Zé Candinho); dislocation of the immigrant in their footsteps and new agricultural period (Humberto); re-

turn of the old landowners to the Capital and new elements
for public officialdom and liberal classes (the Pantojos again).
On the other hand, the spirit of Italian-ness (the "Dante
Alighieri") in combat with the land and the milieu; reactionary movement of traditions and sentiments inherent
in the provisional type formerly outlined (Juvêncio). Mental
aspects. Latent nationalism, embodied in the schoolmaster.
Charlatanism in prevailing politics (Major Feliciano). Alienation of the intellectuals (Eugênio Fortes). Ivan—culminating
character of the book. Synthesis of all the characters. Awareness of all the evils. Action guided by an *a priori* idealism
annulled by cruel skepticisms in the face of surrounding
utilitarianism and overwhelming prejudice. Plethora of con-
trasting and incapable personalities. . . . This book is, above
everything else, a venting of my spleen. It will be apparent
that this book had something to say.

But this is the outline of Oswald de Andrade's *Marco Zero*!
They are two unsuccessful novels based on the same concept, the
same ideas: Plínio Salgado could well hand back to Oswald de
Andrade, with regard to these two books, what João Miramar said
about *O Estrangeiro*. It is clear that there are common themes
and ideals in that generation, notwithstanding all the personal
and artistic antipathies.

One might rightfully think that, besides all that, Plínio
Salgado and Oswald de Andrade were much closer to one another in 1926 and the year following than the two liked to admit
years later. While he was writing *O Estrangeiro* and making a
passably socialistic and messianic Russian the main character in
his book ("synthesis of all the characters"), Plínio Salgado seemed
much more attracted by the preachments of Lenin than those
of Mussolini: "At the red dawn, Christ came forth in armor—
gigantic silhouette of an armored car. It was Lenin. He leaned
over the misty parapet of the ages. . . ." This characterization
of Lenin as the Christ of history is to some, at least, surprising
from the pen of the future founder of Integralism. The picture
was completed in a preview of the great Communist victory over
the world: "Russia remained, like a ridge of ice, which had to

crumble and flood the world. Glacier of future civilization, burning and overflowing the earth."

However, a trip to Paris effected a 180-degree turn in Plínio Salgado's ideas. Just as Oswald de Andrade had created Brazilwood on the Place Clichy, Integralism came, although still disguised in the pages of *O Esperado*, from the banks of the Tiber as viewed from the banks of the Seine: ". . . I finished *O Esperado* in Paris and sketched out the manifesto that I intended to launch for future generations of Brazilians. I had witnessed the political renovation of Turkey, Fascism in Italy, I had read reams of Communist literature circulating in Paris, I had studied German social democracy, I had researched tiny Belgium, meditated on Egypt and English imperialism, I had observed the spiritual anarchy of Spain and the new order in Portugal, and everything indicated to me the death of an old civilization and the advent of a new era in human history." [46]

Once again Plínio Salgado provides documents that serve to contradict him, because the characterization that remains is unquestionably that of a messianic book. Still later, writing a "brief history" of his novels for the *Obras Completas*, he exclaimed regarding *O Esperado*: "This anti-messianic book has always been judged by its title!" In fact, it was as a messianic book that the young Integralists read it in the thirties. In the novel itself there is an opening note to Part III, "O Ofício das Trevas," whose meaning is indisputable: ". . . and until the Long Awaited One arrives, miseries will be multiplied, and the Homeland will have, as in the mournful rites, its Office of Darkness!" Or again, in the last lines, in Edmund's delirium: "Listen . . . I hear footsteps. . . . Brazil is on the march. . . . Its crowds are gathering from all sides. . . . I hear footsteps. . . . Going where?"

The "Hoped For" or "Long Awaited One" was, in the field of the novel, the Cavaleiro de Itararé, of whom the backlanders spoke: "One day the phantom will be disenchanted, because many people will see the invisible horseman." At that time no one doubted, at least not in the belligerent Integralist ranks, that the "invisible horseman" was none other than Plínio Salgado, who thus set himself against the "Knight of Hope," this being the nickname of Luís Carlos Prestes, future chief of the Brazilian Communist Party. We can see that in 1933 the two opposing camps were already well defined. At the same time, the political leader, and not the novelist, conceived of the 1930 revolution as "the phantom bearer of woes of whom the backlanders of the plains of the Paranapanema speak." With this opinion reappeared the old member of the P.R.P. (the Republican Party of São Paulo) who, upon returning to his homeland that year from Europe, immediately took up arms against the revolutionaries.

At that time Plínio Salgado was abandoning his career as a novelist in order to go into politics, which is only of incidental interest to us here. Once again manipulating his dates or his texts (because in the *Psicologia da Revolução* of 1933 he refers to the *first* Great War, an expression which made sense and only really began to be used after 1940), he described all modern forms of art as the "last stage in anarchy and dissolution," and the Dadaist Movement as "spontaneous cretinism." *O Cavaleiro de Itararé* will appear more as a political manifesto than as a work of fiction:

TO ALL CIVILIAN AND MILITARY YOUTH
OF BRAZIL

. . . This book is mainly a heartfelt book. It was written during hours of disappointment, before the panorama of a Homeland debased by ignorance, egoism, and the bad faith of a disgraced generation. . . . The prologue is practically a sociological essay. The novel constitutes an impassioned book. A book of irony and rebellion. A book of sarcasm and violence in which the writer avenges the public man who is misunderstood, harassed, slandered by gangs of charlatans and pigmies. . . . *O Estrangeiro* was a warning. *O Esperado* was a forecast. *O Cavaleiro de Itararé* should be: either a glorification or a curse to our nation. . . . And this book may well be the epitaph of a Fatherland.

Fortunately, it was only the epitaph of a novelist. Technically, it was a backward step with relation to the two former novels and, for many reasons, with relation to the Brazilian novel in 1932. Ideologically, it took up again, for reasons of self-interest, the cathechism of the "heroic life" which Graça Aranha was preaching in mid-1922. It is the unsuccessful novel of young military radicals, just as the revolutions of the twenties never produced a single successful novel in spite of so many ambitious attempts.

Alcântara Machado

Antônio de Alcântara Machado (1901–1935) [47] belongs to
that moment in literary history when Modernism, outgrowing
its first polemical impulse, attempted the esthetic creation of a
specific work. Without having participated in the Week of Modern
Art, which was in the twenties the initiation ceremony by
which the chosen were recognized, he belonged nonetheless to
the Modernist group of São Paulo. If death had not interrupted
his career, he would have been the writer most capable of giving
Modernism a great novelistic achievement, which of course Modernism
never had (when the Movement found its fulfillment in
the novel in the following decade, other factors had modified its
character). Alcântara Machado, to judge from the mutilated
Mana Maria (1936), might have written the urban São Paulo
novel, petit-bourgeois and modern, which was implicit in Modernism's
programs and of which Mário de Andrade's *Amar, Verbo
Intransitivo* (1927) was the prototype par excellence—a novel
which successive generations of fiction writers have been rewriting,
with greater or lesser success, without ever achieving the
complete masterpiece that justifies the existence of literature.

When *Cavaquinho e Saxofone* was published in 1940, Álvaro
Lins, who was the attorney general of the Republic of Letters,

wrote his brief to the effect that Alcântara Machado represented, above all else, a literary "document" and that in prose no one embodied Modernism more thoroughly than he. This was, with some difference in outlook, the opinion of Sérgio Milliet, who pointed out that Alcântara Machado was one of the "representative men" of the Modernist period. Everything depends on what exactly we mean by Modernism. Álvaro Lins, who referred to the Movement by fitting it without the slightest hesitation between two funerary dates—1922 and 1930—was considering a phase of which, in all honesty, Alcântara Machado would not be the typical writer. Mário de Andrade and Oswald de Andrade should be mentioned rather than Alcântara Machado as typical prose artists and conscious practitioners of a specific system. Sérgio Milliet, without dates and unnecessary insistence on chronology, seemed to be referring to the second phase of Modernism, to the years during which the esthetic mystique was being transformed into literary politics, and during which the literary axis began to shift from São Paulo to the Northeast. These are different Modernisms. Alcântara Machado, as I understand it, would have been the Joan of Arc of the São Paulo group if he had not died in 1935.

Here, of course, the historical "situation" of Alcântara Machado seems to me to be of the utmost importance for a true appreciation of his artistry: his talent, Sérgio Milliet writes in *O Sal da Heresia,*

> only truly matured and came to light in 1928 with the publication of *Laranja da China*. From then on his psychological penetration stabilizes, his philosophical thought definitively develops. His very style rids itself of provocative bad habits. Mário de Andrade observed that, in that regard, no one of us was less preoccupied than Antônio about "going modern!" No one was freer of literary idiom. But Mário formed his opinion without carefully rereading our friend's works. That idiom exists in *Pathé Baby,* you find it in *Brás, Bexiga e Barra Funda,* but it is only barely noticeable in *Laranja da China,* and after 1930 it completely disappears and is replaced by a highly personal—but natural—way of being: clean, free of linguistic "gimmickry."

Alcântara Machado was a Modernist beyond a doubt—but of a certain kind of Modernism which is neither the Modernism of the revolutionary decade nor the Modernism of the reactionary decade. He might have been for the Modernism of São Paulo what José Américo de Almeida was for the Modernism of the Northeast in 1928, i.e., the initiator of a properly literary phase which did honor to compromises assumed by manifestoes and manifestations. In the neolithic age in which literary studies still exist in Brazil, we do not know the date of composition of *Mana Maria*, but it would not be rash to place it between 1928 and 1934 or perhaps between 1931, the date of the founding of the *Revista Nova*, and 1933, the date of Alcântara Machado's election to the National Constituent Assembly. Those two or three years represented the apex of Alcântara Machado's intellectual maturity, just as the two or three previous years had constituted his literary adolescence. *Brás, Bexiga e Barra Funda* (1927) and *Laranja da China* (1928), with their undeniable originality and great power of expression, mark the descendant of a school which had produced strong and dominant personalities. *Mana Maria* could have transformed him into the novelist that not one of his masters or friends ever was. As a consequence, there are really two Alcântara Machados, just as there are several Modernisms. Historical vision tends to abolish time and the changes wrought by time and to reason as if the process of spiritual change had not occurred from one age to another. No matter how short Alcântara Machado's life and his literary life may have been, they suffice to reveal him as the only Modernist of São Paulo (among the writers of fiction) who truly transcended Modernism; but, simultaneously, because they were so short, they isolated him in that no man's land which separated the São Paulo trenches from those of the Northeast.

Mana Maria was published posthumously. Studying the paradoxical case of that work which, under normal circumstances, would be of interest only if it were left by a writer of great importance, Álvaro Lins observed that Alcântara Machado's early death was not just fate but the treachery of fate. I do not agree with him, however, when he characterizes the novelist as a "martyr" of the Modernist Movement. It was Alcântara Machado's misfortune that he died prematurely. At heart not one of the great Modernists of the first phase was successful in surpassing Modernism.

Between historical and esthetical significance there is an abyss that few Modernists have succeeded in bridging. Alcântara Machado did not have time to complete his work—I mean, to complete the work of Modernism. And thus this writer, who was destined to surpass it and justify it, was reduced to the role of a trainbearer in a revolution which had mysteriously chosen him as consolidator. In his books the Modernist defects continually neutralize his qualities as a writer.

Since in literature only published works count, and actual defects are more important than potential quality in the light of literary history, Alcântara Machado was the short story writer of São Paulo and not the great novelist of Modernism. As the short story writer of São Paulo, he cannot be compared to Mário de Andrade, from whose domination, moreover, he never completely liberated himself (but who could have in the twenties?). The publisher who in 1961 collected all of Alcântara Machado's works under the title *Novelas Paulistanas* [48] mapped out, as a consequence, the essential critical trajectory of his art. In the adjective "Paulistanas" we should understand the São Paulo of which Mário de Andrade sang in his first books of poetry (more than in the last), just as he had in some of his most characteristic short stories (and even in *Amar, Verbo Intransitivo*): that picturesque São Paulo of the revolutionary decade, saturated with Italian accents and the odor of gasoline, and the honeymoon with easy money which gave no indication of the crash of 1929, creating in the acid notes of machine and cement that "symphony of the metropolis" which was the theme of the entire period. All of this is, from the historical and sociological point of view, a long way off. One aspect of Alcântara Machado's being outdated has nothing to do with literature; it concerns the "date" when his stories were written.

We cannot locate this date precisely. This great defect is, at the same time, his greatest quality: I do not view literature only for its documentary significance, nor do I think that in studying the Modernists, in particular Alcântara Machado, one can properly ignore the "sociological" aspect, the striving for realism and fidelity to the concrete, and, above all, the instinct for urban life. Before Modernism, our urban novels were not really urban. They were mundane. Their action transpired in the salons of high society or the upper bourgeoisie rather than in the streets and bars, in the movie houses or vehicles of public transportation, in modest neighborhoods or among the working classes. Alcântara Machado, who descended from an aristocratic family, was by contrast the writer who represented that new world which was being created by the immigrant population on the foothills of São Paulo, in the districts of "Brás, Bexiga, and Barra Funda," and which finally overflowed to fill the entire city. Before him José de Alencar and Machado de Assis, to cite two significant examples, manifested some nostalgia for "high society"; with Alcântara Machado and the Modernists in general, those writers who vaguely or truly belonged to "high society" had the good sense to know that "high society" is not the same as *society*.

In the first case, it is obvious that idealization was more important than observation; in the second case, if the opposite was true it did not occur without some predilection for the picturesque, for that idealizing tendency which introduced into pure observation a touch of the universal, without which literature cannot exist. It is not without reason that Alcântara Machado's first book should bear the title of *Pathé Baby*: if there is a work in our literature that approximates cinema techniques and profoundly anticipates certain attitudes characteristic of the modern movies, it is certainly this book. Even here Alcântara Machado spontaneously reflected, because he had it in his blood, the dynamism (which is one of the myths of the era) and the desire to create without knowing it what we would today call neo-realism, properly using the vocabulary of the cinema. Italian neo-realism, by coincidence: the characters in his story are street urchins and tenement gangs; they are usually the inhabitants of that strange, threatening, and fascinating suburb which was the Italian district of the twenties. For Alcântara Machado the "real world" existed, and it existed in its urban form under the species of daily life on the sidewalks and of popular types, of street ball and the little human adventure. In *Mana Maria* he went from Brás,

Bexiga, and Barra Funda, let us say, to the Perdizes district, or to what at that time was the Vila Buarque (let us not confuse the São Paulo of today with the São Paulo of half a century ago). Leaving his novel unfinished, in which not only the atmosphere but also the style is modified, Alcântara Machado remained the short story writer with popular appeal.

It would not be proper to assert that his historical value is greater than his esthetic value, and certainly his significance as a "document of Modernism" should not be overrated. But while it is true that nothing would be changed on the face of Modernism if his work had not existed, something would indeed be missing in Brazilian literature had his work not been written. Above all, something would be missing by way of indication of a literary tendency not only possible but also important and which, no matter how surprising it may seem, no one took the trouble to study seriously. Of all the varied Modernist "programs," that of Alcântara Machado (whom we might be tempted to view only as a follower of the programs of others) is still the one that awaits fulfillment. Lacking the vigorous vitality of the Northeastern novel, the urban novel of São Paulo died at the moment of its inception. Years later when the Northeastern novel had exhausted all of its possibilities, São Paulo had its urban novel within the scope of a totally different conception but without that brilliant spontaneity that was the most pleasing aspect of Modernism. Likewise it is possible to think that the ganglionic and appendicular society of the immigrant districts furnished the writer of fiction the meaty materials which the novel required: a rapid plot development growing out of a single episode was perhaps its "necessary genre." Be that as it may, after Alcântara Machado no writer appeared with a disposition to look with sympathy on that great phenomenon which is the immigrant city and express it with epic lyricism. Even in him the picturesque note smothers the human note, just as collective psychology seems to have guided his spirit in the analysis of individual psychology. More complex than he might at first seem, Antônio de Alcântara Machado represents the bitter destiny of a literary vocation which never bore fruit.

José Américo de Almeida

After all that has been said about Antônio de Alcântara
Machado, we can better understand the aptness of A. C. Couto
de Barros's observation regarding *Brás, Bexiga e Barra Funda*.
Only the person who knows São Paulo to the core could understand it thoroughly, he thought, and in this regard "it was a regionalist work." [49] However, Modernism held in its secret places
another unexpected paradox: instead of developing an "urban
regionalism," which was implicit in its very nature, it chose, in
so far as the novel was concerned, rural regionalism—which the
first Modernism had specifically rejected. That, I believe, can be
explained mainly through the change in the historical and social
situation and through the appearance "to the North" of a novelist who exemplified qualities which the novelists of São Paulo
insisted on thwarting. Thus, *A Bagaceira* by José Américo de
Almeida (1887–   ), which was completely alien to Modernism,
took the place of *João Miramar, O Estrangeiro,* and *Macunaíma*
as the source of the greatest Modernist fiction. But that was only
possible, exactly as in the case of *Casa Grande & Senzala* later on,
because the literary milieu had already been conditioned by Modernism and was therefore expecting something of that type.

272

A Bagaceira took its place at once as the novel of social reform, of the collective against the individual, of "class struggle,"
just as the regional novel stood for the local against the ecumenical, the national against the cosmopolitan. Its provincialism,
which today seems so limited to us, was in 1928 the best proof
of its authenticity. What it still retained of romantic and sentimental loquacity seemed, and indeed was, more authentically
Brazilian than Oswald de Andrade's purely "literary" challenge
or the construction—more folkloric than novelistic—of *Macunaíma*. The "class struggle," it seems unnecessary to say, loomed
up in a subtle and quiet way from the heart of the novel; but we
should not forget that *A Bagaceira* was above all else a programmatic novel, that is, it contained a program expressed in the famous
opening statement and also in the aphorisms which fill the text.
For example, in referring to his heroes, the novelist said: "Cane-
trash pariahs, victims of an obstinate organization of labor and
of a dependency which dehumanized them, they were the most
unfeeling in the face of the martyrdom of the drought's migra-
tions." Or again: "And the backlander came out, hugging in his
armful of pitiful possessions four hundred years of servitude
awash in the very substance of his blood."

Regarding *A Bagaceira,* which is so important in the history
of Modernism, I must again say that in spite of the drama of the
droughts which serve as its background (and which is, furthermore, almost totally absent in the novel), it is a story dominated
by the picturesque, by the surface aspect of persons and things.
Departing from the principle that "passion is romantic only
when it is false," José Américo de Almeida endeavors to describe
a passion, or several passions, as though they could be summed
up in the external movements of the characters. The result is
that no matter how paradoxical it may seem, the characters of
A Bagaceira never come to life: they act like vegetables, like
beings governed only by instinct, incapable even of understanding the meaning of their actions. They live more or less voice-
lessly, clinging confusedly to two or three elementary ideas which
make them behave like conditioned reflexes.

With and after this novel, Northeastern literature became the literature of the "picturesque Northeast" and of "type" characters deficient in psychological continuity. They all lack mental coherence, logical development of the emotions, and consciousness of their own feelings: they go through love and through life like animals that protect themselves and reproduce their kind out of a natural urge which they cannot resist. In that way the "regional" drove out the human, and the picturesque became the opposite of the eternal. The novel of the Northeast in general (which dominated Brazilian literature during the entire period of the thirties) is more a novel of the landscape than of the man and more of the "chorus" than of the hero. A group novel without individual development, it is by nature closer to folklore than to literature (but contemporary folklore, not the mythological folklore of *Macunaíma*). One has the impression that all the characters could be endlessly substituted and inexhaustibly multiplied. They are individuals without a name and without a personality, more responsible to their "condition" than to their *persona*. They are the "plantation owner," the "son of the plantation owner," the "migrant girl," the "migrant girl's father," the "boy who wants to marry the migrant girl," the "soldier," the "foreman," the "thug."

I do not say this because I wish to proclaim the undeniable deficiencies of this type of novel, but rather because I wish to emphasize the character that prose fiction assumed in the thirties in the image and likeness of *A Bagaceira*. However, where José Américo de Almeida was superior to his vast following was in his literary refinement, in the elegance of his language, in the deftness of his composition. The Northeastern novel can never deny that it inherited from the Modernists of São Paulo the realistic and socializing tendency and moreover the lack of interest in grammatical correctness or even linguistic correctness. Even there, however, *A Bagaceira* is scarcely Modernist and cannot be taken as one of the representative works of the Movement. But its author is, for the same reasons, one of its basic authors because of the historical role that he played and the influence, neither direct nor literary but rather "moral," esthetically moral, that he came to exert. I refer here to the "moral of novelistic conception," to the unwritten postulates which in every age writers feel obliged to obey. Of course, the novelist typical of that tendency, more than any other, is José Lins do Rêgo. However, would the Sugar Cane Cycle have been written without the example and, above all, without the success of *A Bagaceira*?

Augusto Frederico Schmidt

In 1928—the year of *Macunaíma, Retrato do Brasil, Essa Negra Fulô,* and *A Bagaceira*—the *Canto do Brasileiro* by Augusto Frederico Schmidt (1906–1965) was published. Also the *Serafim Ponte Grande* was probably written in 1928; when he brought it out five years later, Oswald de Andrade said that Modernist literature had degenerated with the economic crisis. We see, then, that this is one of the climactic dates of Modernism. The *Canto do Brasileiro,* whose poetical and historical importance was then and has been since somewhat exaggerated, entered the Modernist ranks, as Tristão de Athayde wrote, "with the new vigor of a spontaneous discontent and of a need to say what it felt." It would be senseless, however, to pretend that it has altered in any way the tendencies clearly evident at that time in the books just mentioned.

The "need to say what it felt," with its immediate satisfaction, was not a new element introduced into literary life by Augusto Frederico Schmidt: since 1922, and even before, that was the first commandment of the esthethic decalogue. That it dealt personally with a "spontaneous discontent," there is no doubt: the poet himself said later, testifying in the already cited *Testamento de Uma Geração,* that "in so-called 'Modernist' literature he had immediately felt 'the taste of the ephemeral, of that which is fed by the transitory, of that which is made only to vanish.' " What was even more decisive was a kind of, let us say, "chronological" disagreement, in part biographical and in part temperamental, which separated him at that time from literary groups. Even in the *Testamento* itself, he said along those lines: "I did not belong to any particular generation, as I said from the start. I was adopted by men older than myself. And immediately I started searching among the younger generations for the place I did not have, that I had not had, and could not have." The *Canto do Brasileiro* was born, as a consequence, more of spiritual unrest than of literary unrest; and, even seen in that light, it was not a new thing. Since the preceding year, *Festa* had initiated the process of "restoration of poetry in Christ" which culminated in 1935 in the work of Jorge de Lima and Murilo Mendes. Schmidt's poems seemed to open like a manifesto against the Modernist picturesque:

> I don't want any more love,
> No more do I wish to sing of my land.
> I get lost in this world.
> I don't want any more Brazil
> I don't want any more geography
> And no picturesque.
>
> What I want is to get lost in the world
> To flee from the world.[50]

Immediately, in the second part, however, it took on the meaning of a religious outcry in which the word "world" was no longer set against "Brazil" but rather against Paradise.

Also the "new vigor" seems considerably overestimated, that vigor with which—in the words of the eminent critic—the great poet emerged. The poem suffers from every inhibition of expression, every prosaism, and from the verbosity that came to characterize his poetry. Mário de Andrade, in his *Aspectos da Literatura Brasileira*,[51] recalled that many of these defects ultimately redounded to the poet's benefit: "In his own phrase, things which are often possibly irritating (the abuse of repetition, the pretentious syntactical complications, religiosity without discretion, patterns not only oratorical but also declamatory, the scanty sense of contemporaneity): all of this, finally, which seems to decrease, actually increases his value." Quod erat demonstrandum, because of all of Schmidt's works during the Modernist period, still his best book is the *Pássaro Cego* (1930), followed distantly by the *Mar Desconhecido* (1942). In all the rest, it is difficult to assert with such certainty that his defects actually increase his value rather than decrease it.

The "novelty" of the *Canto do Brasileiro* could only have that aspect for a critic like Tristão de Athayde, whose mistakes in judgment where poetry is concerned, and particularly where Modernist poetry is concerned, are limitless (Mário de Andrade's correspondence is, in this regard, extremely instructive). In reality here is what Mário de Andrade wrote to Manuel Bandeira on the sixteenth of November in 1930:

> I was really irritated by the *Canto do Brasileiro*, which is a work of such petulance, individualism, and of such tremendous frailty. That's all right: I admit that an individual may copy forms and inventions from other people, but he is obliged to surpass the man he imitated. It is impossible to be angry with Raimundo Correia because of the *Pombas*. But when people do not go beyond, as is the case with Schmidt, and he imitates my intention and copies the form of my *Poemas Acreanos*, then I get mad as hell. And you cannot argue my total lack of antagonism here: when someone bests me, I give him his points and so satisfy my loyalty to true sportsmanship. I must repeat to one and all that a certain kind of verse that I had dreamed of writing, apparently Parnassian because of its musicality and slow rhythm, it was Schmidt who pulled it off when I could not. But I consider my *Poemas Acreanos* abundantly superior to the *Nôvo Canto*, superior as to invention and form. That petulance of Schmidt's, considering himself superior to everybody without the slightest special discernment, gets on my nerves and I get mad as hell. The *Nôvo Canto* is of tremendous frailty, as I said. Besides that nonsense about discovering Brazil, the second part of the poem, good God, *that* is what he discovered!

So it was. And with regard to poetry which we could technically call Modernist, Augusto Frederico Schmidt rejected completely Modernism's spirit and its themes, although through a
tragic mistake he did keep free verse (which he confused with the
versicle). This caused him to dive headlong into discursiveness
and editorializing when inspiration like his required a more severe
and constraining instrument. We need only read this splendid
sonnet from *Estrêla Solitária* (1940) to see this truth clearly:

> This longing for the past is dead and gone.
> The glory I so often sought has fled.
> Our visions of the world and life itself
> And what I held within my palms are smoke.
>
> Each flower that's born most perfect passes on,
> Beauty's gone, with pain, and all storms' rage.
> The anguish of eternal nothing's past.
> Then why, good Lord, does not this moment fly?
>
> From doubt to doubt life runs its dreary course,
> Each passing instant brings a change in us.
> And that which passed itself is sorely changed.
>
> This fleeting love alone flies not away,
> This changing love alone knows nought of change.
> This fickle love alone stands true in me.

Or, still another lovely sonnet, with which he opens *Mar Desconhecido:*

> Alive is an uncharted sea in me,
> And in the wee hours of the night I hear
> The murmur of the waters sunk in prayer:
> Strange prayers are these unsaid in human tongue.
>
> As well I hear ofttimes the unknown sea,
> When horror strikes my lonely heart at night,
> The desperation of the wailing wind,
> The moaning anguish of the sobbing waves.

I feel alive in me a sea of shades,
So rich are they with life and harmony,
I know that's born therein the mystery

Of all the music of my gentle verse,
That music errant as the vagrant breeze
Whose wings birth storms upon the ocean seas.[52]

It is obvious that, with some incongruity between inspiration
and technique, Augusto Frederico Schmidt is a Romantic poet;
but he is a Romantic by temperament, and one who is in search
of a rule. For that reason, he did not understand the romantic
nature of Modernism. In his well-known article on poetry in 1930,
Mário de Andrade observed:

> There is no doubt that Romanticism became a conscious
> rebellion in Augusto Frederico Schmidt from the moment
> when, tired of the themes then popular with Modernism (it
> was he, I think, who first echoed in Brazil the idea of Anti-
> modern, from Maritain . . . , and it was he, through his
> Asiatic lack of agility, who created the *Canto do Brasileiro*,
> a serious . . . copy of the "Vou-me embora pra Pasárgada"),
> he tried, and tried hard, to open a new pathway. To be
> ultramodern, then. . . . But that conscious and moreover
> episodic Romanticism gave to the poet what, it seems to me,
> will most cause him to lose luster with the passage of time:
> beyond a hackneyed vocabulary, which he succeeded neither
> in renovating nor in establishing, certain poems of total or
> considerable imitation (*A Deus, Lira*), visible pastiches whose
> value absolutely escapes me.[53]

Even from the technical point of view, the great Romantic
defect in this poet was the absence of a critical attitude, horror
in face of the labor of polishing and correcting, complacency over
everything that issued from his pen, loosely wrought, wordy: a
flabby mode of expression. As the poet Manuel Bandeira wrote
much later in sentences that might well be considered a definitive
judgment: "Augusto Frederico Schmidt, a strong poet and a weak

versifier. . . . The potential for poetry in Schmidt is considerable. However, not everything that issued from that vast petroleum bed went through the refinery. Sometimes Schmidt weakened a poem by aligning images which, perhaps, were not unpleasant but which were disappointing because they followed one of those brilliant images in which the great strength of the poem seemed to us to be embodied." [54]

Carlos Drummond de Andrade

This third Andrade of Modernism had his literary birth far
from the barricades of 1922. He was fifteen years old when Manuel
Bandeira published *A Cinza das Horas* in 1917, but by the year
1925 he was the Modernist poet in Belo Horizonte's *Revista*.
However, he did not publish *Alguma Poesia* until 1930, thus
symbolically, ideologically, spiritually, and esthetically inaugurating the second phase of Modernist poetry. Carlos Drummond de
Andrade (1902–   ) came upon the revolution after it had sta-
bilized to a certain extent: to him Modernism was no longer a
rebellion, it was a challenge (soon transformed from literary challenge to political challenge).

In 1930, as he proceeded with *Alguma Poesia* to the first stage
of his poetic output, Carlos Drummond de Andrade needed to cry
out, as had Manuel Bandeira:

> I'm fed up with respectful lyricism
> With well-behaved lyricism. . . .

Instead, he proposed a new *ars poetica* under the guise of a symbolic enigma:

> In the middle of the road there was a stone. . . .

From that time on the work of Carlos Drummond de Andrade grew like a flood, and each edition of his collected poems closes one phase and opens another. Each one of them is at one and the same time a reckoning and a testament, if not to a certain degree a repudiation (at least from the chronological standpoint). Thus, the volume of *Poesias* (1942) temporarily brought an end to the the lyrical phase of Drummond's poetry. The age of *engagé* literature and of political poetry was at hand, and *A Rosa do Povo* (1945) is the best example of this aspect in Drummond's corpus. In 1947 the collection of *Poesia Até Agora* was a kind of magistrate's report on the political period then coming to a close. What immediately followed in 1951 was the first statement, in *Claro Enigma,* of the purely esthetic phase of his poetry which will continue alongside his attempt to reconcile regular verse of fixed form with the liberties introduced by Modernism. However, it was *A Rosa do Povo* which brought to a close, in so far as the chronological limits of this study are concerned, the Modernist career of Carlos Drummond de Andrade. And it rounds off this phase well, if we recall that 1945 marks the climax of political and partisan-utilitarian literature which had originated ten years earlier.

It rounds it off even better when we realize that in 1945 the poet had already reached his professional maturity. After that date we can observe a perfection of the poetic instrument and a certain enrichment of inspiration, although nothing truly new was added. Thus the analysis of his work which he gave us in 1962, seen as a whole, was valid at one and the same time for the "Modernist period" and for what followed:

> As he assembled this volume, the author paid little attention, properly speaking, to the selection of poems for their quality or for the phases they may represent in his career as a poet. He was more careful to locate in his published work certain characteristics and tendencies which condition or define his career as a whole. This *Anthology* seemed to him, then, better articulated, a more faithful mirror, all in all.
>
> Because the poems were chosen and arranged according to this criticism, the result was an *Anthology* which was not

divided by books, nor did it obey a strict chronology. The text has been separated into nine sections, each one containing material drawn from different works and arranged according to an internal order. The reader will find, then, as points of departure or poetic materials: (1) the individual, (2) homeland, (3) family, (4) friends, (5) the individual's encounter with society, (6) knowledge of love, (7) poetry itself, (8) trifling exercises, (9) a view, or attempt at a view, of existence.[55]

Thus the work is unified, and the various sections of it do not repudiate one another. In terms of literary history, however, Carlos Drummond de Andrade stands at the juncture of two important changes: the first was the passage from the poetic Modernism of the first phase, more picturesque than profound, less interested in creating than in scandalizing, to the poetic Modernism of the thirties in which, along with and in spite of the political tendencies formerly mentioned, poetry, properly speaking, regained its rights. In the second phase he assured the transition from this new poetic Modernism to the poetry which after 1945 came to take its place, then long past the "Modernist era."

In reality the thirties and forties were predominantly years of prose—fiction and essay; it is not surprising, then, that the remaining basic authors whom we still must study are four novelists and one essayist.

José Lins do Rêgo

Having inherited everything from Modernism—freedom of expression, social interest, predilection for the regional, a reading public whose taste was already developed—José Lins do Rêgo (1901–1957) was nonetheless right to be an enemy of the Movement from the very beginning.[56] The truth is that while the Movement was spiritually drawn to the future, the novelist was always facing the past. His work is somber and pessimistic: from *Menino de Engenho* (1932) to *Fogo Morto* (1943)—to cite only the works which may properly be included in the Modernist period—his novels are the portrait of a society or of beings in a state of disintegration. He will be remembered as the novelist of decadence.

It is difficult in his work to separate memory from imagination—but, in case of doubt, we can always opt for the first over the second. "He is not so much a true novelist as he is a wonderfully lively narrator and reciter of a reality which we can only embrace and revive," Pedro Dantas wrote in a study which was subsequently employed as a preface to one of the editions of *Menino de Engenho*. Viewed in this light, his "Northeastern" novels are intrinsically his recollections of men, because his novels not only indirectly fed on scenes, human types, the milieu in which he spent his childhood, but also took in, just as they were, happenings from real life, along with the names of persons who took part in those happenings and the particular circumstances that surrounded them. It was even said that he lacked imagination, in the sense that novels which are derived from materials alien to their own subject matter do not present the interest, the suggestive force, nor the impression of authentic and spontaneous vitality which are the most striking qualities of novels conceived in a different way.

It is for that reason that the first volume of his memoirs (*Meus Verdes Anos*), published in 1956, literally repeats *Menino de Engenho,* his novel of 1932. Those who spoke of José Lins do Rêgo as a memoirist certainly could not have foreseen how right they were. But it is not only for those external reasons that *Meus Verdes Anos* "explains" *Menino de Engenho* (and, to a considerable degree, the entire Sugar Cane Cycle). This revelation goes much deeper and touches on the most profound depths of sensibility. The book of memoirs provides the key to the interpretation of the novelist and shows to what degree he pawned to literature the very substance of his manhood.

The two fundamental themes in his writing we now know are the two fundamental themes in his life. José Lins do Rêgo is a man who, because of the circumstances of his life, has always lived vitally his *nostalgia for his mother's love* and his *fear of death.* Separated from his mother when he was very young, he lived his entire childhood in the substitute maternal love provided by aunts and relatives. But that is not all: the loss of his mother is confused in his sensibility with death itself, and those two ideas seem to have become symbiotically linked in the depths of his soul. Everyone remembers the first sentence of *Menino de Engenho*: "I was four years old on the day my mother died." Just as in the novel, the death of his mother is the subject of the first chapter of his book of memoirs. In a word, José Lins do Rêgo unconsciously dated his life from the death of his mother: that is the first fact that made him conscious of his own existence. From then on death constantly surrounded him in both the figurative and literal sense. For that little boy, who will be followed to the end by the piercing recollection of a confused paradise forever lost, had to endure a double longing: on the one hand, as an individual he went from one house to another, suffering the hostility of strangers or the indifference of relatives, the deficient or sham interest of the most affectionate; on the other hand, later as an adult member of a community, he witnessed the slow, inexorable disintegration of a world that had been his.

Thus can we explain why all of José Lins do Rêgo's work develops under the sign of death. The exuberant nature of the tropics is accompanied by the inexorable material and moral deterioration of man and society. For the novelist the modern sugar mill is not the symbol of industrial change and, as a consequence, of progress and wealth; rather it is the concrete symbol of the end of a society in which he spiritually continued to live. He introduces and strengthens in Brazilian fiction of the thirties the figure of the failure, of the man who had been chosen for a brilliant future and fell short of it. In general, the novel of that period was depressing and joyless literature which, moreover, denied the reality of the times even when it aspired to portray them most faithfully.

It is a certainty that in the history of the Brazilian novel José Lins do Rêgo is destined to acquire an increasing significance as witness and exemplar and a decreasing significance of an esthetic nature. He, of all the "novelists of the Northeast," was the most typical in his good qualities and his bad; and, being the basic author of a period, he never became a great novelist, if we judge by the universal titles which mark the development of the genre. It is difficult for the present-day reader to understand or even estimate the importance and the popularity of José Lins do Rêgo in the thirties and forties; and when he can, it is even more difficult to explain the phenomenon.

There will be from now on, as I said, a foreseeable tendency to underestimate him as an artist, just as in the past he was unquestionably overestimated. All the disagreement rests on his being a "teller of tales" like the medieval minstrels or, better still, like the blind singers of the Northeast itself. Still his literary tool was obviously inferior and insufficient. He owes his success precisely to the fact that when his best-known novels were produced, literature was ashamed of itself and aspired to be little more than social documentation: the more authentic and worthy of respect the less "literary" it was. That want of literary art now leads us to consider his work extremely poor and frustrated. These books which enjoyed such great success bear up very poorly under rereading.

There are two novelists who could escape this contingency: one of them, Graciliano Ramos, was neither Modernist nor "Northeasterner"; the other, Jorge Amado, having been for many years the elephant driver of our national novel with "a maximum of reality and a minimum of literature," after the Modernist period learned to rise above these limitations in works where these two factors, reality and literature, are no longer in operation as antagonistic forces.

Jorge Amado

The literary career of Jorge Amado (1912–   )[57] has up till now gone through three different phases (and, no matter how paradoxical it may seem, of necessity, complementary phases): the *Lenita* phase (to which *O País do Carnaval* belongs); the phase of his Bahian and political novels; and, finally, the phase I would call *academic*—in the good or bad sense of the word— marked by *Gabriela, Cravo e Canela* (which is the academism of his Modernism and of his Bahianism), by the *Velhos Marinheiros* (which is academic literature in its best sense), and by his election to the Brazilian Academy of Letters (which is purely social academemism or literary establishmentarianism).[58]

The thread that runs through these diverse works, which at one and the same time gives them meaning and explication, is the romantic temperament of the writer, so that the first work, insignificant or deplorable as it may be, serves nonetheless to reveal the spontaneous lines of force of a character (*Lenita*) and, symmetrically, *O País do Carnaval* shows the essential structure of his spirit and accounts for the religious fervor of his adolescence, his militant Communism (much more romantic than realistic), and the kind of liberalization which seems to characterize his ideas after 1955. In his first period, the novelist was a

Modernist without knowing it as, in general, were the writers who came to constitute what later was called the "Northeastern generation." It was the time of the Brunswick Bar, where he and his friends created "in Bahia a review of universalist character which condemned the Greengiltism and the Brazil-mania of the boys from Minas Gerais and São Paulo." [59] *O País do Carnaval* three years later forecast *Os Velhos Marinheiros* in the sense that instead of having "local color," it constituted a program of "intellectual and moral reform." For precisely that reason, in a meaningful preface Augusto Frederico Schmidt, who at that time had turned anti-Modernist, asserted that "the Movement has died and has nothing more to tell us," and thus announced to the novelist that "Christ is the key and the way."

But at that point we were into the thirties. Moving to Rio, the novelist discovered what in the province could only be a laughable sham—true political and intellectual life, in an openly revolutionary atmosphere, in an effervescence in which the political and literary rebellions of the foregoing decade were joined in a common current. Later, claiming in the *Vida de Luís Carlos Prestes* that that "Knight of Hope" exerted great influence on modern Brazilian literature, Jorge Amado made only one mistake. He attributed to the military and romantic idealist of those years preoccupations and literary interests which he did not entertain and, as far as one can see, never came to develop. The fact is that, seen in historiographic and partisan perspective, Luís Carlos Prestes may appear to be the leader of the revolution of 1924 when, in truth, he was only one of the elements in the revolutionary process which originated in 1922 (and lasted until 1935 in the military phase, until 1945 in the political phase), and of which Modernism was the reflection on the intellectual plane. In that light, Jorge Amado was right: "Modern Brazilian literature, that which produced the social novels, the sociological studies, the rehabilitation of the Negro, and historical studies, is a direct result of the cycle of revolutions initiated in 1922; that new literature can come to an end only with the full development of the democratic-bourgeois transformation of 1922, 1924, 1926, 1930, and 1935. These years brought the people to the surface, interested them in the problems of Brazil, gave them a craving for culture of which the present literary movement is the direct result. . . ." [60]

Let us correct the insistent use of the word "result" and its concomitant implications: the fact is that in the thirties there was a "modernism" in politics as there was a "radicalism" in literature; there was a "redemptive Revolution," just as there was a literary redemption. Such was the atmosphere that the student Jorge Amado found in Rio de Janeiro. His generation was conscientiously going to achieve the program of the political revolution (with all the ideological contradictions accruing in the vagueness of its programs) and, unwittingly, the program of the literary revolution. That explains why, when he bore suddenly to the literary and political Left (as Graciliano Ramos did), the Jorge Amado of *Lenita* and of *O País do Carnaval* became the Jorge Amado of *Cacau* (passing, revealingly enough, through the abortive *Rui Barbosa Número 2*).

This was the novelist's Bahian and political phase. Let us take this juncture in its broadest sense: From *Cacau* (1933) to *Os Subterrâneos da Liberdade* (1955), he wrote the political novel in its most deliberate form. In that phase the native qualities of the novelist compensate at once for his limitations as a writer and his intellectual deficiencies. Really, Jorge Amado is the exemplar of the instinctive writer, of the literary "primitive" (like the "primitive" in painting). With the passage of time and the requirements of the dialogue, his general culture was vastly broadened. His trips abroad and his international contacts aided him considerably. But he always remained the spontaneous writer, little given to abstraction and intellectual ratiocination; he was instinctively anti-rationalist and retained his emotional stance in the face of things. Let it be understood that I do not fault him in these matters: I am merely attempting to establish the basis for a correct critical analysis. But if the political keynote came to direct his actions, including his literary actions, if his novel deliberately took on the function of a political tool, it happened that, at the same time, he was forced to accept the Modernist revolution which he had repudiated in the provinces.

Thus contradicting the two postulates of the man who prefaced his work in 1931, he did not consider the 1922 Movement as inexpressive and dead, nor did he seek in Christ the answer to his pressing problems. However, that did not come about all at once. Somewhere between 1936 and 1937 he came suddenly to understand the true significance of a literary reformation of which he was a disciple without knowing it and which up till then he had rejected. As a matter of fact, in an article titled "Literature, Novel, and Politics as Social Consequences," published in *Pan*, in Buenos Aires (March 11, 1936), he wrote among other things:

> An intellectual movement in a purely revolutionary sense, (I speak again as of a literary conception), Modernism destroyed the old literary patterns of the country. But it did not renovate them. It left a blank page. Modernism, which destroyed so many things, built nothing. It produced some great poets and several essayists of worth. Nevertheless, where do we find the great novelist of Modernism? It was not an era of struggles [*sic*], there did not exist in men or in the milieu the turmoil which customarily accompanies great movements so that Modernism might produce the novelist capable of impressing the reading public. And it was necessary for social struggle to flare up so that new Brazilian novelists might emerge, though they have no connection with Modernism [*sic*]. And I add this: it was necessary for the movement of conflict to emerge so that the novelists who in Modernism had gotten lost in allusive poems and Greengilt manifestoes might show themselves. Only after the Movement had been corroborated, also only after the Modernist Movement had ended, did Oswald de Andrade appear with all the strength of his novel. He is the novelist of Modernism, who only showed himself after the Movement was over, when the struggle ceased to be purely literary, in order to become a political struggle.

However, exactly a year later in the *Jornal da Noite* of Pôrto Alegre his point of view was quite altered:

> That which brought new blood to Brazilian literature and especially to the Brazilian novel was the discovery of the true Brazil, a Brazil which only few people had seen before.

That discovery falls to the Modernists, those who around 1922 began to lose faith in the literary taboos of the country. The Modernists destroyed more than they built, that is true. However, they did build. Take Augusto Meyer, for example. But mainly we owe to them the heroic fact of having made Brazil begin to see things differently. They gave rise to all this post-Modernist literature. José Américo de Almeida, the first of all of us to bring out a modern novel, found the path cleared by the Modernists and was thus able to create *A Bagaceira*.[61]

Finally, as we have seen in *A Vida de Luís Carlos Prestes,* he effected the fusion of two currents, the political and the literary, although naturally the first seemed to him to be much more important than the second.

The normal outcome of that period should have been a great political novel, and Jorge Amado did write it, or at least attempted to write it, long after the Modernist era. This was *Os Subterrâneos da Liberdade,* which has remained, and in so far as one can foretell, will remain unfinished. Jorge Amado, as well as he could, rounded out the Modernist period by writing perhaps his worst novel: *Seara Vermelha,* published in 1946. Thus we can say with some surprise that the least significant part of his work was written in that period, since all of his novels paled in the presence of *Gabriela, Cravo e Canela.* The fact is that he was the victim of literature as long as he tried to scorn literature; but already *Terras do Sem Fim* (1942) and *São Jorge dos Ilhéus* (1944) were the unconscious outline of the great *Gabriela* and demonstrate, for that very reason, that around 1945 the literary compass was beginning to turn again.

Gilberto Freyre

Gilberto Freyre (1901–   ) is, *malgré lui*, one of Modernism's basic authors in the thirties and forties (in so far as Brazilian studies are concerned and not literature in the narrowest sense of the word), just as Oliveira Viana had unwittingly been in the twenties (and somewhat into the thirties, since the two streams of thought convened and swelled to a torrent in spite of their irreconcilable antagonisms). This is not the place to study fully the man as a social scientist but only, as Thibaudet said, to place him as a writer in some kind of *order*.

The quality that best identifies him is his originality—accompanied by a very sharp consciousness of himself as originator. It is for that reason that he opposes more and more vigorously any admission of the influence of Modernism on his ideas and frame of mind. It was originality of thought, first of all, which led him to create not only a *Brazilian sociology*—in the broad and narrow sense of that expression—but also to renovate within the international perspective sociological studies which outside of Brazil are now beginning to be prized and valued for their legitimate importance. He is also recognized for the originality of his style, which immediately identifies him incontrovertibly as one of our thinkers whose writing is most engaging, although his manner may often degenerate into mannerism, and although his idiom—*"ondoyante et diverse,"* as Montaigne might say—may frequently annoy the reader because of its peculiar obscurity. Nevertheless, here—as in no other writer—style is the man himself: it reflects the nature of a type of thought which refuses to simplify a complex and contradictory reality. On all sides he "enfolds" the external world, which is hypothetically the social world, and he penetrates its every fissure with all the explosive force of rapidly expanding gases. The mind of Gilberto Freyre could find its natural expression only in that kind of fluid style, with no firm articulation, no rigidity, preferring rather to suggest than to define; a style, if it may be so expressed, which is algebraic rather than geometrical or arithmetical. As Anísio Teixeira has aptly observed: "Nothing in Gilberto Freyre is linear or schematic; his thought reveals itself as rich, multifaceted, and mature, rather psychological than logical, preferring the appearance of contradiction to impoverishing and benighted simplification, as long as no aspect of reality escapes him and he can introduce it in all its extreme, multiple, and delicate complexity, in that *animadísimo tapiz* to which Professor Ayala refers."

So began the comments which I devoted to his "significance" for contemporary Brazilian thought on the occasion of the publication of the *Sociologia* in his *Obras Reunidas*; [62] that attempt at global and literary judgment finds its proper place when we face him as one of the basic authors of the Modernist era. In the always impassioned argumentation over his opinions and the essential significance of his works (always impassioned because the "Gilbertians" and the "anti-Gilbertians" are extremely impassioned), scholars have not only committed noisy injustices in their judgments, but they have also made the mistake, even more unpardonable, of failing to recognize his double originality which is, so to speak, outside of debatable questions and which is, to a certain degree, independent of those questions. If it is true that "it would be useless to expect great things in sociology from a lesser, weak, or mediocre sociologist, no matter how close his methods and techniques were to the methods of the natural sciences," we should add that perhaps in no other man—not only sociologist but thinker in general—is the stamp of the "I" so vital in his science or speciality, that perhaps no other manifests more clearly than he the "power of comprehension, of empathy, let us say even of imagination, scientific and even poetic imagination," which are the proper tools for the grasp of the real, beyond simple "technique of experimentation and measurement." [63]

Gilberto Freyre's sociology, without being in any way less scientific than other sociologies, is also more than anything a projection of his personality upon the external world. Such a "projection of the personality," he says himself, is "inevitable in sociology as in other sciences that deal with man: neutrality or absolute impassivity is impossible in those sciences." If such is the case, if "Cleopatra's nose" must of necessity intervene, if not in destiny, at least on the face of science, if it must inevitably mark it with its shadow or with its shape, then it is preferable that it should manifest itself, as in Gilberto Freyre, under the species of a "nose" that is unmistakable and full of personality, a "nose" that cannot be ignored or despised, instead of getting lost, as do many others, in the uncharacteristic anonymity of so many noses which simply fade away not only on the pathways of sociology but also on the pathways of all the branches of intellectual activity.

Gilberto Freyre is too intellectual to deny that kind of need in the spiritual life. It is his critics who have often not been sufficiently intelligent either to understand or to accept that fact. It is as if in any theory we failed to find not only in sociology but in all the sciences that deal with man—and even with far greater frequency than we might tend to think, even in the so-called natural sciences themselves—that share of subjectivity which is the incomparable and characteristic quality of all great works, of everything of consequence which has been or will be achieved in the history of thought. Everything born of the spirit of man— science "of man" or science "of nature"—whether literature or art, is essentially "style," a way of seeing or feeling the world. And the "world" in itself does not exist; it has already been otherwise expressed by that model of apparent objectivity whose name was Kant: what exists is a spirit which creates the world and, at every moment, imagines that it observes external reality. That does not constitute a denial of the objectivity of scientific observation but only of an objective vision of it as it is: conditioned by sensitivity, imagination, each one's "psychological history" and even by his history, properly speaking. Therefore, Gilberto Freyre says with good reason that there is considerable interest

> in our knowing from a sociologist not only his school, his technique, and his sociological development but also his personality—as thoroughly as possible—including his "Cleopatra's nose" so that we may take into proper consideration his excesses of subjectivity, his possible Freudian or Adlerian complexes, when these latter crop up in his work. The Jewish nose of Durkheim is not an irrelevant detail in a totally objective consideration of Durkheim's work; much less the Jewish nose of Karl Marx. The fact that Professor Sorokin was a Russian, who in his younger days as a university don had fought against Lenin, should never be forgotten when we read his pages of so-called scientific "sociology" on revolutions in which the pamphleteer and the moralist are more obvious than the sociologist. Nor should we forget the fact that the Count of Gobineau had been punished in Brazil by a Brazilian doctor whose wife (perhaps brunette in the Brazilian fashion) the Frenchman had attempted to court, when we read today not only the para-sociological pages of Gobineau on Aryanism or all the sociological literature inspired by those pages.

Gilberto Freyre likewise has his "Cleopatra's noses": one of them is the fact that he is the "son of a land in large part tropical and mestizo, although he descends from a family of European origin with a distant touch of Amerindian blood and no—so it would seem—drop of African blood." In a kind of "psychological reaction" which throws light on one of the essential bases of his work, Gilberto Freyre made of miscegenation—particularly between Negroes and Whites—and tropicalism, the two principles which to him seem to explain Brazil, when they really explain only a part of Brazil in one moment of her history. Later broadening that thesis to an international scale, he went so far as to create "Luso-tropicalism"; that is, he extended to several regions of the globe, where the same natural and human conditions that we observe in Brazil could also be found, the application of the points of view so dear to him. Obviously, those and other assertions have given rise to widely divergent criticisms which run from bad-tempered to polite contradiction. I myself, not so much against his Luso-tropicalist ideas as against his inevitable and deplorable political exploitation (to which he did not mind lending the inestimable value of his support), had the opportunity to oppose him with my reaction, all the more vehement because it seems to me to lessen the prestige and the scope of his observation or of his purely scientific points of view.

Still, these differences of opinion should in no way reach the point, unfortunately all too common, of denying to Gilberto Freyre not only the respect which his work merits but also the recognition of the preponderant role played by him and his work in the evolution of Brazilian sociology and of Brazilian thought in general. Nor should we deny to him the noteworthy place he has won for himself as a writer and a leader of a school of thought. He is the leader of a "Gilbertian" school which concedes to (at least in theory) and even encourages its opponents and their rebuttals and which, more faithful to a complex reality than to the necessary unity of its doctrine, prefers to enlarge creatively the work of the Brazilian sociologist instead of allowing it to languish in the vacuum of an uncompromising and sterile admiration. What I say of the "school" is unfortunately not always applicable to the disciples of the school. The truth is that certain criticisms of Gilberto Freyre rather lessen the critic than the man criticized and reveal Cleopatrically gigantic noses bigger than the face, which in certain cases does not even exist. Now, the fact is that he does not exist on a plane that is higher than his critics, whom he used to tolerate with eminently Britannic discipline and fair play. What must be taken into consideration is the fact that a writer and a thinker of his stature is above a "certain kind" of criticism and moreover deserves and even demands a totally different kind: a creative criticism which comprehends the significance of his work and knows how to put it within its literary and scientific evolution and can mark, with as much certainty as is possible, its scope and fertility.

In the light of that type of criticism, his greatness is beyond question. All the disagreements over detail, even the eventual total repudiation of his points of view, can never justify an ignorance of what Gilberto Freyre represents, not only in himself but also as direct or indirect instigator of numerous Brazilian studies; not only as an observer of social and historical reality but also as a catalytic force which permitted other observations; not only as an inspirer of works similar to his but also as an inspirer of works which are even opposed to his; and not only as the center of purely sociological activities but also as the center of complex intellectual activities whose history has not yet been written. Let us merely indicate that it would have sufficed for him to inspire and, so to speak, delimit in certain aspects the work of a José Lins do Rêgo in order that his influence, not only scientific but also intellectual in the broadest sense of the word, might deserve our individual attention.

Graciliano Ramos

Graciliano Ramos (1892–1953) was the writer of the political revolution of 1930 rather than of the literary revolution of 1922.[64] More than that, his Northeast (speaking in terms of literature) was not the Northeast of José Lins do Rêgo or Jorge Amado. I mean that although in the history of Brazilian publishing he belonged to the same famous generation that produced the so-called Northeastern literature of the thirties (an expression which is only geographical by extension, contrary to the opinion of certain participants of the Congresso de Crítica de Assis), he was truly the great loner and eccentric.

In the bookish and abbreviated retrospect with which we usually perceive literary history, attracted merely by an irresistible temptation to classify, we forget that Graciliano Ramos was born in 1892 and that he was thirty years old at the time of the Week of Modern Art. At that moment he no doubt took no cognizance at all of the great literary event. It is also quite likely that he had heard nothing at all of that other "regional" modernism of 1926, even more limited to Recife than the Modernism of 1922 had been concerned in its first stages with the city of São Paulo. In the twenties Graciliano Ramos was a man of considerable culture, who on his own had undertaken more serious literary and linguistic studies than most of his contemporaries. It appears, however, that he in no way seemed destined for a career as a professional writer, for the national fame as a novelist which came to be his. Moreover, in no way whatsoever did he possess the "Modernist spirit" nor even the modern spirit in the name of which the literary generation of the thirties built their work.

His contemporaries, and in particular the more or less numerous groups of frivolous souls who, in all periods, constitute what we might call "literary circles" and thus influence—indirectly but vigorously—the establishment of critical perspectives, always viewed the grumpy and pessimistic nature of "old Graça" as if it constituted a particular kind of worldly attitude all his own. An unprejudiced reading of his work, and notably of his spontaneous and occasional pages, demonstrates that he was above all a marginal personage in the literature of the day, just as he was a marginal character in the reigning political system and, in a quite obvious way, a marginal personage among the social groups in which he lived. All of this marginalism was conscious and, at the same time, responsible for his remorse and pride: hence the reason for the singular stratification of his character as a man and writer in a paradoxical mixture of pessimism and idealism, of the lure of creativity and the disdain for literature. A more detailed analysis of these contradictions could not ignore a theme which, for the moment, I shall not discuss. This classic individualist became a militant member of the Communist party in which, of course, he saw only the idealistic and programmatic aspects. His travelogue of the Soviet Union is in this respect extremely instructive. To me it does not seem rash to suppose that communist reality, were it installed in Brazil, would be as repugnant to him as republican reality (in the nineteenth-century sense of the word). *Viagem* is from beginning to end a book of evasion: not evasion of Brazil, but of evasion of the very trip which the writer took. We do not require great psychological acuity to see that Graciliano Ramos makes an unconscious attempt not only to accept what they tell and show him but also to stifle any hint of inopportune critical spirit or curiosity. Reaching the Promised Land, he eliminated by an elementary process of psychological sublimation all contact with the immediate world and with himself. Graciliano Ramos did not see the geographical, political, or sociological Soviet Union; he saw the Soviet Union as it was shaped in the mental myth which the Communists of the entire world, and especially those of Brazil, have created slowly over the years of imagined diaspora.

The understanding of the kind of bad literary and political conscience that identified him (ambivalent bad conscience, because it embraced at one and the same time his options and his rejections) depends on knowledge of some of the details of his life, which up till now have been viewed exclusively through the prism of the picturesque, and an objective attitude toward those details. Among these, that of his spiritual development has obviously still not been sufficiently clarified. All that we possess in that regard is the invaluable volume of the *Homenagem,* published on the occasion of his fiftieth birthday in 1943. There we read the well-known story of the "discovery" of Graciliano Ramos by Augusto Frederico Schmidt through the reading of the *Relatório,* now famous, which as mayor of Palmeira dos Índios he had sent in 1929 to the governor of the state of Alagoas. And we also know that when the publisher asked the mayor for a novel, because it seemed to him that the official possessed exceptional writing ability, that novel had already been written in 1926, and it was *Caetés.* More than that: Nineteen chapters of *São Bernardo* had been written in the province, in the "dusty little town," the novelist says, where he might have continued "to play chess and backgammon, attending to my petty chores, listening to the endless arguments on the sidewalks, taking refuge in the afternoon in the hulking cathedral." These qualities, if not of the writer at least of the intellectual, were not recognized by Augusto Frederico Schmidt alone; the governor of Alagoas seems to have recognized them as early as 1930 when after the second—and somewhat unconventional—report, he brought Graciliano Ramos to the directorship of the State Press. The "redemptive Revolution" did not cut short his bureaucratic career because from 1933 to 1936 he was still director of public education in his native state. Thus the future revolutionary adjusted to both the Old Republic and the New Republic. At the same time, after 1933, with the publication of *Caetés,* he enrolled in that Northeastern literature which was, without his knowing it, the novel of São Paulo Modernism. Simultaneously the winds of revolution blew him to Rio de Janeiro, where he established permanent residence in 1936.

Nonetheless in that literature Graciliano Ramos was a writer apart, beginning with his language, as is well known. It is no secret that he repudiated *Caetés*—he repudiated it but continued to republish it. That contradiction, better than any other, serves to substantiate the ambivalences to which I referred. That and the articles collected in *Viventes das Alagoas*. We are in the presence of a man who prepared himself to be a classical and traditional writer, a respecter of the Portuguese language, read of course in the non-conformist text of Eça de Queiroz and who, as he said in his expression of gratitude for the *Homenagem,* "was forced by events to undergo unforeseen displacements." Without expecting it, he was thrown into a career of professional writing; without expecting and without wishing it, he became a "Modernist" writer because in the thirties one tried to be a Modernist or died. If the older Alcântara Machado spoke of Gonçalves de Magalhães as the "repentent Romantic," with regard to Graciliano Ramos, it would be proper to speak of the Modernist *malgré lui,* the Modernist of ill will. In many of his articles, even in the forties, he betrays his disgust in the face of linguistic error and carelessness; in the 1929 *Relatório* (the one in which he mentions the episode of D. Pedro Sardinha "devoured" in the sixteenth century by wild Indians, this with regard to the economics of telegraph expenditures), the erudite placement of objective pronouns betrays the man's cultivated literary taste: "I intend to lengthen it [the Palmeiras de Fora road] to the boundary of Sant'Ana do Ipanema, not in its present condition, because the income from the county would not allow me to undertake a job of that magnitude." This anti-Modernist correctness [65] he retained to the end of his days, just as he practiced to the end a type of prose fiction which bore little substantial resemblance to Northeastern fiction. The basic novelist of this period was, to be sure, José Lins do Rêgo; beside him Jorge Amado represents the second generation, the generation which neither had nor wished to have any connection with literary history prior to 1922. Within the "sociological novel" of the thirties, Graciliano Ramos wrote the "psychological novel": the prestige of ready-made ideas and simplistic views was so great that at the time no one noticed such scandalous behavior. On the other hand, there was no one more alien to "socialist realism" than this Communist writer: even in this regard, Jorge Amado achieved what José Lins do Rêgo and Graciliano Ramos "ought" to have achieved. The latter's "socialist realism" found an outlet in his travel-book, precisely and paradoxically in his least realistic book, and also in the *Memórias do Cárcere,* which are his "notes from underground"—what we might call reality seen through the telescope of a novelist.

None of this escaped the experienced eye of Otto Maria Carpeaux, who wrote one of the most stimulating studies in the *Homenagem.* He justly regards the novelist as a classic, but

> an experimental classic. His extremely tardy appearance as a writer, when he was past forty, ought to have been preceded by the slow preparation of an experimentalist, for even afterward he always continued to experiment. Our friend in common, Aurélio Buarque de Holanda, called my attention to the fact that every one of Graciliano Ramos's works is a different type of novel. In effect: *Caetés* is the product of an Anatole or a Brazilian Eça; *São Bernardo* is worthy of Balzac; *Angústia* has something of Marcel Jouhandeau in it; and *Vidas Sêcas* reminds me of recent North American short story writers.

Otto Maria Carpeaux reminds us that it is not a question of comparison nor even, I would add, of exacting literary assimilation. But these names have the value of a suggestive indication; they bring Graciliano Ramos close to the universal novel in the same measure that they remove him from the "Northeastern literature" of the thirties. I would compare those prestigious allusions to Balzac and Eça de Queiroz to the chess and backgammon which Graciliano Ramos, even if it was only in his imagination, played in Palmeira dos Índios or in Maceió. Actually no Brazilian Modernist of the first decades would admit to a knowledge of backgammon; not one of them was or could be a chess player. If in intellectual life everything responds and corresponds, then one can assert that Northeastern literature was born of minds that no rule of chess ever entered, nor the spiritual conformity which those rules presuppose. By the same token, the chess expert would never have written novels like those of our thirties. Graciliano Ramos was in literature a Northeasterner and a Modernist of *that decade* (be sure to stress those words!); that is, he was gradually and inevitably influenced by the literature which was being produced all around him. It is easy to see that his "experimentalism" has an unconscious meaning and direction. If *Caetés* never was more than a truly literal echo of Eça de Queiroz, *São Bernardo* is then the Northeast seen through the eyes of a Balzac, but a primitive Balzac; *Angústia* is an attempt to surpass the two limitations implicit in these literary coordinates, and it all adds up in my opinion to obvious failure. *Vidas Sêcas* demonstrates a desire for integration into the Northeastern group; it reveals that José Lins do Rêgo's laurels robbed Graciliano of his sleep from time to time.

The inadmissable, shocking, unacceptable, and inevitable conclusion is that Graciliano Ramos's career, after all is said and done, adds up to a frustration, not over what it was but over what it ought to have been. He could not withstand the pressures of his literary milieu and abruptly altered the direction of his work, attempted to conquer his original propensities and the very nature of his mind. *Caetés* is the novel most deserving of criticism of all those which he published (if we take into account that *Vidas Sêcas* is not, properly speaking, a novel), but at the same time it does represent that which he possessed that was truly genuine. Let us be satisfied to say that Graciliano Ramos might have been not our Balzac but our Jean Giono or, at the other extreme, our Caldwell. Literary "events" led him to be a novelist divided between a vocation that opposed dominant currents and a work that sought to reconcile those antagonisms.

Let us add that his Queirozian or Balzaquian side suffered from an obvious weakness: Graciliano Ramos lacked imagination and notably social imagination (which would be inexplicable in a militant Communist if his adherence to Communism had not stemmed from the same kind of misunderstandings as his adherence to literary Modernism). All of his novels begin and end with the individual; they are "stories" of the Northeast composed more or less on the same plane employed by the regional story tellers. In that regard nothing is more typical than the conversations of Alexandre and Cesária; they reveal certain of the novelist's limitations, just as they reveal the effort which was, after all was said and done, his novelesque work and what came from it.

That work was a victory over himself in every sense of the word. It is not by accident that in the "Pequena História da República" he refers to José de Alencar as a "splendid novelist": in the history of the Modernist novel we still have not studied the schizophrenic presence of the writer from Ceará. The subject is too vast to be undertaken at this point. Let us only say that the theoretical fate of Graciliano Ramos, if the direction suggested by *Caetés* had not undergone the abrupt change which the sudden entrance into the world of literary professionalism imposed upon him, would have been that of a modern José de Alencar (much more than an Eça de Queiroz or a Balzac). He took from Alencar the idealizing vision and the sense of the uniqueness of the character. Both understood literature as a linguistic creation and as a national creation; both saw the novel as an essentially epic form of literature. It simply happens that José de Alencar was able to reach fulfillment and become a "splendid novelist," while Graciliano Ramos stifled his native tendencies and took his place in a literary picture which opposed them. At last it was all resolved for the best, since he was warmly and sincerely applauded for being what he was not. But he himself, I hold, was aware of so many confounding errors which, it seemed, could be righted through revolution, a revolution which would destroy the society which opposed him and, with a shining miracle, would restore to him his rightful unity. Graciliano Ramos's revolution was also Alencar's: a romantic revolution. At heart his disturbed and disturbing life could have been the great novel which lay in his power to create and which he almost wrote in the *Memórias do Cárcere*.

Érico Veríssimo

The literary career of Érico Veríssimo (1905–) during the Modernist period goes from *Clarissa* (1933) to *O Resto É Silêncio* (1943). These are ten fertile but uneven years of which the last novel marks, at one and the same time, the high point and the decisive turning point. As a matter of fact, we have here a truly Balzaquian cycle of novels in the sense that the same characters appear and reappear in different perspectives, living out their history in chronological progression. The indisputable failure of *Saga* seems to have forced the novelist to finish off his "Clarissa cycle" and come back immediately with one of his strong books, *O Resto É Silêncio,* whose last pages, beyond other small indications, forecast the great novel which he wrote after the period under study here.[66]

During that entire phase Érico Veríssimo was certainly the most popular of all the modern Brazilian novelists and the most wronged by the critics. They maintained a kind of reserve toward him, if not outright hostility, which is explained before all else by the marginalism which placed him outside the literary currents then in vogue. Really as much as Graciliano Ramos, but for totally different reasons, Érico Veríssimo was an eccentric with relation to literary history. Without living in Rio de Janeiro,

307

he wrote the urban novel of customs when the fashion was to write novels of social protest, Northeastern rural novels, written in the heat of the streets of Rio. At a time of bigoted political options to the Right or to the Left, he was a classical democrat preaching the creed, truly a little simplistic, of fraternity and humanitarianism and indicting (here is the chink in his armor) the bad conscience of the intellectual because he was not a man of action.

On the other hand, surrendering to the snobbery typical of the vanguardists, the Brazilian critics of the thirties tacitly decided that the novelist's success was the proof of his lack of quality. Literary history has now had time to demonstrate that the critical success of many other writers is not necessarily a proof of their high quality. The truth is that, of all the novelists of this period, Érico Veríssimo was truly the one with the greatest technical resources, the one with the greatest capacity for renewal and the one, at last, to whom the mission of reinvigorating the Brazilian novel fell, placing him on an incomparable universal and literary plane. It is possible that his virtuosity, sometimes too obvious, has annoyed the cultivators of a literature that was primitivist and stylistically unqualifiable, partisans of the monolithic and tongue-tied character, rather symbol than human being, living out his wretchedness and moral decay as in a Russian novel, and automatically repeating exactly what he was expected to say.

Disturbed, so it would seem, by the limitations imputed to him by the critics each time he brought out a new novel, Érico Veríssimo frequently committed the error of devoting long stretches in his books to theoretical discussion of politics or social philosophy. These are out of place, and furthermore they reveal his lack of talent for that kind of reasoning. The credo of this novelist is not composed of commonplaces (on the contrary, there was nothing less trivial in the thirties and forties) but of basic truths, which many do not wish to accept as true, while others face them as self-evident. Thus, as a thinker, as an intellectual defending an ideology which seemed to him correct and salutary, Érico Veríssimo suffered the unpleasant fate of displeasing everyone. At the same time those alien materials weakened his novels, either because they introduced into them an element of unevenness or inferiority, or because they caused a break in their profound unity. In many of his books of that period Érico Veríssimo simply lacked the courage to be himself: I mean, a novelist cast in the classical mold, ready to tell on the level of esthetic invention the daily life of the common man.

He was the novelist of the middle-class city and of the middle-class man in Brazil. The provincial capital or the character from the urban bourgeoisie, struggling against poverty and never against misery, the wealthy upper middle class, dramas of the conscience, the unknown gamut of sensibility: these were his favorite and specific domains. When he tried to write a "political novel" on the ideological level of leftist-rightist debates, it turned out to be the frustrating experience of *Saga*. Ten years later, after the Modernist period, when he wrote the "political novel" viewed through the eyes of the man of Rio Grande do Sul, he attained with no difficulty the extraordinary level of the masterpiece.

In Modernist perspective, belonging to the consolidating generation, he is one of the basic authors of the Movement because he did outside of São Paulo what none of the revolutionaries of 1922 could do. He wrote a modern urban novel more interested in interpreting man faithfully than in amazing his reader with the novelty of his style. But at the same time we must take into account the fact that style in the novel is something more than the well-turned phrase: it is structure, conception of character, view of the world, narrative reliability, control of the technical instrument. All of these matters considered together force us to place him with the strictest of critical correctness among those who have given to the Modernist novel precisely what it lacked (and what the death of Alcântara Machado kept it from achieving): a true style.

If we divide his career into two clearly recognizable phases (the phase of the urban and petit-bourgeois novel represented by the "Clarissa cycle," and the epic phase represented by *O Tempo e o Vento,* both materially and novelistically separated by that unique work which is *O Resto É Silêncio*), then we perceive that only the first phase belongs to us, this last work included in it, and that it contains the most unequal and at the

same time most typical novels by this writer. The more demanding readers have already made their choice and have set *Clarissa*
aside in the series for its ingenuous and simple freshness;
Caminhos Cruzados as a successful example of a technique which
the novelist repeated with variations in other books; and, finally,
O Resto É Silêncio, which would have occupied an eminent
position in the hierarchy of our novel if the readers, including
the critics, had had some technical understanding of literary art
close to that of the novelist when he wrote it.

If, in general, in the history of Modernism the most common
spectacle is that of overestimated writers (even in so far as the role
they played in the emergence and evolution of the Movement
was concerned), Érico Veríssimo was the sole example of the under-
estimated writer, waiting for great critical essays, exhaustive analyses, and the "recognition" of what he truly represented. As for
conception and technique, his work has no "Modernist" traits;
but, like many others, it would not have appeared outside the
milieu introduced by the Movement without the catalytic action
which it exercised. He himself in one of the books of this first
phase said that the difference between old and modern literature
resided in the fact that in the old the sun was the "king-star,"
while after Modernism the sun was simply referred to as the sun.
That small image says more than it appears to say, and might clarify the situation, at first sight paradoxical, of the Brazilian novel of
the thirties (Northeastern or otherwise): it was Modernist fiction
which in the best authors fulfilled itself in a natural flowering of
the programs outlined ten years earlier.

The long march at last came to an end, the march which since
1922 had led Brazilian literature from Modernism to the modern,
that is, from the circumstantial to the present. At the same time,
through a characteristically dialectical process, doors were opened
for the still unknown *-isms* which lay hidden in the future.

Notes

1. Mário da Silva Brito, *História do Modernismo Brasileiro* (São Paulo: Saraiva, 1958). Only the first volume, *Antecedentes da Semana de Arte Moderna*, has been published as of this writing.

2. João do Rio, *Psicologia Urbana* (Rio de Janeiro: H. Garnier, 1911), pp. 185 ff. The title of this small collection of works is, incidentally, significant of the process of urbanization which was growing in intensity and became one of the catalytic sources of Modernism.

3. At the time, the best attempt to locate Modernism within the current of civilization, which on one hand quietly affirmed its *new* but *necessary* character and on the other hand aimed at pacifying the excessive fears of the traditionalists, was the book by Rubens Borba de Moraes, *Domingo dos Séculos* (Rio de Janeiro: Candeia Azul, 1924). This was Sérgio Buarque de Holanda's intention when he reviewed the volume in *Estética* (II, January–March, 1925, p. 222) and observed that "the small volume . . . is not *properly speaking* [my italics] a concession that a Modernist artist makes to a public which does not read Modernist writers." The critic adds that it is necessary to bear one fact in mind in order not to miss the true meaning of the essay: "But the concession which Senhor Rubens de Moraes makes to the public never grows so great that he sacrifices his more daring ideas to that simple pleasure."

   The lecture by Ronald de Carvalho (1925) has that same "reactionary" meaning: "As Bases da Arte Moderna" (cf. *Lanterna Verde*, Rio de Janeiro, III, February, 1936, pp. 14 ff.).

4. "50 Anos de Literatura Brasileira" in the *Panorama das Literaturas das Américas* (From 1900 to the Present), ed. Joaquim de Montezuma de Carvalho (Angola: Município de Nova Lisboa, 1958), I, pp. 103 ff.

5. Homero Senna, *República das Letras* (Rio de Janeiro: Livraria São José, 1957), p. 76.

6. Oswald de Andrade, *Poesias Reunidas* (São Paulo: Edição Gaveta, 1945).

7. The frantic desire to replace Modernism, to kill it off and bury it, brought on a multiplicity of "generations" after a certain point. In that regard Oswald de Andrade maliciously observed: "That surely was the cause of a young man's demanding for himself the prestige of belonging to the generation of August 12, 1939, because such was the condition of things: after the generation of 1922, which had come after the generation of Machado de Assis, the generation of 1930 had painfully appeared, followed by the generation of 1935, then 1936, then the first semester of 1937, then the second semester, and finally the young man's own generation. When I asked him what all those generations had done, he answered: 'Studied problems.' " (*Ponta de Lança*, p. 59.)

8. *Ibid.*, p. 6.

9. Oswald de Andrade, "Manifesto Antropófago," originally published in the first number of the *Revista de Antropofagia* (May, 1928). Now available in a more accessible edition in the *Revista do Livro*, XVI (December, 1959), pp. 192 ff.

10. "Urupês" in *Urupês, Outros Contos e Coisas* (São Paulo: Companhia Editôra Nacional, 1943), pp. 125 ff.

11. Marques Rebêlo, Introduction to the *Poemas Completos of Murilo Araújo* (Rio de Janeiro: Pongetti, 1960).

12. Mário da Silva Brito, *História do Modernismo Brasileiro*, I, 45 ff.

13. *Ibid.*, 36 ff.

14. "One Saturday"—it is Anita speaking here—"two young men came in out of a downpour. They began to laugh outrageously and one of them could not stop. I was furious and demanded satisfaction. The more angry I grew, the wilder the laughter of the one fellow. Finally he calmed down a bit and, as he left, he introduced himself: 'I am the poet Mário Sobral' (Mário de Andrade's youthful pseudonym). Some days later, as he said good-bye, he presented me with a Parnassian sonnet on my painting 'The Yellow Man.' " Statement to the *Diário Carioca* (February 24, 1952), cited by Mário da Silva Brito, *op. cit.*, p. 55. Mário da Silva Brito asserts that this visit occurred on December 15, 1917. The same version of the events is reproduced in an interview with Anita Malfatti in the *Correio Paulistano* of April 5, 1959.

15. Guilherme de Almeida, "Idéias de 1922" in RASM (*Revista Anual do Salão de Maio*), I (1939). No page numbers.

16. Menotti del Picchia, *Correio Paulistano* (1920). Also recorded in the *Revista do Brasil* (July, 1920).

17. Pär Bergman, *"Modernolatria" et "Simultaneità."* Investigations into two trends in the avant-garde literatures of Italy and France on the eve of the First World War. (Uppsala: Svenska Bokförlaget, 1962), p. viii.

18. *Ibid.*, p. 161. Tutto si muove, tutto corre, tutto volge rapido. Una figura non è mai stabile davanti a noi ma appare e scompare incessantemente. Per la persistenza della immagine nella retina, le cose in movimento si moltiplicano, si deformano susseguendosi, come vibrazioni,

nello spazio che percorrono. Cosi un cavallo in corsa non ha quattro gambe: ne ha venti e i loro movimenti sono triangolari.
The "technical manifesto" was not included by Graça Aranha in the book *Futurismo* (Manifestoes by Marinetti and his companions) (Rio de Janeiro: Pimenta de Mello & Cia., 1926).

19. *Ibid.*, p. 97.
20. *Ibid.*, pp. 13 ff.
21. *Ibid.*, pp. 55 ff.
22. Renato Almeida, *Velocidade* (Rio de Janeiro: Schmidt, 1932).
23. *Ibid.*, p. 62. Still serving at the Futurist altars in 1932, Renato Almeida fell into the same anachronism as the master, Graça Aranha, when six years later he published the Marinettian manifestoes. At that time the Italian school had not only been entirely surpassed in Brazil, as well as in the rest of the world, but it had also been expressly repudiated by the Brazilian Modernists, as we shall see. The same insensitivity to subtle Modernist transformations, if not actually ignorance of the facts of literary history, is exhibited by Mário Guastini (*a hora futurista que passou* . . . published in São Paulo by the Casa Mayença, the firm which published Mário de Andrade's *Paulicéia Desvairada*). Also in 1926 Guastini called the Modernists' "disappointment" over Marinetti a recent occurrence. Moreover, to write a book in that year against Modernism, equating it with madness, is ample proof of intellectual anachronism; even more so, to call the Week of Modern Art a "teratological week."
24. Jean Epstein, *La Poésie d'Aujourd'hui* (Paris: Editions de la Sirène, 1921), p. 169.

25.   Quisera ser ás para voar bem alto
         Sôbre a cidade de meu berço!
         Bem mais alto que os lamentos de bronze
         Das catedrais catalépticas:
         Muito rente do azul quase a sumir no céu
         Longe da casaria que diminui
         Longe, bem longe dêste chão de asfalto . . .

26.   Se um dia
         O meu corpo escapasse do aeroplano,
         Eu abriria os braços com ardor
         Para o mergulho azul na tarde transparente . . .
              .   .   .   .   .
         Riscando o céu na minha queda brusca

         Rápida e precisa,
         Cortando o ar em êxtase no espaço
         Meu corpo cantaria
         Sibilando
         A sinfonia da velocidade . . .

27.   Ah! le siècle automobile
                  aéroplane
              .   75
              Rapidité surtout RAPIDITÉ

28. Paulo Mendes de Almeida was kind enough to call my attention to this address by João do Rio. For the complete "meaning" of the writer, cf. Luís Martins, "João do Rio e a Vida Vertiginosa" in the "Suplemento Literário" of the *O Estado de São Paulo*, No. 347 (September 14, 1963).

29.   Não se lembram do gigante das botas de sete léguas?
Lá vai êle: vai varando, no seu vôo de asas cegas,
as distâncias . . .
    E dispara,
        nunca pára,
            nem repara
para os lados,
    para frente,
        para trás . . .
            Vai como um pária . . .
E vai levando um novêlo embaraçado de fitas:
fitas
    azuis,
        brancas,
            verdes,
                amarelas . . .
                    imprevistas . . .
Vai varando o vento: —e o vento, ventando cada vez mais,
desembaraça o novêlo, penteando com dedos de ar
o feixe fino de riscas,
                tiras
                    fitas,
                        faixas,
                            listas . . .
    E estira-as,
        puxa-as,
            estica-as,
                espicha-as bem para trás:
E as côres retêsas, sobem, descem DE-VA-GAR,
paralelamente,
    paralelamente,
        horizontais,
sôbre a cabeça espantada do Pequeno Polegar.

30. Ilse and Pierre Garnier, *L'Expressionnisme Allemand* (Paris: Editions André Silvaire, 1962), p. 8.
31. *Ibid.*, p. 17. In Brazil, for example, the influence of Whitman is quite apparent in Ronald de Carvalho while Rubens Borba de Moraes and Mário de Andrade call Rimbaud the fountain source of all modern poetry. A thread of baroquism runs subtly through Modernist poetry from the publication of the *Paulicéia Desvairada*. This baroque flourished without inhibitions after 1945.
32. Mário de Andrade, *Cartas a Manuel Bandeira* (Rio de Janeiro: Organização Simões Editôra, 1958), pp. 339–340.
33. Epstein, *op. cit.*, p. 53.
34. Garnier, *op. cit.*, p. 61.
35. Mário de Andrade, "Elegia de Abril," *Clima*, I (May, 1941), p. 11. This

essay may also be read now in *Aspectos da Literatura Brasileira* (Rio de Janeiro: Americ-Edit, 1943), pp. 237 ff.

36. Cf. Menotti del Picchia, Plínio Salgado, Cassiano Ricardo, *O Curupira e o Carão* (São Paulo: Editorial Helios Limitada, 1927), pp. 43 ff.

37. Epstein, *op. cit.*, pp. 57 ff.

38. Mário de Andrade, *O Movimento Modernista* (Rio de Janeiro: Casa do Estudante do Brasil, 1942).

39. *Ibid.*, p. 52.

40. Alceu Amoroso Lima, "Êxodo," *Revista do Brasil* (September, 1917).

41. Bergman, *op. cit.*, p. 51.

42. *Ibid.*, p. 55.

43. Mário da Silva Brito, *op. cit.*, p. 151.

44. Mário de Andrade, "Open Letter to Alberto de Oliveira," *Estética*, III (April–June, 1925). Cf. n. 2 of Pt. Two.

45. Mário da Silva Brito, *op. cit.*, pp. 157 ff.

46. Paul Mendes de Almeida, "A Cigarra Literária" in the "Suplemento Literário" of the *O Estado de São Paulo* (June 6, 1964).

47.   alta, direita, fina e esguia
        com teus ombros em linha reta erguidos,
        dás, a quem te vê,
        a impressão de um grande T.

48. Plínio Salgado, *Críticas e Prefácio*, in *Obras Completas* (São Paulo: Editôra das Américas, 1955), XIX, 144 ff.

49. Pedro Costa, *Alaor e Ocede* (Ed. Loester & Cia., 1922).

50.   "Estala" o canário!
        —Trinos! Trinos! Trinos!
            Repentinos!
            Peregrinos!
        E a cuiúba "chilreia" . . .
            (É bardo de aldeia!)
        Mas outro alado voa, e repete um "rosário":
        —Marido! . . . Marido! . . . Marido-é-dia?! . . .
            Ma-ri-do-é-dia?! . . .
            Ma-ri-do-é-dia?! . . .
        (E como "dêle" o canto com a hora condiz!)
            E lá está uma que à luz diz:
            —Surgi! Surgi! Surgi!
            E enquanto êste assim clama,
            Acolá já um outro exclama:
            Bem-te-vi! bem-te-vi! bem-te-vi!

            Ah! desperta a Natureza
            Almoxarifado da beleza! . . .

51. Di Cavalcanti, *Viagem da Minha Vida* (Rio de Janeiro: Civilização Brasileira, 1955). "I suggested to Paulo Prado that our Week would be one of literary and artistic scandal, one that would give hell to the petty *bourgeoisie* of São Paulo" (p. 115).

52. Renato Almeida, "Ronald de Carvalho e o Modernismo," *Lanterna Verde,*
IV (November, 1936), p. 70. In 1924 Léo Vaz transmitted the idea that
Graça Aranha had selected São Paulo because he needed to go there to
settle a business transaction involving coffee sales for the firm to which
Paulo Prado belonged (cf. Mário da Silva Brito, "Café e Modernismo" in
the "Suplemento Literário" of *O Estado de São Paulo,* No. 269 [February
17, 1962], a special number commemorating the fortieth anniversary of
the Week of Modern Art). Many years later on December 31, 1941,
Nazareth Prado granted a sensational interview to Joel Silveira (cf.
Diretrizes, No. 80 of that date) and publicly revealed what initiates
already knew: that she had been Graça Aranha's lady friend and that he
had been seeking any pretext to visit her in São Paulo. In her own words:
". . . the truth is that, more than any other reason, I was the main cause
of the 'Week of Modern Art.' Let me explain: In 1922 I was living with
my family in São Paulo. Graça Aranha needed some reason to come see
me. The 'Week of Modern Art' was a splendid pretext . . . I do not mean
that I was the indispensable cause of the Brazilian literary revolution. The
truth is that if the 'Week' had not taken place in 1922, it would have
happened later and would have originated under the guidance of someone other than Graça Aranha. But, I repeat, the fact that it occurred in
1922 was because of me."
  So, between the Marxist interpretation (proposed at the same time
with vilification and innocence by an ultraconservative to demoralize the
Modernists) and the unintentional "vaudeville" interpretation, it appears
that the Week had an extra-literary origin. Writing about "O Poeta Mário
de Andrade" in the *Anuário Brasileiro de Literatura* (VI, 1942, p. 28),
Moacir Werneck de Castro seems reluctant to accept Nazareth Prado's
version. It has been confirmed, however, by an unexpected eyewitness,
Rubens Borba de Moraes. Cf. "Memórias de um sobrevivente de *Klaxon,*"
in *Anhembi,* São Paulo, Year XII, Vol. XIV, No. 138 (May, 1962), p. 494.
  On my part, I find that life is somewhat more complex than these
explanations would have it. The coffee deal and the amorous intrigue
could very well have coexisted with a purely esthetic interest.
53. See Fernando Góes, "História da 'Paulicéia Desvairada,'" *Revista do
Arquivo Municipal* (São Paulo), CVI (January–February, 1946), p. 101.
54. If we omit Mário de Andrade's "no endorsement" interjected at a certain
point in Graça Aranha's address, which was the source of a subsequent
development, as we shall later see.
55. Cit. by Mário da Silva Brito, "Café e Modernismo."
56. Afrânio Coutinho, ed. *A Literatura no Brasil,* Vol. III, Part I (Rio de
Janeiro: Editorial Sul Americana, 1959), 446.
57. Transcribed by Mário da Silva Brito, *História do Modernismo Brasileiro,*
pp. 205 ff.
58. See Mário de Andrade, "Carta Aberta a Alberto de Oliveira," *Estética,*
III (April–June, 1925): "It was not to imitate Apollinaire or Marinetti
(the first I had not as yet read and the second I simply did not like) that
in December of 1919 I wrote in its entirety the first version of the
Paulicéia."

59. Carlos Chiacchio, *Modernistas e Ultramodernistas* (Bahia: Progresso, 1951). Articles collected posthumously.
60. Confirmed by Mário Guastini: "I fully expected to find at his side on the stage the dwindling number of Futurists in our land; I expected to find one of those *innovators* with the courage of Graça Aranha introducing him. I also thought I would witness deafening uproar. I was deceived in part. At first, Marinetti by himself. Not a sign of the Futurists. Almeida, *op. cit.,* pp. 116–117.
61. See *Cartas a Manuel Bandeira,* pp. 100 ff. For the booing of Marinetti, cf. Mário Guastini, *op. cit.,* pp. 115 ff.

62.
    Um dia uma revista
    Conheci então Cendrars
    Apollinaire
    Spire
    Vildrac
    Duhamel
    Todos os literatos modernos
    Mas ainda não compreendia o modernismo

63. When Mário de Andrade wrote against Mallarmé, he was merely echoing Epstein, as was so often the case in the *Escrava*: "We can already see the vast difference which separates modern writers from Mallarmé. He could never conceive of the notion that one might for one moment do without intellect for the benefit of that very intellect, in order to provide it with some new and truly fresh food. An imperturbable logician, he never departed too far from the support of grammar." Epstein, *op. cit.,* p. 115.
    It was Epstein who called Rimbaud the "model" for modern writers. In a final letter of the volume, Cendrars considered the two poets to be symbols of two distinct epochs: before the war, Mallarmé; after the war, Rimbaud. "A change of proprietor," he added.
64. See Renato Almeida, "Ronald de Carvalho e o Modernismo," *Lanterna Verde,* IV (November, 1936), p. 79.
65. Joaquim Inojosa, *A Arte Moderna* (Recife: Of. Graf. do "Jornal do Comércio," 1924), p. 6.
66. Eduardo Frieiro, *O Clube dos Grafômanos* (Belo Horizonte: Ed. Pindorama, 1927).
67. Oswald de Andrade?
68. *Cartas a Manuel Bandeira,* p. 45.
69. *Ibid.,* pp. 71–72.
70. See Mário Neme, *Plataforma da Nova Geração,* p. 71.
71. It is difficult to believe, but Catulo da Paixão Cearense was then considered the bard of the race and the greatest Brazilian poet of all time. In November, 1918, for example, the critic on the *Revista do Brasil,* in reviewing *Meu Sertão,* wrote: "the greatest poet in this country, the poet's poet, the poet whose compositions are inspired in music and are sung on all lips from north to south, awakening the most gentle emotions in every man's breast . . ."
    Such exaggeration provoked unfavorable criticism of the backlands bard, which was supported by the young Alceu Amoroso Lima in the same

journal (January, 1919): "Criticism of the poet, I think, came as a reaction against those who would make him our Greatest Poet. In that regard, the criticism was totally justified. Catulo was more than a regional poet, but less than a national poet, and much less than the Greatest Poet."

In spite of that, however, in March of 1922, the *Revista do Brasil* reaffirmed what appears to have been its official point of view: "A cyclic poet, the Brazilian poet par excellence. We contemporaries have still not granted his proper worth to the great rhapsodist who is supreme and unique. . . ." (Review of *Poemas Bravios*.)

Our surprise will be lessened if we recall the extraordinary success (editorial and critical) of *Alma Cabocla* by Paulo Setúbal, published by the *Revista do Brasil* itself in 1920. Regionalism, in all its guises, is the Brazilian's favorite genre; the only one, at heart, to which he spontaneously gives himself with no mental reservations (and I am not speaking only of the popular reader).

72. Oswald de Andrade, *Pau Brasil* (Paris: Au Sans Pareil, 1925).
73. Plínio Salgado, *Obras Completas*, X, 14–15. "Breve História Dêstes Escritos," *Despertemos a Nação!*
74. Domingos Carvalho de Silva, *Modernismo* (special number, *Revista Branca*, Rio de Janeiro, 1952, p. 137).
75. Cassiano Ricardo, *Revista Anual do Salão de Maio*, cit.
76. "Terra Roxa e Outras Terras," I (January 20, 1926). This text may be consulted with the other Modernist manifestoes in the *Revista do Livro*, XVI.
77. We must not be deceived by the Manichaean tone adopted *a posteriori* by the National Leader: Plínio Salgado was a regular contributor to the *Revista de Antropofagia*, which published his articles on the Tupi language.
78. *O Movimento Modernista* (Rio de Janeiro: Ministério da Educação e Cultura [Os Cadernos de Cultura], 1954).
79. Adopted without reservation by Afrânio Coutinho, *Introdução à Literatura no Brasil* (Rio de Janeiro: Livraria São José, 1959), pp. 290 ff.
80. Sérgio Milliet, *Testamento de Uma Geração*, pp. 241–242.
81. *Modernistas e Ultramodernistas* (see footnote 59 above).
82. Cf. Homero Senna, *República das Letras*, pp. 143 ff.
83. See *Testamento de Uma Geração*, p. 22.
84. Peregrino Júnior, *O Movimento Modernista*, pp. 5–10.

85.   FOGOS
                        (Impressões de uma noite de S. João)
            Tátá . . . Chiii . . . Quetá! . . .
            Prráá . . . Bumbum!!! Búbú! . . .
            Chiii . . . Toque tá! Prrráá . . .
            Tique bum! Bambam . . . Bá . . .
            Chóóó . . . Xiii . . . Viut . . . ú . . .
            Brra . . . Chiiin . . . Papàu!
            Crro óóó . Xin . . . Bóbó! . . .
            Ti bum! Crr . . . Fiáu . . .
            Crro óóó . Xin . . . Bóbó! . . .

Prr . . . Brrrá . . . Chiii . . . Tibão!
—O'i o balão! O'i o balão Santos Dumão! . . .

86. *Modernistas e Ultramodernistas,* p. 121.
87. Francisco I. Peixoto, "Mestre Tasso, otimista impenitente," *Verde,* No. 5 (January, 1928).
88. See *Definição do Modernismo Brasileiro* (Rio de Janeiro: Edições Forja, 1932), final note.
89. Renato Rocha, *Modernismo, Revista Branca,* p. 59.
90. Tasso da Silveira, *Modernismo, Revista Branca,* pp. 19–20.
91. *71 Cartas de Mário de Andrade.* Coligidas e anotadas por Lýgia Fernandes (Rio de Janeiro: Livraria São José, n. d.), pp. 83 ff. Cf. also the letter dated 5/11/1929 to Manuel Bandeira, *op. cit.,* p. 217.
92. Cecília Meireles (1901–1964) was indisputably *Festa's* crowning ornament; however, for that very reason it may be proper to think that the group owed her more than she owed the group.
93. Cf. *Definição do Modernismo Brasileiro,* pp. 79 ff.
94. Cf. Gilberto Freyre, "Notas sôbre Gilberto Freyre," *Região e Tradição* (Rio de Janeiro: Livraria José Olympio Editôra, 1941), p. 11.
95. *A Arte Moderna.* p. 7.
96. Cf. *Testamento de Uma Geração,* p. 84.
97. Probably the book mentioned here was *A Escrava Que Não É Isaura.*
98. Cf. Jorge de Lima, *Obra Poética* (Rio de Janeiro: Aguilar, 1950), notes by Otto Maria Carpeaux.
99. Cf. Gilberto Freyre, *Manifesto Regionalista de 1926* (Recife: Edições Região). I refer to the 1952 edition because, judging from the style, the author has practically rewritten his work here. Moreover, he himself admits that the *Manifesto,* which had previously been published only in part in the *Diário de Pernambuco,* appeared in this more recent edition with some addenda to the *reconstitution* of the manuscript abandoned some years back." (Italics mine.) Cf. *op. cit.,* pp. 15–19.

If Gilberto Freyre for so many years neglected the text of the *Manifesto,* it is proof that quite late he conceived the idea that it possessed the importance of a historical document, of a precursor of all modern literature called "Northeastern." Joaquim Inojosa's previously mentioned book confirms the fact that in 1926 there was no "regionalist manifesto" and that the text which we have is of a much later date. Gilberto Freyre himself admits that "at the time" such a document "had not been called the 'regionalist manifesto.' " And he adds: "I have sometimes expanded and retouched older articles for recent publication without making any alteration in the essential ideas, rather frequently preserving the very personal and erratic punctuation of the original articles; and, in the expanded versions, I have added ideas that were expressed at the time of the original publication of other similar articles of mine (ideas less important than my fundamental and basic notions)—these are the practices I have followed." Cf. Gilberto Freyre, "Carta de Pernambuco" (Recife: *Jornal do Comércio,* 4/21/1968 and Rio de Janeiro: *O Jornal,* 4/30/1968). Cf. also Joaquim Inojosa, *No Pomar Vizinho* (Rio de Janeiro: Guanabara, 1968).

100. *Manifesto*, pp. 7–8.
101. Osman Lins, "Gilberto Freyre e o Manifesto Regionalista" in the "Suplemento Literário" of the *O Estado de São Paulo* (August 1, 1959).
102. José Aderaldo Castello, *José Lins do Rêgo: Modernismo e Regionalismo* (São Paulo: EdArte, 1961), pp. 19, 29–30.
103. *Ibid.*, p. 67.
104. Manoel de Abreu, "Acabou o modernismo no Brasil?," *Lanterna Verde*, pp. 33 ff.
105. Homero Senna, *op. cit.*, p. 79.
106. Mário Neme, *op. cit.*, pp. 32 ff.
107. Bergman, *op. cit.*, p. 65.

> "Les temps héroïques du futurisme, 'l'età d'oro del movimento,' comme écrit Paolo Buzzi, se placent dans l'avant-guerre. A cette époque le monde entier est regardé comme le domaine du futurisme. Après le début de la guerre le futurisme devient de plus en plus nationaliste, et après l'élection de Marinetti à l'Académie de Mussolini le futurisme devient presque un mouvement officiel, professant une idéologie et un art fascistes."

108. Cf. Graça Aranha's preface to *Futurismo: Manifestos de Marinetti e seus companheiros*, pp. 8–9.
109. The word "almost" was omitted, as we can see, in the review's text.
110. As a matter of fact, Alceu Amoroso Lima had said in his "Indicações Políticas": ". . . I confess that I can see no other party which can, like Integralist Action, so completely meet the demands of a Catholic conscience . . . I think that our stance before the Integralist Movement—if it should be neither hostile nor confused—can only be one of COOPERATION." (Cit. by Plínio Salgado, *Obras Completas*, IX, 157 ff.)

     In a doctoral thesis in Theology (University of Texas) on religious thought in Alceu Amoroso Lima, J. M. Stout observes: "*Preparação à Sociologia* . . . was published in 1931 at a time when Fascism was looked upon by Amoroso Lima and others as the 'saviour' of the church in church-state relations" (p. 41).
111. Olavo Bilac, "Afonso Arinos," *Revista do Brasil* (January, 1917).
112. Mário da Silva Brito, *op. cit.*, pp. 176 ff.
113. *Estudos Brasileiros*, II, p. 118.

114.
> Perambulando pelo pampa enorme,
> Para ânsias de amplidão satisfazê-las,
> Vive a correr, no seu corcel, conforme,
> O pampeiro das lendas e novelas.
>
> O gaúcho, por entre a massa informe
> Dessas campinas, verdes, amarelas,
> Se a noite o pega, no deserto dorme
> Coberto pelo poncho das estrêlas . . .
>
> É portador dum ar de quem domina.
> Seu sangue forte vibra e rumoreja,
> Ao troar da pistola ou da clavina.

Quando à morte, a garrucha aperta e beija,
E morre revivendo na retina
A epopéia crioula da peleja.

115. MADRUGADA

A noite amadureceu a madrugada
e o dia vai abrir os lábios vermelhos da manhã,
para engolir a sombra
numa grande risada
de sol.

Sinto a alegria verde da manhã do Pampa!
O campo está todo enfeitado de miçangas,
porque a noite enfiou as continhas brancas do sereno
nas hastes lisas da flechilha.

Eu saio de pés descalços para a sanga
e vou amassando sob os pés molhados
os desenhos do orvalho sôbre a grama fôfa.

116. Rubens Barcellos, *Estudos Rio-Grandenses* (Pôrto Alegre: Globo, 1955).
117. *Revista do Brasil* (April, 1940).
118. *Testamento de Mário de Andrade e Outras Reportagens* (Rio de Janeiro: Ministério da Educação e Cultura, 1954), p. 15.
119. Sílvio Elia, "A Contribuição Lingüística do Modernismo," in *Uma Experiência Pioneira* (Pôrto Alegre: Faculdade de Filosofia da URGS, 1963), pp. 81 ff., for a good inventory of this problem.
120. *Cartas a Manuel Bandeira*, p. 76.
121. *Ibid.* (May 11, 1920).

122.   Sou môço e forte, adoro a fôrça e o valor,
            Abomino o temor,
            Amo o orgulho hostil e a maldade bravia . . .

123.   . . . ágil como um poldro e forte como um touro:
            no equilíbrio viril dos seus membros possantes
            há audácias de coluna e a elegância dos barcos.

124. Homero Prates, "Alguns Novos do Rio Grande do Sul," in *Revista do Brasil* (October, 1917).

125   E a vila que se fundara
            por trás do muro da Serra
            (a princípio eram só três)
            logo é um covil de Gigantes.

126. Mário de Andrade forgot, among others, the João do Carmo of *Alma* (Vol. I of *Os Condenados*) and Jorge d'Alvellos of *A Estrêla de Absinto*. He also forgot Lúcio, from *A Bagaceira*, and others.
127. In the text of the review *Clima*, and also in his *Aspectos da Literatura Brasileira*, Mário de Andrade mistakes the title of the novel by Oswaldo Alves. An interesting Freudian slip. Of course, Oswaldo Alves's novel is called *A Man Inside the World* and not *A Man Outside the World*.

PART TWO—REPRESENTATIVE WORKS

1. These documents are currently in the possession of Antônio Cândido. The first version of certain chapters of the novel was published by the literary journal, *A Cigarra*, throughout 1917. See Paulo Mendes de Almeida, "A Cigarra Literária," in the "Suplemento Literário" of the *O Estado de São Paulo*, No. 383 (June 6, 1964).
2. See Fernando Góes, "História da *Paulicéia Desvairada*" in *Revista do Arquivo Municipal* (São Paulo), CVI, 89 ff.
3. Ângelo Guido, *Ilusão*. Essay on *"A Estética da Vida"* (Santos: Institute Esch. Rosa, 1922). Ângelo Guido's incompatability with Modernism is evident from the first line of the volume: "I see in Graça Aranha's latest book the point of departure of a new orientation in our national literature."
4. Cf. *Cartas a Manuel Bandeira*, p. 293.
5. *71 Cartas de Mário de Andrade*, p. 29.

6.   Hũ certo animal se acha também nestas partes
        A que chamam Preguiça
        Tem hua guedelha grande no toutiço
        E se move com passos tam vagarosos
        Que ainda que ande quinze dias aturado
        Não vencerá a distância de hũ tiro de pedra

7.   Dê-me um cigarro
        Diz a gramática
        Do professor e do aluno
        E do mulato sabido

        Mas o bom negro e o bom branco
        Da Nação Brasileira
        Dizem todos os dias
        Me dá um cigarro

Echoes of this jocular mode may also be heard in the Modernist poetry of Cassiano Ricardo. In this case the "joke" of the poem does not admit of translation, as the final line involves a nuance of Brazilian syntax.

8.   Minha terra tem palmares
        Onde gorjeia o mar
        Os passarinhos daqui
        Não cantam como os de lá

        .   .   .   .   .

        Não permita Deus que eu morra
        Sem que volte pra São Paulo
        Sem que veja a Rua 15
        E o progresso de São Paulo

9. This was first published under the title "Um Grão Senhor" in the "Suplemento Literário" of the *O Estado de São Paulo* on October 26, 1963.

10. Paulo Prado, *Retrato do Brasil,* 6th ed. (Rio de Janeiro: Livraria José Olympio Editôra, 1962), pp. 151–152.
11. *Ibid.,* pp. 152–153.
12. *Ibid.,* p. 162.
13. *Ibid.,* p. 163.
14. *Ibid.,* pp. 164–165.
15. Wilson Martins, *op. cit.,* pp. 151 ff.
16. Cavalcanti Proença, *Roteiro de Macunaíma* (São Paulo: Anhembi, 1955), p. 237.
17. See *Estudos Brasileiros,* II (Rio de Janeiro: Briguiet, 1931), p. 151.
18. See *Cartas a Manuel Bandeira* (July 13, 1929), p. 227.
19. *Ibid.,* pp. 169 ff.
20. See *71 Cartas de Mário de Andrade,* p. 30.
21. Alfredo Ellis, *Raça de Gigantes* (São Paulo: Novíssima, 1926).

22.
I
Meu pai era um gigante, domador de léguas.
   Quando um dia partiu, a cavalo
no seu dragão de pêlo azul que era o Tietê dos
   /bandeirantes,
lembro-me muito bem de que me disse: olhe, meu filho,
eu vou sururucar por esta porta e um dia voltarei trazendo
   /umas duzentas léguas de caminho e umas dezenas de
   /onças arrastadas pelo rabo a pingar sangue do focinho!
E dito e feito! lá se foi dando empurrões no mato dos
   /barrancos
por entre alas de jacarés e de pássaros brancos.
Quando veio o Natal meu pai estava longe,
em luta com os bichos peludos, com os gatos grandes de
   /cabeça listrada e com as mulas-de-sete-cabeças que
   /moram no fundo das árvores espêssas.
No planalto batia um sino perguntando: êle não vem? êle
   /não vem?
Um outro sino de voz grossa respondia: não . . . e não dizendo
   /"Nãão" e repetindo "nãão" e não.

II
E eu me lembrei de procurar um par de botas
das que meu pai usava e pôr o par de botas
atrás da porta do sertão que resmungava entocaiado no
   /arvoredo.
Como fazia frio aquela noite!
Fiquei com tanto mêdo . . . Um gato corrumiau
passeava pelos vãos da telha-vã . . .
Mas chegou a manhã, linda como um tesouro!
e eu fui achar, com o coração aos pulos de alegria,
   as duas botas de couro
   abarrotadas de ouro!

III
Passou mais um ano e meu pai não voltou.
Botei meus sapatões atrás da porta novamente
   e no outro dia
fui encontrar meus sapatões abarrotados de esmeraldas!

Minha vovó, uma velhinha portuguêsa com cabelo de garoa e
/xale azul-xadrez me garantia:
—"Foi o papá Noel quem trouxe." Até que um dia
fiz que não vi mas vi; acordei da ilusão.
Meu pai era um Gigante, caçador de léguas,
   um feroz domador de onças pretas,
   terror do mato, assombração das borboletas
mas tinha um grande coração.

Por fim cresci. Hoje sou gente grande.
Sou comissário de café. Tenho viadutos encantados.
Minha cidade é êsse tumulto colorido que aí passa
levando as fábricas pelas rédeas pretas de fumaça!
   Barulho fantástico
de um mundo que saiu da oficina.
Grito metálico de cidade americana.
Vida rodando fremindo batendo martelos
   com músculos de aço.

E o Tietê conta a história dos velhos Gigantes
que andaram medinho as fronteiras da pátria,
ao tempo em que S. Paulo colocava os sapatões atrás da porta
e os sapatões amanheciam cheios de ouro . . .

E os sapatões amanheciam cheios de esmeraldas . . .

E os sapatões amanheciam cheios de diamantes . . .

23. Cf. *O Curupira e o Carão*, pp. 71 ff.

24.   Vou andando caminhando caminhando
       Me misturo no ventre do mato mordendo raízes

25.   Aqui é a floresta subterrânea de hálito podre parindo cobras

       Rios magros obrigados a trabalhar.
       As raízes inflamadas estão mastigando lôdo

       Batem martelos no fundo
       soldando serrando serrando

       Estão fabricando terra . . .
       Ué Aqui estão mesmo fabricando terra!

Part Three—Basic Authors

1. Cf. José Lins do Rêgo, "Notas sôbre um caderno de poesia," *Jornal de Alagoas* (December 15, 1927). These notes were reprinted as a postface to the *Poemas* (1927) and to the *Poemas Escolhidos* (1932). This clearly indicates that the poet himself substantiated the story.
2. Writing about "A Voz da Terra" in *Lanterna Verde*, No. 4 (November, 1936), p. 21, Jorge de Lima observed: "It is assuredly true that the great Ronald de Carvalho sang of all America. But later a lesser poet published 'his America' . . ."

3.
CIDADE DE CUSCO. HACE FRÍO.
Lá vem a procissão do Senhor dos tremores de terra
Viva El Señor de los temblores! Viva El Perú!
Há flôres de ñuchos pelas ruas.
Há meninas rotundas nos balcões.
Há namoros vermelhos nas esquinas.
Há borrachos a aguardente e chicha!

De repente tinem sinos,
carrilhões
da Capilla del Triunfo. Blão! Blão!

.   .   .   .   .

4.
U. S. A.
Indústrias gigantescas, trustes colossais,
Massachussetts [sic]
New Hampshire,
Rhode Island,
Connecticut,
Pensylvania [sic]
Estados Unidos da América!
Todos os ritos alegres e assombrosamente numerosos:
Cultos, conferências, o congresso eucarístico
de Chicago distribuindo hóstias a 2 milhões de bôcas:
O maior record de distribuição do Corpo do Senhor!
Mas acima de tudo a suprema alegria marca U. S. A.:
—O amor divorciado 20 vêzes glorificado,
sempre jovial e tempre nôvo como a própria
alma alegre dos Estados Unidos
da América do Norte.

5.
G. W. B. R.
VEJO ATRAVÉS da janela de meu trem
os domingos das cidadezinhas,
com meninas e môças,
e caixeiros engomados que vêm olhar
os passageiros empoeirados dos vagons.
Esta estrada de ferro Great Western
feita de encomenda para o Nordeste
é a mais pitoresca do universo,
com suas balduínas sonolentas
e seus carrinhos de caixa de fósforos marca ôlho.
Houve um tempo em que os rebanhos se assustavam
aos apitos dêsses trens;
hoje os passarinhos olham das linhas ribeirinhas do
telégrafo,
o pitoresco que ela tem,
aos vaivéns, aos arreganhos,
rangendo e ringindo interminàvelmente.

6. See Tristão de Athayde, "As Quatro Etapas de Jorge de Lima," *Jornal de Letras* (December, 1963).

7. This section was first published in the "Suplemento Literário" of the

O Estado de São Paulo (November 1, 1958), under the title "Um Tísico Profissional."
8. Manuel Bandeira, *Poesia e Prosa* (Rio de Janeiro: Editôra José Aguilar, 1958).
9. Menotti del Picchia, "Futurismo," *Correio Paulistano* (December 6, 1920).
10. Cit. by Mário da Silva Brito, *op. cit.*, p. 146.
11. Menotti del Picchia, *A Tormenta* (*Obras* III) (São Paulo: Martins, 1958), p. 89.
12. *Cartas a Manuel Bandeira* (May 3, 1926), pp. 140 ff.
13. See *a hora futurista que passou* . . . , pp. 59 ff.

14.   Creio que há no charco uma festa veneziana
        em honra da Senhora Lua Nova.

                    .   .   .   .   .

        E o crescente de fósforo navega
        na água morta do brejo,
        Bucentauro dogal num canal de Veneza.

15.   Senhora, por quem sois, não sejais minha
        que o bem que aspiro é um mal para nós dois

16.   ". . . on my lyre"!

17.   Um grito pula no ar como um foguete.
        Vem da paisagem de barro úmido, caliça e andaimes hirtos.
        O sol cai sôbre as coisas como placa fervendo.

        Um sorveteiro corta a rua.

        E o vento brinca nos bigodes do construtor.

18. See Mário de Andrade's review in *Klaxon*, No. 7 (November, 1922).

19.   Como é linda a minha terra!
        Estrangeiro, olha aquela palmeira como é bela:
        parece uma coluna reta reta reta
        com um grande pavão verde poisado na ponta,
        a cauda aberta em leque.
                    E na sombra redonda
        sôbre a terra quente . . .
                    (Silêncio!)
                    . . . há um poeta.

20.   ("Maxixe")
        O chocalho dos sapos coaxa
        como um caracaxá rachado. Tudo mexe.

        ("Cateretê")
        batuque
                batepé
                        saracoteio.
        Pulam pingos brutos pelas telhas pardas

("Samba")
        E o samba estronda
    rebenta
        retumba
            rebomba.

21. This statement by Tasso da Silveira, *Modernismo, Revista Branca,* is cited merely as an indication of his frame of mind. By its very nature it is a subjective statement; beyond that it contradicts what he himself had written in *Definição do Modernismo Brasileiro:* "Senhor Ronald is a first-rate writer. Great poet, however, he is not. Nor even a poet, in the strictest sense of the word . . . All of his finest pages are devoted to popularization." (P. 26.)

22. Cited by Renato Almeida, "Ronald de Carvalho e o Modernismo," *Lanterna Verde,* No. 4 (November, 1936), pp. 76–77.

23.   Europeu!
    Nos tabuleiros de xadrez da tua aldeia,
    na tua casa de madeira, pequenina, coberta de hera,
        .   .   .   .

    tu não sabes o que é ser Americano!

24.   América dos cafèzais, dos seringais e dos canaviais,
    América das locomotivas e das carrêtas de bois, dos
            /elevadores
        e dos guindastes, das porteiras de peroba e das
            /comportas
    de aço cromado de Pittsburgh
        .   .   .   .

    Onde estão os teus poetas, América?
    Onde estão êles que não compreendem os teus meios-dias
            /voluptuosos,
    as tuas rêdes pesadas de corpos eurítmicos, que se balançam
        nas sombras úmidas

25. Wilson Martins, "Nos Domínios da Ucronia," in the "Suplemento Literário" of the *O Estado de São Paulo* (November 8, 1958).

26. This section was published on April 5, 1956, in the "Suplemento Literário" of the *O Estado de São Paulo,* under the title "Esquema Para Um Livro."

27. Although he declared in a moving moment that his merits as a participant had in reality been borrowed from others.

28. Or, if we should like to identify one *faculté* at the expense of all others, it would have to be his *experimentalism,* as he himself recognized when he said that he had devoted all his labors to that end. At least, it was in that light that these pages were written.

29. When it is finally published, Mário de Andrade's general correspondence will be of greater importance in our literature than that of Flaubert in French literature, simply because his letters frequently go beyond limits that are strictly personal. The same is true of his literary marginalia, which Antônio Cândido intends either to publish or to have published.

30. See Mário de Andrade, *Obras Completas* (São Paulo: Livraria Martins, 1955).

31. See Mário de Andrade, "Farauto," *Klaxon,* No. 7 (November 30, 1922).

32.   XXXIII
Meu gôzo profundo ante a manhã Sol
            a vida carnaval . . .
        Amigos
            Amôres
    Risadas
Os piás imigrantes me rodeiam pedindo retratinhos
de artistas de cinema, dêsses que vêm nos maços de cigarros.
Me sinto a Assunção de Murillo!

Já estou livre da dor . . .
Mas todo vibro da alegria de viver
    Eis porque minha alma inda é impura.

                XXXIII No. 2
Platão! por te seguir como eu quisera
Da alegria e da dor me libertando
Ser puro, igual aos deuses que a Quimera
Andou além da vida arquitetando!

Mas como não gozar alegre quando
Brilha esta alva manhã de primavera
—Mulher sensual que junto a mim passando
Meu desejo de gozos exaspera!

A vida é bela! Inúteis as teorias!
Mil vêzes a nudeza em que resplendo
À clâmide da ciência, austera e calma!

E caminho entre aromas e harmonias
Amaldiçoando os sábios, bendizendo
A divina impureza de minha alma.

33. Mário de Andrade, "A Poesia em 1930," *Aspectos da Literatura Brasileira* (Rio de Janeiro: Americ-Edit, 1943), p. 42. "It is a little amazing, if painful, to observe that bold little dunghill of schoolboys' books, useless, more or less rosy-cheeked, all promise but, after all: folly that will not withstand the ravages of time."

34. Oswald's riposte concerns Mário's patronymic: Mário Raul de Morais Andrade. The first element, Morais, was lacking in Oswald's full name which was José Oswald de Sousa Andrade. Hence, they were separated by a question of *morais* (morals).

35. Oswald de Andrade, *Um Homen Sem Profissão*, I, "Sob as Ordens de Mamãe" (Rio de Janeiro: Livraria José Olympio Editôra, 1954), p. 84.

36. Jean Cocteau, *Les Mariés de la Tour Eiffel,* theatrical satire first performed by the Swedish Ballet with music by Les Six and costumes and sets by Cocteau and Valentine Hugo (Paris, 1921). Poetry by Cocteau, of course.

37. *Um Homem Sem Profissão,* pp. 124–134.

38.   Eu quero fazer um poema
Rachado e sentimental
Como as bandas de música
De meu país natal

Eu quero fazer um poema
De todo o amor que sinto
Pelas palmas e bandeiras
Do meu país musical

39. See Samuel Rawet, *Modernismo,* special number of the *Revista Branca,* pp. 106–107.
40. Antônio Cândido, *op. cit.,* pp. 12 ff.
41. Plínio Salgado, *Espírito da Burguesia, Obras Completas,* XVI, 173.
42. *Ibid.,* p. 127.
43. Plínio Salgado, *O Estrangeiro* (São Paulo: Editorial Helios Ltda., 1926).
44. Plínio Salgado, *O Esperado* (São Paulo: Companhia Editôra Nacional, 1927).
45. Oswald de Andrade, "Dois Emancipados: Júlio Ribeiro e Inglês de Sousa," *Revista do Brasil* (May, 1941). However, Plínio Salgado states that *O Estrangeiro* was written in 1923, which would seem to contradict Oswald de Andrade's line of reasoning. On the other hand, it does serve to prove that "novelesque expressionism" was in the air.
46. Plínio Salgado, *Despertemos a Nação!, Obras Completas,* X, 20.
47. This section was published under the title "Uma Vocação" in the "Suplemento Literário" of the *O Estado de São Paulo* (July 22, 1961).
48. Alcântara Machado, *Novelas Paulistanas* (Rio de Janeiro: Livraria José Olympio Editôra, 1961).
49. A. C. Couto de Barros, "A propósito de *Brás, Bexiga e Barra Funda,*" *Verde* (Cataguases), No. 2 (October, 1927), p. 12.

50.   Não quero mais o amor,
Nem mais quero cantar a minha terra.
Me perco neste mundo.
Não quero mais o Brasil
Não quero mais geografia
Nem pitoresco.

Quero é perder-me no mundo
Para fugir do mundo.

51. Mário de Andrade, *Aspectos da Literatura Brasileira* (Rio de Janeiro: Americ-Edit, 1943), p. 54.

52.   Passa a saudade do que foi e é morto.
Passa a glória que eu quis e me fugiu.
Passam as próprias visões do mundo e a vida,
E é sonho quanto tive em minhas mãos.

Passam as flôres nascidas mais perfeitas,
Passa a beleza, e a dor, passam tormentos.
Passa essa angústia diante do eterno nada.
Que não passa, Senhor, todo momento?

De incerteza em incerteza, a vida corre,
E nos mudamos nós, de instante a instante.
O que foi, êle próprio, sofre muda.

Só não passa êste amor tão passageiro.
Só não muda êste amor que é tão mudável.
Só êste amor incerto é certo em mim.

Sinto viver em mim um mar ignoto,
E ouço, nas horas calmas e serenas,
As águas que murmuram, como em prece,
Estranhas orações intraduzíveis.

Ouço, também, do mar desconhecido,
Nos instantes inquietos e terríveis,
Dos ventos o guaiar desesperado
E os soluços das ondas agoniadas

Sinto viver em mim um mar de sombras,
Mas tão rico de vida e de harmonias,
Que dêle sei nascer a misteriosa

Música, que se espalha nos meus versos,
Essa música errante como os ventos,
Cujas asas no mar geram tormentas.

53. "A Poesia em 1930," *Aspectos da Literatura Brasileira*, pp. 56–57.
54. Manuel Bandeira, "O Caminho do Frio," in the "Suplemento Literário" of the *O Estado de São Paulo* (May 30, 1964).
55. Carlos Drummond de Andrade, "Informação," *Antologia Poética* (Rio de Janeiro: Editôra de Autor, 1962).
56. See the best comprehensive work on the novelist to date, José Aderaldo Castello, *José Lins do Rêgo: Modernismo e Regionalismo*. Cf. also Wilson Martins, "A língua simbólica de José Lins do Rêgo," introduction to *Usina*, 6th ed. (Rio de Janeiro: José Olympio Editôra, 1967).
57. This section, under the title "Uma Carreira," was published in the "Suplemento Literário" of the *O Estado de São Paulo* (June 30, 1962). It is reprinted here with a few alterations since this book deals only with the Modernist period.
58. This last phase does not correspond to the chronological limits of the present volume.
59. See Miécio Tati, *Jorge Amado: Vida e Obra* (Belo Horizonte: Editôra Itatiaia Limitada, 1961).
60. *Ibid.*, p. 112.
61. The two passages above by Jorge Amado *apud* Miécio Tati, *op. cit.*, pp. 91–92.
62. Wilson Martins, "Gilberto Freyre" in the "Suplemento Literário" of the *O Estado de São Paulo* (March 22 and 29, 1958).
63. Gilberto Freyre, *Sociologia* (Rio de Janeiro: Livraria José Olympio Editôra, 1957), pp. 69–70.
64. This section was published under the title "O Velho Graça" in the "Suplemento Literário" of the *O Estado de São Paulo* (June 2, 1962).

65. Graciliano Ramos had employed the continental syntactical construction "me não permitiriam . . ." rather than the customary Brazilian usage "não me permitiriam . . ."
66. Érico Veríssimo, *O Tempo e o Vento* (Rio de Janeiro: Editôra Globo, 1949–1962).

Bibliography of Works Consulted

Alcântara Machado, Antônio de. *Novelas Paulistanas*. Rio de Janeiro: Livraria José Olympio Editôra, 1961.

Almeida, Guilherme de.
  Natalika. Rio de Janeiro: Candeia Azul, 1924.
  Meu (livro de estampas). São Paulo: n. pub., 1925.
  Do Sentimento Nacionalista na Poesia Brasileira. São Paulo: Casa Garraux, 1926.

Almeida, José Américo de. *A Bagaceira*, 8th ed. Rio de Janeiro: Livraria José Olympio Editôra, 1954.

Almeida, Renato. *Velocidade*. Rio de Janeiro: Schmidt, 1932.

Alomar, Gabriel. *Verba*. Madrid: Biblioteca Nueva, n. d.

Alves, Osvaldo. *Um Homem Dentro do Mundo*. Curitiba: Guaíra, 1940.

Amado, Jorge. *Obras*. São Paulo: Martins, 1944.

Amaral, Amadeu. *O Dialeto Caipira*. São Paulo: "Revista do Brasil," 1916.

Amoroso Lima, Alceu.
  Afonso Arinos. Rio de Janeiro: Anuário do Brasil, 1923.
  Estudos (5 series). Rio de Janeiro: Terra do Sol, A Ordem, Civilização Brasileira, 1927–1935.
  Contribuição à História do Modernismo. I: *O Pré-Modernismo*. Rio de Janeiro: Livraria José Olympio Editôra, 1939.
  Primeiros Estudos. Rio de Janeiro: Agir, 1948.

Andrade, Mário de.
  O Movimento Modernista. Rio de Janeiro: Casa do Estudante do Brasil, 1942.
  Aspectos da Literatura Brasileira. Rio de Janeiro: Americ-Edit, 1943.
  Obras Completas. São Paulo: Martins, 1944.
  Cartas (. . .) a Manuel Bandeira. Rio de Janeiro: Organização Simões, 1958.

334   The Modernist Idea

71 Cartas (. . .). Coligidas e anotadas por Lygia Fernandes. Rio de Janeiro: Livraria São José, n. d.

Andrade, Oswald de.
Memórias Sentimentais de João Miramar. São Paulo: Independência, 1924.
Serafim Ponte Grande. Rio de Janeiro: Ariel, 1933.
Os Condenados. Pôrto Alegre: Globo, 1941.
Marco Zero. I: A Revolução Melancólica. Rio de Janeiro: Livraria José Olympio Editôra, 1943.
Poesias Reunidas. São Paulo: Gaveta, 1945.
Marco Zero. II: Chão. Rio de Janeiro: Livraria José Olympio Editôra, 1945.
Ponta de Lança. São Paulo: Martins, 1945.
Um Homem Sem Profissão. I: Sob as Ordens de Mamãe. Rio de Janeiro: Livraria José Olympio Editôra, 1954.

Araújo, Murilo.
Quadrantes do Modernismo Brasileiro. Rio de Janeiro: Ministério da Educação e Cultura (Os Cadernos de Cultura), 1958.
Poemas Completos. 3 Vols. Rio de Janeiro: Pongetti, 1960.

Bandeira, Manuel.
Poesias Completas. Rio de Janeiro: Americ-Edit, 1945.
Apresentação da Poesia Brasileira, 3rd ed. Rio de Janeiro: Casa do Estudante do Brasil, 1957.
Poesia e Prosa. Rio de Janeiro: Aguilar, 1958.

Barbosa, Francisco de Assis. Testamento de Mário de Andrade e Outras Reportagens. Rio de Janeiro: Ministério da Educação e Cultura (Os Cadernos de Cultura), 1954.

Barcellos, Rubens de. Estudos Rio-Grandenses. Motivos de história e literatura, coligidos e selecionados por Mansueto Barnardi e Moisés Vellinho. Pôrto Alegre: Globo, 1955.

Bastos, Abguar. Terra de Icamiaba. Romance da Amazônia. Rio de Janeiro: Adersen, 1934.

Bergman, Pär. "Modernolatria" et "Simultaneità." Recherches sur deux tendances dans l'avant-garde littéraire en Italie et en France à la veille de la première guerre mondiale. Uppsala: Svenska Bokförlaget, 1962.

Bopp, Raul. Cobra Norato. Nheengatu da margem esquerda do Amazonas. São Paulo: Irmãos Ferraz, 1931.

Borba de Moraes, Rubens. Domingo dos Séculos. Rio de Janeiro: Candeia Azul, 1924.

Cândido, Antônio. Brigada Ligeira. São Paulo: Martins, 1945.

Carpeaux, Otto Maria. Pequena Bibliografia Crítica da Literatura Brasileira, 3rd ed. Rio de Janeiro: Letras e Artes, 1964.

Carvalho, Flávio de. Os Ossos do Mundo. Rio de Janeiro: Ariel, 1936.

Carvalho, Ronald de.
Tôda a América. Rio de Janeiro: Anuário do Brasil, 1926.
Estudos Brasileiros, II. Rio de Janeiro: Briguiet, 1931.
Pequena História da Literatura Brasileira, 5th ed. Rio de Janeiro: Briguiet, 1935.

Castello, José Aderaldo. *José Lins do Rêgo: Modernismo e Regionalismo.*
     São Paulo: EdArt, 1961.
Cavalheiro, Edgard. *Testamento de Uma Geração.* Pôrto Alegre: Globo, 1944.
Chiacchio, Carlos. *Modernistas e Ultramodernistas.* Salvador: Progresso, 1951.
Coutinho, Afrânio (ed.).
     A Literatura no Brasil, 4 Vols. Rio de Janeiro: Sul-Americana e Livraria
     São José, 1956.
     Introdução à Literatura no Brasil. Rio de Janeiro, 1959.
Cavalcanti Proença. *Roteiro de Macunaíma.* São Paulo: Anhembi, 1955.
Costa Filho, Odilo. *Graça Aranha e Outros Ensaios.* Rio de Janeiro: Selma,
     1934.
Di Cavalcanti, E. *Viagem da Minha Vida* (memórias). I: O Testamento da
     Alvorada. Rio de Janeiro: Civilização Brasileira, 1955.
Drummond de Andrade, Carlos.
     A Rosa do Povo. Rio de Janeiro: Livraria José Olympio Editôra, 1945.
     Antologia Poética. Rio de Janeiro: Editôra do Autor, 1962.
Elia, Sílvio. "Contribuição Lingüística do Modernismo," in *Uma Experiência
     Pioneira.* Pôrto Alegre: Faculdade de Filosofia da URGS, 1963.
Ellis, Alfredo. *Raça de Gigantes.* A civilização do Planalto Paulista. São Paulo:
     Novíssima, 1926.
Epstein, Jean. *La Poésie d'Aujourd'hui.* Un nouvel état d'intelligence. Paris:
     Editions de la Sirène, 1921.
Freyre, Gilberto.
     Manifesto Regionalista de 1926. Recife: Edições Região, 1952.
     Região e Tradição. Rio de Janeiro: Livraria José Olympio Editôra, 1941.
     Casa Grande & Senzala, 5th ed. Rio de Janeiro: Livraria José Olympio
     Editôra, 1946.
     Sociologia. Rio de Janeiro: Livraria José Olympio Editôra, 1957.
Frieiro, Eduardo. *O Clube dos Grafômanos.* Belo Horizonte: Pindorama, 1927.
Garcia, Othon Moacyr. *Cobra Norato,* O Poema e o mito. Rio de Janeiro:
     Livraria São José, 1962.
Garnier, Ilse e Pierre. *L'Expressionnisme Allemand.* Paris: Editions André
     Silvaire, 1962.
Graça Aranha.
     O Espírito Moderno. São Paulo: Monteiro Lobato & Cia., 1925.
     (ed.). *Futurismo.* Manifestos de Marinetti e seus companheiros. Rio de
     Janeiro: Pimenta de Melo & C., 1926.
Guastini, Mário. *a hora futurista que passou* . . . São Paulo: Casa Mayença,
     1926.
Guido, Ângelo. *Ilusão.* Ensaio sôbre *A Estética da Vida.* Santos: Instituto
     Esch. Rosa, 1922.
Inojosa, Joaquim. *A Arte Moderna.* Carta literária dirigida a Severino de
     Lucena e S. Guimarães Sobrinho, diretores da revista "Era Nova," da
     Paraíba do Norte. Recife: Of. Graf. do "Jornal do Comércio," 1924.
     O Movimento Modernista em Pernambuco. 2 Vols. Rio: Guanabara,
     1968.
     No Pomar Vizinho . . . Fraudes literárias de Gilberto Freyre, Rio:
     Guanabara, 1968.
Leoni, Raul de. *Luz Mediterrânea,* 5th ed. São Paulo: Martins, 1943.

Lima, Jorge de. *Obra Poética.* Rio de Janeiro: Aguilar, 1950.

Lins do Rêgo, José. Novels: *Menino de Engenho, Doidinho, Bangüê, Moleque Ricardo, Usina* and *Fogo Morto.* Rio de Janeiro: Livraria José Olympio Editôra, 1932–1943.

Magalhães, Adelino. *Obras Completas,* 2 Vols. Rio de Janeiro: Zélio Valverde, 1946.

Martins, Wilson. "A língua simbólica de José Lins do Rêgo." Introdução a *Usina,* 6th ed. Rio de Janeiro: José Olympio, 1967.

Meireles, Cecília. *Mar Absoluto.* Rio de Janeiro: Livros de Portugal, 1945.

Mendes, Murilo. *Mundo Enigma.* Pôrto Alegre: Globo, 1945.

Menotti del Picchia.
  Obras. 14 Vols. São Paulo: Martins, 1958.
  O Curupira e o Carão (with Plínio Salgado and Cassiano Ricardo). São Paulo: Helios, 1927.

Milliet, Sérgio.
  Ensaios. São Paulo: Soc. Impressora Brasileira, 1938.
  O Sal da Heresia. São Paulo: Departamento de Cultura, 1940.
  Panorama da Moderna Poesia Brasileira. Rio de Janeiro: Ministério da Educação e Cultura, 1952.

Monteiro Lobato. *Urupês, Outros Contos e Coisas.* São Paulo: Companhia Editôra Nacional, 1943.

Montezuma de Carvalho, J. de (ed.). *Panorama das Literaturas das Américas* (De 1900 à atualidade). I Vol. Angola: Edição do Município de Nova Lisboa, 1958.

Motta Filho, Cândido.
  Introdução ao Estudo do Pensamento Nacional (O Romantismo). São Paulo: Novíssima, 1926.
  Notas de um Constante Leitor. São Paulo: Martins, 1960.

Neme, Mário. *Plataforma da Nova Geração.* Pôrto Alegre: Globo, 1945.

Oliveira Viana.
  Populações Meridionais do Brasil. São Paulo: Monteiro Lobato & Cia., 1922.
  Evolução do Povo Brasileiro. São Paulo: Monteiro Lobato & Cia., 1924.

Pederneiras, Mário. *Poesia.* Ed. Rodrigo Octavio Filho. Rio de Janeiro: Agir, 1958.

Peregrino Júnior. *O Movimento Modernista.* Rio de Janeiro: Ministério da Educação e Cultura (Os Cadernos de Cultura), 1954.

Prado, Paulo. *Retrato do Brasil,* 6th ed. Rio de Janeiro: Livraria José Olympio Editôra, 1962.

Ramos, Graciliano. Novels: *Caetés, S. Bernardo, Angústia, Vidas Sêcas.* Rio de Janeiro: Schmidt, Ariel, José Olympio, 1933–1938.

Ricardo, Cassiano.
  Borrões de Verde e Amarelo. São Paulo: Helios, 1926.
  Vamos Caçar Papagaios. São Paulo: Helios, 1926.
  Martim Cererê. São Paulo: Revista dos Tribunais, 1928.

Rio, João do. *Psicologia Urbana.* Rio de Janeiro: H. Garnier, 1911.

Saldanha, Coelho, ed. *Modernismo.* Estudos Críticos. Rio de Janeiro: Revista Branca, 1954.

Salgado, Plínio.
  O Estrangeiro. São Paulo: Helios, 1926.
  O Esperado. São Paulo: Helios, 1927.
  Obras Completas. 20 vols. São Paulo: Editôra das Américas, 1955.
Salles Cunha, Dulce. *Autores Contemporâneos Brasileiros.* (Depoimento de uma época.) São Paulo: Cupolo, 1951.
Schmidt, Augusto Frederico. *Poesias Completas* (1928–1955). Rio de Janeiro: Livraria José Olympio Editôra, 1956.
Senna, Homero. *República das Letras.* Rio de Janeiro: Livraria São José, 1957.
Setúbal, Paulo. *Alma Cabocla.* São Paulo: Revista do Brasil, 1920.
Silva Brito, Mário da. *História do Modernismo Brasileiro. I: Antecedentes da Semana de Arte Moderna.* São Paulo: Saraiva, 1958.
Silveira, Tasso da. *Definição do Modernismo Brasileiro.* Rio de Janeiro: Forja, 1932.
Stout, John M. *Religion's Influence in the Writings of Alceu Amoroso Lima.* Reproduced by the author. Austin, Texas, 1934.
Tati, Miécio. *Jorge Amado.* Vida e Obra. Belo Horizonte: Itatiaia, 1961.
Thiollier, René. *A Semana de Arte Moderna.* São Paulo: Cupolo, n. d.
Vargas, Netto. *Tropilha Gaúcha e Gado Xucro.* Pôrto Alegre: Globo, 1929.
Veríssimo, Érico. Novels: *Clarissa, Caminhos Cruzados, O Resto É Silêncio.* Pôrto Alegre: Globo, 1933–1943.
Veríssimo, José. *História da Literatura Brasileira,* 3rd ed. Rio de Janeiro: Livraria José Olympio Editôra, 1954.
Victor, Nestor.
  Cartas à Gente Nova. Rio de Janeiro: Anuário do Brasil, 1924.
  Os de Hoje. Figuras do Movimento Modernista Brasileiro. São Paulo: Cultura Moderna, 1938.

PERIODICALS

  Anuário Brasileiro de Literatura
  Clima
  Estética
  Festa
  Klaxon
  Lanterna Verde
  O Estado de São Paulo
  Revista de Antropofagia
  Revista do Arquivo Municipal de São Paulo (1946)
  Revista do Livro
  Revista Nova
  Verde

Name Index

This is the first global critical appraisal of *Modernismo,* the most important Brazilian artistic and literary movement in the twentieth century. Putting under scrutiny both the key authors and the representative works, it tries to define the "modernist idea" and to estimate its accomplishments and shortcomings. It should be noted that *Modernismo* in Brazil stands for the avant-garde currents called Modern Art, Surrealism, Expressionism, and so on, in European countries. That is, in short, the literature and arts of the Twenties and Thirties.

However, Brazilians added to the cosmopolitan flavor of those European currents a strong note of artistic nationalism: the music of Villa-Lobos, or the painting of Portinari, for example, stem from modernist roots and are linked to them. The same is true for the so-called Northeastern novel of the Thirties, which has been an outstanding experiment in the *social,* if not socialist, literature. Poetry followed the same line of cosmopolitan-nationalist oscillation, with a most surprising emphasis on the technical aspects of verse writing.

Evidencing its organic nature, the movement is also related to the large effort of modernization of Brazilian society during that period; it is not an overstatement to say that it shaped all ulterior developments, even after its decline and disappearance in the mid-Forties.